Starting Over

Critical Perspectives on Women and Gender

Critical Perspectives on Women and Gender brings books on timely issues and controversies to an interdisciplinary audience. The series explores gender-related topics and illuminates the issues involved in current debates in feminist scholarship and across the disciplines.

Titles in the series

Michelle Fine
Disruptive Voices: The Possibilities of Feminist Research

Susan D. Clayton and Faye J. Crosby
Justice, Gender, and Affirmative Action

Janice Doane and Devon Hodges
From Klein to Kristeva: Psychoanalytic Feminism and the Search for the "Good Enough" Mother

Jill Dolan
Presence and Desire: Essays on Gender, Sexuality, Performance

Judith Newton
Starting Over: Feminism and the Politics of Cultural Critique

Starting Over

Feminism and the Politics of Cultural Critique

Judith Newton

Ann Arbor

THE UNIVERSITY OF MICHIGAN PRESS

1997   1996   1995   1994   4   3   2   1

A CIP catalogue record for this book is available from the British Library.

Library of Congress Cataloging-in-Publication Data

Newton, Judith Lowder.
    Starting over : feminism and the politics of cultural critique /
Judith Newton.
        p.   cm.—(Critical perspectives on women and gender)
    Includes bibliographical references.
    ISBN 0-472-09482-3 (alk. paper).—ISBN 0-472-06482-7 (pbk. :
alk. paper)
    1. Feminist literary criticism. 2. Criticism. 3. Feminism and
literature.   I. Title.   II. Series.
PN98.W64N49   1994
801'.95'082—dc20   94-10225
                                                              CIP

Methuen & Co. for excerpts from *Feminist Criticism and Social Change*,
edited by Judith Newton and Deborah Rosenfelt, © 1986. Routledge for
excerpts from *Rewriting the Victorians*, edited by Linda Shires, © 1992.
"History as Usual" originally appeared in a slightly different form in
Cultural Critique #9, © 1988 Oxford University Press, *Cultural Critique*.
Used with permission. "Learning Not to Curse" originally appeared in a
slightly different form in *Cultural Critique #25*, © 1993 Oxford University
Press, *Cultural Critique*. Used with permission. "Historicisms New and
Old: 'Charles Dickens' Meets Marxism, Feminism, and West Coast Fou-
cault" was originally published in FEMINIST STUDIES, volume 16, num-
ber 3 (Fall 1990): 449–70, and is reprinted here, in a revised version, by
permission of the publisher, Feminist Studies, Inc., c/o Women's Studies
Program, University of Maryland, College Park, MD 20742.

To my families

Contents

Preface

These essays, written between 1981 and 1992, represent a series of interventions in the discourses of mainstream feminist and leftist cultural criticism over the last decade. Each essay is marked by the limitations, stakes, and strategies of my insertion into specific historical moments, my membership in different and sometimes conflicting communities, my participation in and reaction against complex and changing configurations of shared discourse, and by the peculiarities of my own (always constructed) life history. These essays were not written, or rewritten, as a series of chapters (or as a systematic performance or definition of a critical approach), nor are they meant to be read in that way. Although they are linked by recurring concerns and preoccupations, those concerns shift in relative importance, are reformulated, or sometimes give way altogether. There is movement here but hardly ever in a direct line.

These essays were also written for myself as a way of clarifying what strategies and methodologies I might employ in writing a book on the culture of the nineteenth-century British middle class. It is this effort at self-help that accounts for the dominance here of materials on the nineteenth century, the British, the white, and the middle class, for it made sense to me to think critically about strategies and methodologies in relation to scholarship on the culture that I was also officially writing about. Like several of my most deliberate projects, however, this one had some unexpected and unintended effects. I did not finish my book on nineteenth-century British culture, and, though my reflections on contemporary cultural criticism did eventually inform my nineteenth-century work, the nineteenth-century work began equally to construct my reading of the present. That is, my work on the construction of nineteenth-century cultural narratives and on competing forms of social expertise began to intersect with and even guide my reading of the contemporary U.S. critical scene. The two essays focused most directly on nineteenth-century themes, "Sex and Political Economy in the *Edinburgh Review*" and

" 'Ministers of the Interior': The Political Economy of Women's Manuals," are included, therefore, not as purloined chapters from another work but, like the rest, as readings of the politics of cultural critique.

Like all the essays in this collection, the nineteenth-century essays are engaged with cultural criticism as a terrain of power, a terrain in which some voices, themes, and reading strategies are more successfully authorized than others, in which traditional forms of expertise are both criticized and reconstructed on new grounds, in which the reading strategies deployed in cultural narratives are both shaped by and also shape political and other investments and desires, and in which struggles over resources and unequal relations of gender, class, nationhood, and race enter into the production of competing public knowledges and expertise. These essays attempt to map and, more important, to intervene in these struggles by critically exploring the ideological resonances and political potentialities layered into the meaning-making practices of some forms of cultural criticism that I have cared about and participated in.

Rereading these essays from the perspective of 1993 I can construct their limitations in ways that were not so available to me when they were being written. I can see these essays, for example, as interventions in the discourses of those who were primarily white, professional, and middle-class (but feminist, leftist, and/or antiracist as well.) Specifically, these essays sought to intervene in the discourses of (1) mainstream feminist literary criticism in the early 1980s, (2) largely male-authored Marxist and post-Marxist cultural criticism of the same decade, and (3) the reinventions of male-authored post-Marxist cultural criticism represented by popular forms of new historicism and cultural studies. These discourses circulated in critical communities to which I also belonged and within which I felt variously authorized to speak. As communities, they were predominantly white.

These essays, of course, also attempted to intervene in and further construct the critical tendency in which I mainly located myself— that of materialist-feminist criticism. But while the work of feminists of color was very much a part of the way I constructed materialist-feminist criticism—indeed, some of it provided the most coherent models—and while my interventions in the discourse of this community were more broadly aimed, here too I felt most authorized to exhort white feminists, not excluding, of course, myself. It is only in my last essay, "Learning Not to Curse" (co-authored with Judith Stacey in 1992), in my preface, and in my afterword, that I have consciously addressed myself to a broader audience. For I am differently situated in communities now. I work within a multiracial women's studies program that I helped to build. I also participate in several cross-gender and cross-racial communities or networks. As with many white feminists in the 1990s, then, there has been movement, but uneven movement as I will suggest.

The first essay in this collection, for example, "Toward a Materialist-Feminist Criticism," drafted in 1981 and rewritten in 1985, was addressed to mainstream feminist literary criticism as it was often practiced in the early 1980s. It was addressed, that is, to the tendencies in mainstream feminist literary criticism to privilege literary texts and gender division, to read literary texts in isolation from other material practices, and to focus on an undifferentiated women's nature and on an unchanging "patriarchy." In that essay my co-author, Deborah Rosenfelt, and I evoke a different critical configuration, materialist-feminist literary criticism, which we define as an approach based on ideological critique, on the analysis of meaning in the service of power, and one that positions its readings of literary texts in relation to other forms of public written representation and other forms of the material, in relation to (always constructed) social and economic relations. We evoke, as well, a criticism that works along more than one axis of analysis, that works with gender in relation to class, racial, sexual, and national identities, an approach that emphasizes difference among women and among men. We evoke a criticism that retains notions of agency and the possibility of progressive social change and that defines the latter as change within interlocking oppressions and as change requiring broad alliance.

That we attempted in this essay to name, define, give examples of, and indeed further construct such a literary critical configuration had to do with our shared political trajectories, but here I will refer only to my own. As I suggest in the afterword, I had come to feminism through antiracist politics and socialist cultural criticism and to feminist literary criticism first through my classroom teaching of works by radical back men and then my teaching of nineteenth-century British culture, as seen primarily through the lens provided by the work of Raymond Williams. Gender politics became a part of this larger configuration in 1971, and it has been the dominant part for many years, but my construction of "being feminist" has always implied a location of myself in several related struggles. There was for many years, however, a cleavage between my larger politics, my work in classrooms and in radical faculty groups on campus, on the one hand, and my writing on the other. In my teaching (at La Salle University in the 1970s and 1980s), for example, I often worked on nineteenth-century and contemporary U.S. culture and consistently emphasized race along with gender and class. ("Too much on women!" "Too much on blacks!" my evaluations sometimes read. My students either did not notice or else felt at home with class analysis.) But in my published work on nineteenth-century middle-class British culture, race—in this case whiteness in a largely white society—was hard to see. Indeed, whiteness in a mixed-raced society like my own was hard to see unless I was directly examining white-nonwhite relations. (And since I grew up in Compton, now a black-run city near South Central Los Angeles, and lived in Philadelphia for twenty years, this meant almost entirely black-white relationships to me.) Although I dealt with British and U.S. imperialism in my classrooms to some degree, it was also a long while before I could approach these themes in my written work. Postcolonial critique emerged in the early 1980s, but there was a lag of many years before I felt sufficiently pressed and confident enough to take it on. As with many white feminists in the 1990s, therefore, there is an emerging focus in my published work on race and postcolonial analysis. These concerns are foreshadowed in "Toward a Materialist-Feminist Criticism," my essays on the nineteenth century included here, and "History as Usual," but my latest collaborative project, represented by the essay "Learning Not to Curse," marks the most deliberate beginning of this move.

The stakes and limits of my writing on nineteenth-century British culture shaped the interventions that I felt authorized to make in the critical discourse of male cultural critics on the Left. A primary concern in my own work, that is, was for many years to revise Marxist accounts of the nineteenth-century British past, to write gender into these accounts, for women and for men, to write middle-class and working-class women into history too, to write middle-class women, in particular, into the construction of dominant forms of nineteenth-century British culture alongside men, and to alter what *class, culture, politics,* and the *state* could mean. These are the concerns that inform "Sex and Political Economy" and "Ministers of the Interior."

In a demonstration of the truism that our readings of the present intersect with, shape, and are shaped by our readings of the past, my essays on contemporary Marxist, post-Marxist, and new historicist work also concerned themselves with gender, and specifically with reading strategies that inhibit the investigation of gender as a category of analysis and the investigation of women's as well as men's participation in the construction of culture in both the present and the past. A related focus of these essays has been upon the tendency to erase twentieth-century feminist work, in all its variety, from the contemporary critical scene—from footnotes, from the genealogies of the discourses or approaches that are being authorized and installed, from intellectual history over the last twenty years. It is this erasure that forces feminists to "start over" in the sense that they must "erase the erasure" and write themselves back into the latest histories of theory and of the critically "new."

Since the mere argument for inclusion has never seemed a sufficiently powerful argument (rhetorically speaking at least) to make, my concern in these essays has also been to suggest the difference that multiple axes of analysis make or might make in our readings of culture and in the construction of categories that have always seemed crucial, from my perspective, to anyone engaged in efforts to change the world—human agency, the instability of dominant ideologies, the fluidity of social relations, and the possibility of progressive change. These concerns are most fully represented in "History as Usual? Feminism and the New Historicism" (written in 1987), *"Family Fortunes:* History and Literature in Materialist-Feminist Work" (written in 1988), and "Historicisms New and Old: 'Charles Dickens' Meets Marxism, Feminism, and 'West Coast Foucault'" (written in 1989).

A recurring characteristic of the latter essays has been their focus on the close reading of literary critical texts. Indeed, I have sometimes returned to the same texts more than once in order to position them and their approaches somewhat differently, to see them from another angle, or to throw the outlines of a competing approach into greater relief. My focus on texts is in part an attempt to test out theory by examining its operations in specific reading practices, for, like many others, I think of theory as a "tool kit" that we rifle through for whatever serves us, for what it can afford us in the way of "explanatory power." There is in this focus on the close reading of critical texts a trace of my formalist training as well, which, for all my criticism of its political tendencies, I still value for teaching me this preoccupation and this skill. There is an expression too of a continuing element of my (constructed) subjectivity—that I am fond of the specific, am given to making charts and drawing idea trees. There is a reflex of the fact that I wrote these essays in a self-improving vein and that, like the students I have taught, I learn better if given an example.

My attention to the specific and concrete, however, also comes out of my political history and desires. It comes from a sense that intervention works better if you take pains to make yourself understood, and it comes from a related impatience with a move in post-Marxist, and some feminist, work, toward ever greater obscurity and abstraction, to the deployment of a language so specialized that it is available only to groups of academics. Although I have learned from such writing, have patiently translated it for my students as well, and believe that there is room for politically engaged writing in many modes, I have always desired a broader audience than the norms of such writing would allow. In the context of the neoconservative colonization of many public intellectual spheres, the largely unprotested dismantling of U.S. universities, in the context of the continuing domestic crisis, and a more global and international focus for our work, this desire for a broader audience—and for broader alliances— seems more pressing even than before.

Alliance, of course, has been a recurring concern for me, as for many others, since my days at Berkeley in the 1960s, and, in gathering my contemporary essays together for the first time, it struck me that I evoke the dream of broad alliance at the end of more than one. This concern with alliance, however, has deepened over the last three years, years that I have spent "in the field" directing a women's studies program at University of California, Davis. My sense of who alliance might be with has also been revised, as I have found myself working not only with white feminists and feminists of color, which I had set out very consciously to do, but with men of color as well and with some mainly liberal white males. During these same three years, other developments that bear on the question of broad coalition have taken place. Major forms of socialism collapsed, and the

U.S. Left began a series of reflections upon itself; the backlash against political correctness emerged, U.S. cultural studies, and radical multiculturalism rose to prominence; and a Democrat was elected president. Each in its own way has positioned white feminists, feminists of color, gays, radical men of color, and Left/liberal, white, heterosexual men in some version of alliance politics—whether demonized, idealized, or "actually existing." These developments and others have prompted me to rethink the bases for and potentialities of collective political work.

One fruit of this rethinking is the project that I have begun with Judith Stacey on the political and intellectual trajectories of radical academic men (white men and men of color, gay and straight men) over the last twenty-five years. The project focuses upon the relation of radical academic men to critical discourses on race, gender, class, sexuality, and neocoloniality. İt focuses, that is, on what Sandra Harding calls the formation of "traitorous identities," a willingness to take on the knowledges that call the privileges of one's own position into question, or on what others refer to as the process of becoming a counterhegemonic collective subject (Hennessy 1993, 96). To study male "others" in this way, however, to gather life histories as we planned to do, has meant revising some long-cherished attitudes and preoccupations. In relation to white men, for example (as subjects whom we had often exhorted and written critically about), we realized that the genres we had adopted in the past—the feminist report card, the nagging text—would not do. If we could manage no greater openness than that, we might not secure interviews in the first place, or worse, we might end up with an unhelpful collection of exceedingly well-defended narratives.

Our first experiment with interviews, moreover, made us newly aware of the folly of presuming to read the politics of a career out of a written text. Written texts are only one site of self-presentation and political behavior, and, indeed, we know from constructing histories of ourselves that gender, racial, and sexual politics in the classroom, in department meetings, or in the kitchen may be different and different once again from the politics implied in a written text. Studying men renewed in us a sense of the uneven ways in which political commitments and alliances are forged, renewed in us a sense of the complexities of reading others, and, I should say, often heartened us about the possibilities for alliance.

One impact of our early interviews has been to make more room in our critical writing for appreciation as well as for critique, to make room for the acknowledgment of greater complexity and contradiction in our academic others than we had been willing to accord them in the past. A related consequence was to make room for greater humility about ourselves. This greater humility, of course, had been under construction for the past ten years, a product of age, of political conditions during the Reagan-Bush era, and of our long immersion in critical assessments of white feminism by women of color. It was critique by women of color, to a large degree, that prepared us to see in the contradictions, lapses, and efforts of male colleagues a reflection of our own—and that made it possible for us to move beyond certain historical resentments. Like many feminists of color whose public discourse toward white feminists has shifted in the last few years, we are thinking less about victimization these days and more about collective desire, about the politics of what needs to be done.

Our intervention in our own discourse as feminists, of course, is more broadly aimed. It is aimed in some ways at all of those with whom we seek alliance, but, for me at least, it has particular resonance with respect to white feminists in their critical discourse with one another. As other feminists like Nancy Miller, Jane Gallop, and Marianne Hirsch have noted, the incidence of careless reading, caricature, and reduction, dismissive and contemptuous critique, the use of club words like *essentialism,* the disinterest displayed in accounting for the larger aims of an essay or for the limits of its historical location, and the adoption of implicitly transcendent theoretical positions are no longer reserved for the historical "enemy," white men, but have multiplied in the discourse of feminists in relation to one another over the last few years. As a result, Hirsch notes, people are more careful and circumspect and are writing out of "hurt and fear" (Gallop, Hirsch, Miller 1990, 365). As a (young, white, lesbian, poststructuralist) feminist put it privately at a recent conference, tears often follow dismissive critique, and a lot of energy is wasted "mopping up."

This discourse of dismissal casts a strange light upon the prospects for "alliance" (a concept everywhere evoked these days) unless this means, for some white feminists, alliance only with feminists of color (respectfully regarded but sometimes as an undifferentiated group) and with white feminists who share one's own theoretical perspective. To the extent that feminists seek broader alliances than this—with men, for example, and with other feminists who entertain competing theoretical vantage points—we would do well to remember that contempt and one-upmanship are not firm foundations for political union. We need, as Jane Gallop has put it, an "ethics of criticism" once again, an emphasis upon what others have to offer as well as upon their limitations, a sense of humility as well as rigorous argument and critique (Gallop, Hirsch, Miller 1990, 368).

My work with my collaborator on the intellectual and political trajectories of radical academic men, our interviews with feminists of color—for we are trying to secure the stories of our feminist others as well—and the complexities of reading narratives about careers and trajectories that are not my own have produced in me, again, an interest in telling my own story as well. Age, too, has revived this interest, and so has an investment in having my own version of this story on the record. I am not alone. I have read with interest several recent essays on personal writing, have seen more than one new volume of academic life stories, and know of several ethnographic projects with relation to Judith Stacey's and my own. Does this reversion to life story come in waves through generations? Or is it that those of us who were students in the 1960s, who were "there" for the beginning of the current revolutions, want to construct our narratives for the future before it is too late?

I have chosen in "Starting Over: An Afterword" to tell my own story, or at least one story of myself as author of this book. I deliberated about taking this (decided) risk for quite a while, and I take it now only with some trepidation, for it is always distressing to have "unfriendly readers," but it is particularly so when the topic is oneself. Like many others, nonetheless, I find the critical discourses that many feminists have permitted ourselves of late (especially those of us in literature and theory) impoverished and politically undesirable as well. As I respond to the oral histories I am currently collecting from radical men and feminists of color, as I alter my way of reading others in response to them, I find myself wondering about the potential impact on critical exchanges of "locating" oneself in academic and political discourses alone, as if our subjectivities had that purity, that rigor, that innocence. I am thinking of the contradiction implied in texts that emphasize the multiplicity and fluidity of identities and that locate the author, with elegant brevity, as, say, "white, lesbian (or heterosexual), female, and middle class," as if these categories were unified and self-evident.

I am wondering what the impact might be on our textual relations, on the norms of critical discourse, if we were to describe ourselves with more complexity than this, if more of us were to acknowledge the discourses, the languages that, in our nonwritten representations of ourselves, we also share. (I am thinking here of the languages that I particularly enjoy—discourses of desire, of community, of home.) I am wondering if a fuller presentation of the self might play a role in writing for, in speaking to, a wider audience both within the academy and without. (These are questions, not answers. This is less an argument than a venture into unmarked space.)

In a critic like myself, moreover, one who has returned again and again to the necessity of moving beyond public written texts to constructions of daily behavior, familial relations, and desires in studying others of the past, it would be a contradiction to omit them from any attempted location of myself. These are areas, after all, that women's and ethnic studies have added to our sense of the material. I have chosen to experiment, then, in "Starting Over" with a layering of different discourses in my narrative of this book. The story is not whole. It conceals perhaps as much as it lays bare, but it is a gesture in the direction of what Nancy Miller calls "the personal material," a modest effort to "recognize the resistance that particularity offers to the grandiosity of abstraction" (1991, 24, xiii).

Some might see a danger, of course, for white feminists in particular, of writing about themselves only to resecure their subjectivities on a discursive center stage. But, structurally speaking, we are on this stage already, and we lay claim to it anew, perhaps most forcefully of all, when we assume the transcendence of being within a series of academic discourses alone, of being without an individual, idiosyncratic, desiring history, of being white, heterosexual, and middle class—no explanations needed. Alliance, moreover, requires that we recognize the zones and boundaries that are "the very condition of exchange with another limited other" (Miller 1991, xiv). Finally, there is the opportunity here to see ourselves more critically as well, to grasp the evanescent meaning of our whiteness, for example, in trying to think through the specificities of our own (constructed) lives. As Patricia Williams puts it:

What is "impersonal" writing but denial of self? If withholding is an ideology worth teaching, we should be clearer about that as the bottom line of the enterprise. We should also acknowledge the extent to which denial of one's authority in authorship is not the same as elimination of oneself; it is ruse, not reality. And the object of such ruse is to empower still further, to empower beyond the self. . . . The other thing contained in assumption of neutral, impersonal writing styles is the lack of risk. It is not only a ruse, but a warm protective hole to crawl in, as if you were to throw your shoe out the front door while insisting that no one's home." (Williams 1991, 92–93)

Acknowledgments

These essays, written between 1981 and 1992, were begun, revised, and finished in so many different communities and locations that it is hard to recall the many people who exercised a beneficial influence upon them. There are those, however, who have been so long a part of my intellectual and personal life, who have so generously read and reread my manuscripts (giving me, in the process, much excellent, though not always followed, advice), who have, in some instances, co-authored essays with me, and in whose friendship I have taken such long-standing delight that they are inextricably a part of this book's history. My special thanks then to Deborah Rosenfelt, Judith Stacey, and Judith Walkowitz, and my thanks, in memory, to Richard C. Newton, who lives on in me and in many of these pages.

I am also deeply grateful to my other co-editors at *Feminist Studies* between 1978 and 1989 for years of intellectual, political, and personal intensities. (I miss our close connection and our work. I miss "drinking wine together in the twilight.") I am indebted, as well, to the women and men of MLG from whom I have learned, and continue to learn, much—not all of it strictly theoretical or political. And I owe much to friends who came later into my life—Jane Caplan, Mary Poovey, Leonore Davidoff, Susan Landau, Suad Joseph— whose thinking, in different ways, stimulated my own and whose friendship helped me feel at home in the world. I also wish to acknowledge a grant from the National Endowment of Humanities, which, during the academic year of 1983–1984, gave me respite from my eight courses a year and allowed me to write.

Finally and most profoundly, I am grateful to my daughter Anna, whose coming into the world has been the occasion for my most life-enhancing, and most fun, "starting over."

Toward a Materialist-Feminist Criticism

With Deborah Rosenfelt

(1985)

This essay, as I mention elsewhere, was begun in 1981 as a short talk on the relations between mainstream, largely white, feminist criticism and post-Marxist literary critical assumptions and methodologies. In 1984 Deborah Rosenfelt and I recast the essay as an introduction to a collection of "materialist-feminist criticism." What had begun as an attempt to bridge mainstream feminist criticism and post-Marxist work became a different sort of intervention. It became an attempt to construct—through naming, defining, and citing it—a literary critical configuration that drew upon critical gender, antiracist, post-Marxist, and poststructuralist work without being positioned solely in any of these discourses or locations.

Although the essay indirectly addresses some forms of poststructuralist feminist literary criticism, which we felt overprivileged gender division and public written representation, it is much more directly an intervention in mainstream, largely white, feminist literary criticism as much of it was practiced in the early 1980s. The essay focuses, for example, on the tendency of much mainstream feminist criticism to privilege literary texts, gender division, an undifferentiated women's nature, and an unchanging patriarchy. It evokes, instead, an approach or tendency that we choose to call materialist-feminist literary criticism, an extension of the term materialist feminism *as employed by British cultural critics such as Annette Kuhn and Michele Barrett. This approach, as we defined it, focused, like much mainstream feminist work, on the interests at stake in the construction of social identities and knowledges, but it positioned its readings of literary texts in relation to other forms of public written representation and other forms of the material, such as (always constructed) social and economic relations. We evoked a criticism that worked along more than one axis of analysis—that worked with gender in relation to race, ethnicity, sexual and national identi-*

ties, and class—and that emphasized difference not just between women and men but among women and among men. We evoked a criticism, finally, that retained some notion of agency and of the possibility of progressive social change, and we defined the latter as change within interlocking oppressions, as change requiring broad, cross-gender, cross-racial, cross-class alliance.

I have made very few changes either in the body of the essay or in the footnotes because I think it is of interest to see both the essay's historical limitations and the ways in which it prefigured contemporary articulations of materialist-feminist and feminist cultural studies work. Among the most central of its limitations are its essentially additive view of race, class, and gender and its lack of attention to the global and neocolonial scholarship (which was then emerging in the United States). Nonetheless, in its evocation of an ideology critique that focused on knowledge and power and that drew on critical gender, antiracist, post-Marxist, and poststructuralist work, it prefigured many current formulations of materialist feminism, materialist-feminist criticism, and feminist cultural studies work.

Lillian Robinson once said that the most important question we can ask ourselves as feminist critics is "So what?" Implied in that question was a view that most of us shared—that the point of our work was to change the world. But to begin with the question "So what?" is to take on the task of asking other questions as well, such as what is the relation of literature and therefore of literary criticism to the social and economic conditions of our lives? Most feminist critics still work within a central insight of the women's movement—that gender is socially constructed and that its construction has enforced unequal relations of power. From that insight it is a relatively short step to the assumption that other products of consciousness, like literature and literary criticism, are also socially constructed and that they too are political. Like women's studies, generally, in fact, feminist criticism began with the assumption that we make our own knowledge and are constantly remaking it in the terms that history provides—and that, in making knowledge, we act upon the power relations of our lives.[1]

As feminist critics, for example, we speak of making our knowledge of history, choosing to see in it not a tale of individual and inevitable suffering but, instead, a story of struggle and relations of power. We speak of making our notion of literary texts, choosing to read them not as meditations upon themselves but as gestures toward history and gestures with political effect. Finally, we speak of making our model of literary criticism, choosing to see in it not an ostensibly objective reading of a text but rather an act of political intervention, a mode of shaping the cultural use to which women's and men's writings will be put.[2]

This reconstruction of our knowledge, however, has been a form of struggle, a political action carried out upon our culture and ourselves, for to assert that literature and culture are political is radically to challenge modes of thinking that are dominant in our world. For those of us trained as 1960s-style literary critics, moreover, these modes of thinking are apt, after long apprenticeship, to become so deeply ingrained that our struggle with our culture seems a struggle with ourselves.[3] For literary studies, more than most other disciplines in the 1960s, had divorced the study of ideas and language from the study of other material conditions and had fostered a view of intellectual activity as a solitary individual enterprise rather than as a project with social origins, ideological alliances, and political consequence.[4] As feminist critics, therefore, many of us have implicitly committed ourselves to resist a view of literature, formalism, that sees literature and literary critics as divorced from other material conditions, from social and economic totalities, a view still perpetuated—despite their air of currency—by many of the poststructuralist criticisms now dominant in the United States.[5] Many have also committed ourselves to resist a view of history once beloved by humanities departments throughout the land, the view that history, especially modern history, is the essentially tragic story of individual suffering, a suffering often universalized and guaranteed permanency as part of the human condition. This is a view, of course, that permits us to "see" literature and the rest of history in relation but that nullifies what is potentially radical in such a vision by denying the possibility of meaningful change.

But given that knowledge is constructed and that remaking knowledge is a form of struggle against our culture and ourselves, and given the training of some of us as formalist critics in particular, it is not surprising that we should still be immersed in critical practices that it is against our interests as feminists to maintain, that our primary assumptions and our theory, our theory and our practice, have not always developed hand in hand.[6] Thus, despite the assumption that ideas, literature, and culture are socially constructed, that psychic forms of oppression are rooted in the social and economic conditions of our lives, much of our literary theory implies a version of the world in which all women are oppressed, for the most part, by literary constructs or in which female countermyths are more powerful than (or as powerful as) economics.[7] Rather than elucidating the complex web of relations—social, economic, symbolic—of which literature is a part, we disassociate public written representation from other kinds of discourse and from other (discursively organized) social and economic conditions. This disassociation replicates and enforces a habit of mind already dominant in the culture at large and blunts the radical edge of feminist critical intervention. As Lillian Robinson observed in 1970, there is "a kind of idealism to which we become susceptible when we explore the question of feminine consciousness. For we, too, have a tendency to ignore its material basis" (8).

This looseness of hold upon what is not literary, or upon what is not public written representation, is also reflected in the fact that applied feminist criticism frequently offers little else as "history" and by the fact that the constructions of history it does offer tend unwittingly to recapitulate the tragic politics of the English departments and the culture in which many of us were trained. Much white, middle-class feminist criticism, in particular, although it begins at least by assuming the existence of systematic and unequal gender-based relations of power, implicitly constructs those relations in such a way as to render them tragic—unchanging, universal, monolithic. Many white, middle-class feminists, that is, still evoke a universal and unchanging "patriarchy." Yet insofar as this construction of patriarchy obscures historical change, women's agency, and cultural complexities (such as those represented by the intersections of gender with race, nationalism, and class), they themselves replicate the habits of thought they intend to challenge. They produce, in fact, a feminist version of "the" human condition.[8] This tendency to tragic essentialism in regard to male domination is the obverse of an inclination to comedic essentialism on the other side of the equation. This essentialism, for example, subsumes women into the sisterly category of "woman," despite pronounced (and also constructed) differences of race, ethnicity, class, and historical condition, or posits "women's" nurturing and relational qualities as, in themselves, a sufficient counter to male domination.[9]

These inclinations in some feminist criticism, of course, are part of larger currents in feminist theory and politics as a whole. Polarization of the masculine and the feminine, or of male and female; denigration of the masculine, or the male as violent and possibly irretrievable; valorization of male power into a "monolithic and unchanging out there"; the construction of women as at once totally dominated and essentially good; and the celebration of a unifying women's nature have in varying ways characterized the discourse of cultural and radical feminists in England and the United States, some women in sectors of the peace and antipornography movement, and some French poststructuralist feminists as well.[10] These theoretical tendencies, of course, have been expressed in a variety of political actions, including "Take Back the Night" marches, ritual theater at military bases, and campaigns for more stringent laws against pornography. Such actions, whether one completely sympathizes with them or not, have been visible, dramatic, and sometimes effective.[11] But more than ever—in a context of backlash and cutbacks, the absence of a unified progressive movement, the rise in the United States of the New Right and Moral Majority, and economic hard times—the theoretical constructions of history on which they rest seem too simplistic adequately to analyze the possibilities and priorities for long-term political struggle.

In the United States, where feminist poets have powerfully influenced feminist politics, this tendency has sometimes expressed itself in poetic language imbued with a kind of wishful thinking. In an article about the role of feminist poets as theoreticians and political spokeswomen, for example, poet and critic Jan Clausen writes of three poems by Judy Grahn, June Jordan, and Susan Sherman that, while their optimistic conclusions about women's power are strong and moving, "their impact seems to rest more on our *desire* to believe their closing assertions than on the intrinsic credibility these assertions possess based on what we know of the world." Clausen then warns feminist poets and leaders to avoid "the rote chanting of slogans we are unable to make real, the temptation to dish up to the audience what it wants or has learned to expect in the way of exhortation and uplift" (1982, 26). It is, of course, the nature of poetry to work better as rhetoric than as analysis, and we need poetry to inspire just as we need analysis to guide us. Still, Clausen advises us not to confuse inspiration with theory.

There have been many challenges to this polarization of male domination and female powerlessness and to this utopian celebration of female virtue, with the essentialism or universalism that so much of it implied. A dialectic of criticism and self-criticism has continued to characterize feminist debate over pornography, peace, the gender gap, poststructuralist feminism, race, and sexuality. New work by feminist scholars, moreover, continually reworks our history and theory. New theories of gender construction have reemphasized the idea that gender identity and ideologies of gender, as part of a sex-gender system, are socially and symbolically constructed rather than innate, that they are created by women as well as by men, despite women's lesser access to cultural power, and that gender is multiple, fluid, and discursively organized.[12] Feminist history has, in addition to its other contributions, countered the ahistorical quality of some feminist psychoanalytic theory by illuminating the ways in which constructions of gender and sexuality have changed with changing historical situations.[13] Writings by women of color, working-class women, and lesbians have powerfully challenged the notion of an undifferentiated and implicitly white, middle-class, and heterosexual women's nature.[14] Finally, a growing literature by postcolonial critics and feminist anthropologists has begun correcting the ethnocentric bias of many white Western theories about the subordination of women, women's culture, and women's nature in the present.[15]

In feminist literary criticism similar tendencies have challenged us further to interrogate the tragic conceptions of history we have inherited and to tighten our hold upon the specific, the different, the local, not just in written texts but also in social and economic relations, institutions, and daily behaviors. These tendencies appear most consistently and consciously in the work of radical women of color and of many white feminists who are also socialists, but we refer to work in which such currents dominate as "materialist-feminist" rather than, for example, "socialist-feminist" or "radical." We do so because the former term is more inclusive and because it reminds us that materialist analysis appears, however unevenly, in the work of many feminist critics who are not radical women of color or who do not consider themselves socialist (especially in the United States, in which Marxism and socialism are marginalized and negatively viewed by the culture as a whole).[16]

The boundaries between materialist-feminist criticism, therefore, and other feminist criticisms are fluid. What this means is that our analysis and critique will inevitably be self-analysis and self-critique as well. What it also means, since all of us are situated in and limited by history and since we and our work change with changing circumstances, is that analysis and critique must address themselves not to individuals, or at least not to individuals whom we confidently assume to be politically fixed and wholly available for analysis in their written texts; criticism must address itself to the (presumably changing) tendencies of their work.

Despite this fluidity of boundaries, however, we can make distinctions that help define and further construct a materialist-feminist critical practice. We have said that most feminist criticism begins with a materialist assumption: that gender is socially and/or discursively constructed and that its construction enforces unequal relations of power. Most feminist criticism may be said to engage in a form of ideology critique as well, in that feminist criticism often explores the complex and hidden ways that contesting interests shape the construction of social identities and relations. But materialist-feminist criticism is, for the most part, multiply committed to materialist analysis and ideology critique. It is committed out of its concern with gender relations, and it is committed out of its concern with race, economics, and national and sexual identities. Barbara Smith's early essay on "A Black Feminist Criticism" is a classic example of this multifaceted approach:

> a black feminist approach to literature that embodies the realization that the politics of sex as well as the politics of race and class are crucially interlocking factors in the work of black women writers is an absolute necessity. (1970, 5)

Understanding the intersections of multiple oppression, however, as June Howard reminds us, is not "a simple choice of perspective but a long labor" (1983, 1). And to most materialist-feminist critics the labor of constructing and using theoretical positions entails a multiple shift: work on the power relations implied by gender and simultaneously on those implied by class, ethnicity, race, and national and sexual identification; an analysis of literature and an analysis of what is not literary; an analysis of the circumstances of cultural production and an analysis of the complexities with which, at a given moment in history, they are inscribed in the written text.

Like other feminists, materialist feminists are concerned with the importance of culture and symbolic systems to women's oppression. This emphasis on culture and on the symbolic, indeed, is one of the central contributions of the women's movement—along with the black liberation movement that preceded it—to political thought.[17] What a materialist-feminist criticism tends to mean, therefore, aside from more work than one was used to as a formalist reader, is more focus on the nonliterary than in most other feminist criticisms and more power granted to culture and the symbolic than in much traditional Marxist criticism (that is, in much Marxist criticism written before the 1970s.)

For the materialist-feminist critic this analysis of culture frequently takes the form of discussing ideology and of performing ideology critique. The term *ideology,* a staple of critics working within a Marxist tradition, or at least of critics familiar with that discourse, has been defined in various ways. Terry Eagleton, for example, in *Marxism and Literary Criticism,* provides a familiar working definition: ideology is "that complex structure of social perception which ensures that the situation in which one social class has power over the others is either seen by most members of the society as 'natural' or not seen at all" (1976, 5–7). Ideology, however, is not simply determined by the economic and the political but may be thought of as having a relative power and life of its own. What this means, in the words of Annette Kuhn, is that "ideology is not necessarily a direct expression of ruling-class or gender interests at all moments in history and that at certain conjunctures it may even move into contradiction with those interests" (1978, 63). Ideology, then, is not a set of deliberate distortions imposed on us from above but, rather, a complex and contradictory system of representations (discourse, images, myths) through which we experience ourselves in relation to one another and to the social structures in which we live. Ideology is a system of representations through which we experience *ourselves* as well, for the work of ideology is also centrally to construct coherent subjects: "The individual thus lives his or her subject-ion to social structures as a consistent subjecti-vity, an imaginary wholeness" (Coward and Ellis 1977, 71).[18]

In materialist-feminist and in much current Marxist work, as the preceding paragraph suggests, ideology is granted "relative autonomy" from economic conditions.[19] This tendency to view ideology as functioning somewhat independently parallels and has been shaped by poststructuralism and by the tendency of feminist criticism as a whole to examine the power of images, myths, cultural ideals, and linguistic categories over our thinking and, therefore, our lives. But where a materialist-feminist criticism still insists upon the intersection of public written representation with other (discursively constructed) forms of the social and historical, reminding us that "we can't look to culture alone to liberate us," much current feminist criticism implies the *primacy* of the psyche as the essential terrain on which political struggle is waged, viewing public written representation as the *major* armaments in that struggle (Barrett 1980, 112). Gilbert and Gubar's *Madwoman in the Attic*, for example, a rich and perceptive work, focuses almost entirely on the entrapment of women in male-authored literary or mythic constructs and on women's literary resistance and, in so doing, emphasizes the power of the literary, a power that materialist-feminist criticism would seek to qualify (1979, xxi, xxii, 16).

Nina Auerbach's perceptive *Woman and the Demon* takes a similar tack when it suggests that freedom from Victorian constructions of womanhood, which, she argues, granted women an almost mythic power, produced more loss than gain for women of the 1880s and 1890s, despite the fact that middle-class women of this period had greater access than before to work, higher education, and the vote (1982, 222). In a sense Rachel Brownstein's *Becoming a Heroine* takes this propensity in feminist criticism and in other book-loving females as its study, but, while Brownstein points out some of the dangers for feminists of giving too much power to literary texts, of seeking to become the "integral self" that literary heroines represent, she does not see inattention to other social and economic conditions as one of the problems (1982, 295).

Clausen has questioned this tendency to valorize the transformation of the symbolic as in itself a sufficient political transformation. Citing examples from criticism by Adrienne Rich and Judith McDaniel, she writes that "it is hard to come away from a reading of the works in which the passages I have quoted appear without feeling that for these writers the politics of language actually take prece-

dence over other politics" (Clausen 1982, 24). Clausen feels that the
blurring of distinctions in the United States between literary prominence and political leadership has meant that "sometimes feminist
theory and practice have been skewed in the direction of too much
stress on the transformation of the spoken and written, too little
emphasis on other sorts of transformations which a political movement that hopes to succeed in the material world must undertake."
Or perhaps (she goes on) the causal relationship goes the other way:

> Perhaps it is in part precisely because of what a Marxist would
> call an "idealist" bent in our movement, a weakness for mind-
> over-matter approaches, that poets have emerged as leaders.
> This would help to account for the popularity of such feminist
> thinkers as Mary Daly, who has focused almost exclusively on
> language as a vehicle for feminist transformation. (1982, 24, 25)

Those in leftist communities who have emphasized the relative
autonomy of ideology have done so for different reasons from those
of feminist poets and critics such as Rich and Daly, who have emphasized the primacy of language. For Rich and Daly the transformation
of language seems virtually synonymous with social change. Some
Marxist critics, in contrast, have emphasized the autonomy of ideology in an effort to avoid the pitfalls of a narrow economic determin-
ism, but they have remained within a leftist materialist tradition that
critics such as Rich have explicitly attacked. Michele Barrett, however, feels that elements of the leftist community in England have
privileged discourse almost to the exclusion of anything else and
have gone too far. Her criticism of these elements for overprivileging
discourse echoes Clausen's criticism of cultural feminism in the
United States:

> There is a world of difference between assigning some weight
> to ideological struggle and concluding that no other struggle is
> relevant or important. The relief with which the intellectual left
> has seized upon these ideas as a justification and political legiti-
> mation of any form of academic work is in itself suspicious and
> alarming. For although I would not dispute the political
> significance of such activity, a distinction must be retained be-
> tween this form of struggle and the more terrestrial kind. Are

we really to see the Peterloo massacre, the storming of the winter palace in Petrograd, the long march, the Brunswick picket, as the struggle of discourses? (Barrett 1980, 95)

Materialist-feminist criticism, then, while acknowledging the importance of the written, the spoken, and, more broadly, the discursive and symbolic as a site of political activity, is skeptical of the isolation of it from other ways of thinking about struggle. While suspicious of an unrelenting focus on the symbolic and of theorizing for its own sake, however, materialist-feminist criticism is committed to theory and to symbolic analysis. It is particularly committed to the difficult task of exploring the making of meaning as a struggle over resources and power and the changing relationships among public written representation and discursively constructed social conditions and relations.[20]

One need not, however, use the terms and categories of a specifically Marxist discourse to undertake a materialist-feminist reading of history and literary texts. Barbara Christian's *Black Women Novelists* is a nuanced discussion of the connections among the "public dream" of the plantation as happy family, the relations among whites and blacks, male and female, in the antebellum South, and the portrayals of black women in the literature of the era. Christian's "public dream" is essentially synonymous with what we mean by "ideology"—a structure of perception that helps maintain a particular set of social and economic relations at a particular juncture in history and that centrally shapes the way all of us (for Christian, antebellum southerners, black and white, male and female) construct our own subjectivities (1980).

This sustained attention to the complex ways in which many kinds of discourse and discursively constructed social conditions intersect, and this concern with the process of historical change, means that materialist-feminist work also aspires to be "dialectical."[21] One of the key aspects of both dialectical art and dialectical film criticism, as defined by materialist-feminist film critic Julia Lesage, is that they elucidate "the relation of human consciousness to historical and social process and change." Thinking dialectically has as its end "elucidating its object, the concrete world, in terms of that world's all-sidedness, contradictions, determinations and necessities. Dialectics explains process and change." This way of thinking, as Lesage asserts in her analysis of the Cuban film *One Way or Another*, locates movement, transformation, and process in the incompatible development of two necessarily related entities (such as labor and capital) or in the contradictory aspects of a single phenomenon—such as the contradictory implications of women's work in the domestic sphere. Lesage acknowledges that feminist art and criticism cannot directly change power relations, cannot alone effect the transformation of relations between public and private spheres that she sees as one goal of feminism. But she argues that the greater self-awareness and imaginative capacity fostered by such art, when linked with a social movement, is an essential component of revolutionary change (Lesage 1979, 1, 2, 5, 8).

This kind of dialectical, as opposed to a static and linear, mode of analysis distinguishes feminist-materialist criticism from many other feminist criticisms. It is a way of seeing that prompts us to locate in the same situation the forces of oppression and the seeds of resistance, to construct different groups of women in a given moment in history simultaneously as victims and as agents. One might compare, for example, Sonja Ruehl's analysis of Radclyffe Hall's *The Well of Loneliness* with Catherine R. Stimpson's discussion of the same novel in "Zero Degree Deviancy" (Ruehl 1986 [1982]; Stimpson 1981). Both Ruehl and Stimpson locate their analysis historically, analyzing the origins of "lesbian" as a social category and tracing the emergence of homophobia as a historical phenomenon. But whereas Stimpson finds in the novel a tale of damnation that helped, along with the controversy surrounding its publication, to "submerge, screen, and render secondary" a more progressive consciousness about the possibilities of lesbian experience (1981, 372), Ruehl argues that the novel is the start of a "reverse discourse," a process by which the

> category of lesbianism derived from a medical discourse is firstly adopted and then eventually transformed by those defined by it. . . . Hall's intervention can be seen as a contribution to the formation of . . . political self-consciousness; later generations of lesbians were to follow her model of public identification even if they repudiated her particular views. (1986 [1982], 170).

Thus, the novel, in accepting and propagating the rigid segregation of lesbians, of "congenital inverts," as a separate group, lays the basis for a "later political solidarity." The moment of extreme categorical rigidity, which is codified in the text, becomes a moment of birth and change as well.

Materialist-feminist work demonstrates this capacity to embrace contradiction. It interprets history not as an assortment of facts in a linear arrangement, not as a static tale of the unrelieved oppression of women seen as an undifferentiated group or of their unalleviated triumphs, but, instead, as a process of transformation. It reads the act or artifact of cultural production as an intervention in that process, usually with contradictory implications of its own. This dialectical approach enables us to view ideological struggle and social change as possible, for through it we may examine and understand the tensions and contradictions within both ideology and society.

Literature and culture, of course, as sites at which ideology is produced and reproduced, are also sites on which the outlines and contradictions of ideology may be made visible. Materialist-feminist criticism does not assume that literature and cultural production "reflect" history in a simple mimetic moment. Since history is "in" representation, there can in fact *be* no reflections of it. Literature, rather, draws upon various ideological productions of history or discourses about history to make its own production. What a literary text does not say, therefore, becomes as interesting as what it does say. The discourse suppressed tells us as much as the discourse expressed, for omission throws the margins of a text's production into relief, allowing us to see the limits and boundaries, the gaps and incoherences, of what it posits as "the real."[22] In Catherine Belsey's essay on "Constructing the Subject," the scientific rationality of the Sherlock Holmes stories is revealed as ideological precisely because the stories mystify and thereby marginalize what they cannot at this moment in history subject to a positivist approach: the sexuality of white middle-class women. "The presentation of so many women in the Sherlock Holmes stories as shadowy, mysterious, and magical figures," Belsey argues, "precisely contradicts the project of explicitness . . . and in doing so throws into relief the poverty of the contemporary concept of science" (1986, 62). Since positivism is linked with classic realism as a literary mode, and since the haunted treatment of genteel women in the Holmes stories defies a positivist approach, they ultimately undermine the very mode in which they are cast as well as the very assumptions they ostensibly endorse. Here the gaps

and fissures, the incoherence, of the text are located as signs of contradiction and breakdown in a larger social imagination.

Materialist-feminist work also frequently emphasizes the way
in which a text is reproduced by its readers, and reproduced differently in changing historical situations. There is an articulation here
between currents in materialist criticism and the body of work
known as reader theory or reader-response criticism. Not all reader-
response criticism is materialist or feminist, but this approach does
accommodate a materialist and feminist perspective more easily
than many other tendencies in contemporary criticism. What is in-
herent in the text is not a fixed verbal structure but, rather, in
Belsey's words, "a range of possibilities of meaning" (1986, 20).
Specific interpretive communities, to use Stanley Fish's helpful
phrase, will share common readings of the same text, but different
interpretive communities, with different (constructed) experiences
and different understandings of aesthetic and cultural codes, will
produce widely different meanings (Fish 1980).

Janice Radway, for example, in "Women Read the Romance,"
argues that feminist critics who have written about the romance and
its supposed effect on readers come from interpretive communities
utterly different from those of romance readers themselves. Thus,
they have produced different meanings from those produced by
readers whose behavior they are trying to explain: "They have sev-
ered the form from the women who actually construct its meaning
from within a particular context.... This assumption has re-
sulted...in an incomplete account of the particular ideological
power of this literary form." Radway herself uses ethnographic meth-
ods to investigate how a specific community of female readers interprets the texts of romance novels (1983, 53–78). Since readers in
different historical situations will produce different versions of the
text, each with its own political effects, the political functions of a
text will change along with the goals and strategies of readers in
different historical situations.[23]

Although most feminist criticisms regard literary canons as socially constructed, materialist-feminist criticism is more likely to insist
on the social and historical relativity of aesthetic standards.[24] It also
analyzes the interest that those standards serve, considering race,
class, sexual and national identity, and gender. Paul Lauter, for example, in "Race and Gender in the Shaping of the American Literary

Canon," examines the historical process by which white female and also black writers were eliminated from the American literary canon in the 1920s. He shows how our very conceptions of literary history are derived from the experience of elite white men, at the expense of all women and at the expense of men of color. Our traditional focus on Puritanism, for example, has "led to the study of the ideology by which a narrow group of male divines construed and confirmed their dominant roles in New England society," distorting, among other things, our understanding of "colonial family and sex life, and the systematic extermination of 'Indians'" (Lauter 1983, 453).

In materialist-feminist criticism, moreover, a more sustained focus on the process of social and discursive construction means that the category of literature itself is more consistently regarded as a historical construction and that literature is apt to be seen in relation to, rather than in isolation from, other forms of discourse such as advertising or film. From this perspective cultural production and discourse at large are opened up to a radical revision in which representation on every level is seen as a site of struggle over resources and power and in which literary—now cultural—studies become a mode of intervening politically in a much wider field.[25]

This emphasis on cultural studies as opposed to purely literary ones has characterized much contemporary Marxist and post-Marxist criticism. Yet the commitment of materialist-feminist criticism to articulating the relation between discourse, ideology, and other material conditions in terms of gender, race, and sex enforces a somewhat different view of literature and culture from that maintained by traditional and post-Marxist criticism and by other feminist criticisms as well. Materialist-feminist criticism differs from most Marxist criticisms in emphasizing difference among women and among men and in foregrounding the extent to which cultural discourse is gender and race as well as class specific. It gives emphasis, say, to the way in which white, middle-class women are constructed differently from white, middle-class men, refusing to see them as just one more bourgeois subject. Criticism that is solely within a traditional Marxist or socialist perspective fails to account for the specific oppression of women within gender relations and gender ideology. Thus, it is likely to register the desire for autonomy or achievement in a white, middle-class woman's text as one more example of bourgeois individualism.

This is true, for example, of Eagleton's *Myths of Power*, which, despite its theoretical recognition of women's oppression, is, in its readings, a prefeminist book. Failing to grasp the radical thrust in Bronte's *Villette* of Lucy Snowe's desire for self-fulfillment, the book dismisses her desire as "an overriding need to celebrate bourgeois security" (Eagleton 1985, 71). A materialist-feminist reading, in contrast, might register the socially transforming potential of a desire for autonomy and achievement even in a white woman of the middle class. Thus, Cora Kaplan's essay on *Aurora Leigh* cautions that we should remember that "the description of Aurora as an independent author living and working in London is possibly the most 'revolutionary' assertion in the poem, the item most likely to corrupt the daughters of gentry" (1986b, 158).

But if materialist-feminist criticism differs from traditional Marxist criticism in its emphasis on gender, race, and sex relations, and the transforming potential of even white middle-class female desire, it also differs from other feminist criticisms in its refusal to valorize that desire almost to the exclusion of other values. The work of a materialist-feminist, indeed, reminds us how inadequate that desire is as a single response to a social formation fractured by inequities not only of gender but also of race and class. Many feminist readings of *Villette*, for example, tend to focus exclusively on and to give unmediated value to Lucy's desire for self-development or to the text's fantasies of power. Materialist-feminist readings like that of Mary Jacobus, in contrast, qualify the value we can give to such individualist longings: "The drive to female emancipation, while fueled by revolutionary energy, has an ultimate conservative aim in successful integration into the existing social structure" (1979, 57). Similarly, Kaplan reminds us that "the strains in *Aurora Leigh* which prefigure modern radical feminism are not only those which appear in the heroine's relation to art, but those which surface in Barrett Browning's manipulation of her working-class figure, Marian Erle" (1986b, 140).

Materialist-feminist criticism, moreover, differs from many other feminist criticisms in its assumption that men as well as women are ideologically inscribed. It is likely, therefore, to examine the similarities between men and women of the same class or racial group as well as their differences. And where much white middle-class feminist criticism refers to men and male domination as if all men really were the free agents proposed by bourgeois and patriarchal ideology, materialist-feminist criticism stresses men's relative imprisonment in ideology and in other material conditions. In so doing, it works against the notion that men are a monolithic, totally different, and controlling "out-there."

While materialist-feminist criticism, like other feminist criticisms, examines men's imagined superiority, real dominance, and undeniable exploitation of women, it views men not in terms of gender ideology and relations alone but also in terms of class, racial, national, and sexual ideologies and class, racial, national, and sexual relations. Thus the relative powerlessness of working-class men, gays, and men of color, and men's divisions from one another along the lines of racial, class, or sexual identification, become part of the critical perspective.[26] Since women, too, are seen in terms of class and racial ideologies and relations, they appear in situations of relative power to others. Since their ideological investment in these relations is generally explored, women are not viewed as an unalloyed force for good, as a unified sisterhood, or as having a unified nature. Women, like men, appear divided from one another, enmeshed not in a simple polarity with males but, rather, in a complex and contradictory web of relationships and loyalties.

Materialist-feminist criticism by women of color is most likely to be conscious of the racial and class differences among women, although obviously not all criticism by women of color is explicitly materialist. Some of it, for example, posits a universalized "black woman" or "Chicana"—concepts that reflect an inclination toward cultural nationalism that runs parallel as a tendency to cultural feminism.[27] Some of this work explores, often quite usefully, the textual integration of myth, folklore, and oral tradition, but it tends not to interpret the political implications of this contemporary recuperation of traditional materials or to consider in depth the changes in social fabric that demarcate the time of origin from the moment of adaptation.[28] In contrast, work by critics such as Barbara Smith (1977), Mary Helen Washington (1979a, 1979b), Barbara Christian (1980), Gloria Hull (1982), Elaine Kim (1982), Sherley Anne Williams (1982), and Gloria Wade Gayles (1984) offers rich interpretations of the dynamic of oppression and liberation as lived by women of color and as mediated in literature.

A materialist-feminist criticism, in short, a criticism that explores

the relation of knowledge and power, by combining feminist, socialist, and antiracist perspectives, is likely to assume that women are
not universally the same; that their relations are determined by race,
class, and sexual and national identification; that social change cannot be conceived of in terms only of women who are white and
privileged; that integration into existing social structures is not likely
to liberate even white, middle-class women; and that unequal relations of power in general must be reconstructed, not only for women
but for all the oppressed.[29] It is because of assumptions such as these
that a materialist-feminist criticism is more likely than a simply feminist one to analyze working-class and other nontraditional litera-
tures[30] or, like Deborah Rosenfelt's analysis of Tillie Olsen's relation
to feminism and the Left, to consider women writers as agents in
social transformations not limited to those determined by gender
alone.

    This emphasis on transforming power relations that extend be-
yond those of gender accounts for the fact that materialist-feminist
criticism is more likely to think of working not just in opposition to
but in relation to men. The transformation of all power relations
cannot be achieved without such collaboration—however difficult
this alliance has often proved for individual women in their political
and personal lives, however awkward and painful the contradictions.
A materialist-feminist critic, therefore, is less opposed to using male-
authored theories for her own purposes than many cultural feminists. She is likely to perceive such labor less as a form of "ladies'
auxiliary" than as "fruitful alliance" or revolutionary activity—though
she is likely as well to wince at the persistence in such theories of
assumptions about gender that she has long ago learned to question.

    For these reasons, too, a single focus on women and women's
culture may be of less interest as a critical imperative to materialist-
feminist than to other feminist work, although other feminist criticisms have begun to express restiveness with prolonged residence
in communities of women. To a materialist-feminist, writing about
men may well seem essential both to an understanding of women
and women's culture and to an understanding and transformation
of our gender systems. A focus on women's culture, moreover, might
well seem to work against an exploration of the real class, racial,
sexual, and national divisions among women, divisions that must be
encountered before any real sisterhood, that is, any sisterhood that

extends beyond women who are white, Western, and middle-class, can be established. Bonnie Thornton Dill, for example, calls for the "abandonment of the concept of sisterhood as a global construct based on unexamined assumptions about our similarities" and calls for a "more pluralistic approach that recognizes and accepts the objective differences between women": such an approach, she continues, "requires that we concentrate our political energies on building coalitions around particular issues of shared interest, through joint work on another's needs and perceptions and begin to overcome some of the suspicions and mistrust that continue to haunt us" (Dill 1983, 146). Perhaps a more compelling critical imperative should be to explore communities of women, to compare the experiences and visions of female writers of color and white, working-class writers with the experience and visions of women who are white and middle-class.[31]

Like other feminists, materialist-feminists have long understood that the ideas and structures we wish to transform are not just "out there" but also within our movement and within ourselves. It is the desire to account both for the *persistence* of oppressive structures and ideologies *and* the possibilities of change that has led some materialist-feminist critics to explore psychoanalytic theories of the way in which gender is constructed on the most basic levels of consciousness. In Britain and France, particularly, the theories of Jacques Lacan, despite criticism of their lingering phallocentrism, have seemed helpful. According to Lacan, it is in language that we come to consciousness, that a sense of identity is imposed upon us, for language offers us a series of subject positions, a range of discourses in which we are constructed. In the language of bourgeois society, in particular (according to a materialist-feminist application of Lacan), we are constructed as fixed, autonomous, and coherent beings. In reality, however, the ego is "necessarily *not* coherent," for language cannot fully formulate unconscious desire. Because there is no continuity of psychic life, according to Jacqueline Rose, "there is no stability of sexual identity, no position for women (or for men) which is ever simply achieved." This, indeed, is at the bottom of what Rose sees as an affinity between feminism and psychoanalysis, the "recognition that there is a resistance to identity which lies at the very heart of psychic life" (Rose 1983, 11, 9).

In addition, the range of positions from which we are liable to grasp ourselves as subjects may be incompatible. White, middle-class women, according to Belsey, "participate both in the liberal-humanist discourse of freedom, self-determination and rationality and at the same time in the specifically feminine discourse offered by society of submission, relative inadequacy and irrational intuition." This, in turn, creates intolerable pressures and may lead to a number of responses from falling sick to seeking "a resolution of the contradiction in the discourses of feminism" (Belsey 1986, 50).

As Rose suggests, however, this construction of women's identity is in some ways a difficult one to maintain for women whose goal as feminists is to establish a strong sense of ego and identity. It is equally difficult for women trying to forge a political movement to feel at home with a relentless focus on the social construction of knowledge, on the necessary partialness of truth (Rose 1983, 5–21). For if we accept the logic of a materialist position, how can we privilege materialist-feminist readings of culture and history over readings that are not? Do we end up with a world that is ultimately arbitrary and inscrutable and in which one discourse (and therefore one mode of action) is as good as any other? How do we extricate ourselves from an intellectual and political pluralism that validates no higher value than that of the right to choose?

Changing the world requires a set of values and perceptions that we can commit ourselves to, a set of values, moreover, that is compelling to others. If as feminists together we are to transform our readings of culture and the ideological and material structures of our social life, can we afford to designate ourselves as one more critical approach in the marketplace of ideas? On the other hand, how do we confront the necessary partialness of knowledge and the reality of diversity within the women's movement, for it is these realities, too, that Kolodny's notion of "playful pluralism" was meant to address? (1980, 19).

One answer, perhaps, is that absolute knowledge is not necessary for political action, since absolute knowledge is impossible and yet political transformation has taken place. A second is that seeing knowledge as a form of historical practice does not mean we cannot lay claim to degrees of its relative coherency and completeness while maintaining all the while a vision of its inescapable provisionality, its ongoing process of being transformed (Ryan 1982, 213). This is a view of knowledge that befits a women's movement that is changing and diverse and that has consistently imposed challenges to what has seemed to be "nature." It is a view of knowledge that leaves room for unity and diversity as well. Unity, at any rate, cannot finally be achieved through appeals to some final knowledge, for the provisionality of our vision assaults us at every corner. Nor can we expect to rally women against a monolithic male out there. Men and male domination are too complex. Nor, finally, can unity be achieved through idealist proclamations about woman's nature and her unmediated capacity for good. For as Ann Rosalind Jones asks, in her analysis of French poststructuralist feminism, "if we concentrate our energies on opposing a counterview of Woman to the view held by men in the past and present, what happens to our ability to support the multiplicity of women and the various life possibilities they are fighting for in the future?" (1981, 256).

A materialist-feminist analysis offers a more complex and, in the end, less tragic view of history than one polarizing male and female, masculine and feminist; constructing gender relations as a simple and unified patriarchy; and constructing women as universally powerless and universally good. A materialist-feminist analysis actively encourages us to hold in our minds the both-ands of experience: that different groups of women at different moments in history have been both oppressed and oppressive, submissive and subversive, victim and agent, allies and enemies, both of men and of one another. Such analysis prompts us to grasp at once the power of ideas and literature, their importance as a focus of ideological struggle, and their simultaneous embeddedness in and difference from other material conditions of our lives. Such an analysis, of course, does not offer us simple answers. Indeed, the uncompromising complexity of its vision may sometimes discourage those who long for certainty and simplicity. Nonetheless, in its insistent inclusiveness, in its willingness to embrace contradictions, materialist-feminist analysis seems to us the most compelling and potentially transformative critical approach to culture and society, offering us theory for our practice as we work toward a more egalitarian world.

NOTES

We are deeply indebted to Elizabeth Abel, Jane Caplan, Darlain Gardetto, Cora Kaplan, Paul Lauter, Caryn Musil, Leslie Rabine, and Judith Stacey for their thorough and incisive readings of this introduction. Although we have not always followed their suggestions, we have been consistently challenged and educated by them.

1. See, for example, the essays of Florence Howe (1984) on both interdisciplinary women's studies and feminist literary criticism; the essays in Hoffman, Secor, and Tinsley (1976), *Female Studies VI;* and the essays in the first anthology of feminist literary criticism, Koppelman Cornillon 1972.

2. For early feminist work that reflects these assumptions to varying degrees, see, for example, Millett 1970; Howe 1972; Fetterley 1978; Robinson 1978; Belsey 1980; Rich 1979; Christian 1980; Kolodny 1980; Spender 1981; and Hull and Smith 1982.

3. For three accounts of the changing and unchanging relation between developments in literary criticism and dominant modes of thought in England and America, see Belsey 1980; Eagleton 1983; Lentricchia 1980. See Kolodny 1980 for an interesting account of the way in which critical training socializes us to dominant notions of literary value.

4. This generalization is not, of course, universally applicable, nor is this critique new. See, for example, the essays in Kampf and Lauter 1972. According to Eagleton (1983), "It is the *extremism* of literary theory, its obstinate, perverse, endlessly resourceful refusal to countenance social and historical realities, which most strikes a student of its documents, even though 'extremism' is a term more commonly used of those who would seek to call attention to literature's role in actual life." Eagleton sees this reduction of literary criticism to a private contemplative act as an equivalent in the literary sphere "to what has been called possessive individualism in the social realm" (196–97).

5. For early feminist critique of formalism, see the essays in Koppelman Cornillon 1972, especially that of Stoker; and the essays in Donovan 1975, especially Donovan's afterword. For critiques of many forms of poststructuralism as a new variety of formalism, see Lentricchia 1980, Ryan 1982, and Lauter 1984.

6. Kolodny (1980), for example, writes of "our reticence at taking full responsibility for the truly radicalizing premises that lie at the theoretical core of all we have so far accomplished" (7). Howard (1983) continues this feminist self-critique by citing Kolodny's work as one example of the way in which feminist criticism has not always lived up to its own potential. Writing of black feminist criticism in particular, Hull and Smith (1982) note that "much of the current teaching, research, and writing about Black women is not feminist, is not radical, and unfortunately is not always even analytical" (xxi).

7. Archetypal feminist criticism, for example, posits countermyths of female heroes and female quests that oppose the "life-denying myths of female inferiority, virginity, romantic love, and maternal self-sacrifice" without, as a rule, concerning itself with the social conditions that generate or impede the imagining and experiencing of "heroism" in daily life. Such work includes Christ 1980, Pearson and Pope 1981 (quote from p. 48), and Pratt 1981.

Even feminist criticism focused on a particular historical era often tends toward a history of ideas, even when the *conflicts* among ideas are foregrounded. Brilliant as their readings are, these are the implied histories of much of Gilbert and Gubar 1979 and of Auerbach 1982 as well as of such fine and often politically impassioned readings as Kolodny 1975 and Fetterley 1978.

8. Both de Beauvoir (1961 [1949]) and Millett (1968) have influenced this tendency, although the works of each have materialist dimensions. De Beauvoir offers something close to an essentialist vision of women's nature, Millett a universalist vision of patriarchal power, both of which lock women in our places. Rich (1979, 49), who has contributed significantly to our critical understanding of the importance of material circumstances, including race and class, in women's lives, has tended increasingly to posit an omnipresent and ahistorical patriarchy whose "creative energy" she insists is running out (9).

9. See Jones 1981 on the way in which *femininité*, as defined by French feminists such as Irigaray and Cixous, implies these assumptions. Among the most eloquent American writers who express these assumptions are Rich 1979 and Griffin 1978.

10. Kate Ellis (1984, 115) sees this trend in regard to the construction of the masculine, or of men, in the discourse of the antipornography movement. This discourse, she argues, surrounds us "with a monolithic world 'out there,' a patriarchal system of which all the parts are equally developed and fit perfectly together." Such discourse, she continues, despairs of the process of "finding fissures and weak points in the armor of patriarchy." The same trend is apparent in some sectors of the peace movement. See, for example, Warnock 1982; and see Echols 1983 on the tendency to simplify and celebrate women's nature in the discourse of the antipornography movement and of cultural feminism generally: "If the source of the world's many problems can be traced to the dominance of the male principle, its solution can be found in the reassertion of the female principle" (442). See Rosenberg 1984 on this same tendency among sectors of the peace movement: "The gender gap has been taken as evidence that women are inherently more benevolent and caring than men, and even as heralding the long-awaited appearance of a force large enough to form a major peace movement" (453). See Jones 1981, finally, on both tendencies in French poststructuralist feminism.

11. Although socialist feminists view some of the actions springing from cultural or radical feminist analysis as wrongheaded, it would be erroneous to argue that the cultural or radical feminist tendency has led to withdrawal from the political sphere. Indeed, in a recent forum among four women associated with socialist feminism—Barbara Haber, Judy McClean, Barbara Epstein, and Deirdre English (1985)—all the participants except English expressed the belief that radical and liberal feminists had been more engaged and successful as activists than leftist feminists and that the connection of radical feminists with the peace movement suggests a displacement of socialist feminists to the periphery of political struggle. According to English et al. 1985: "Socialist feminism has become part of academia and has been killed

by it" (107). Yet socialist feminists (including these four) have been active in the peace movement, in anti-imperialist work, in the struggle for reproductive rights, and so on. The question here is, What kind of *theory* can best guide us in the long run?

12. For early work on the construction of gender and subjectivity, see Rubin 1975; Dinnerstein 1976; Coward and Ellis 1977; Chodorow 1978; Flax 1978; Belsey 1980; Haraway 1983. For later work, published after this essay and emphasizing the multiple, fluid, performative nature of a discursively organized gender, see, among many others, de Lauretis 1984, 1986, 1987; Martin and Mohanty 1986; Riley 1988; Smith 1988; Fuss 1989; Butler 1990; and Hennessy 1993.

13. See Ryan 1981; Walkowitz 1980; and Weeks 1981.

14. For early work, see Cade 1970; Moraga and Anzaldúa 1981; Davis 1981; Jones 1982; Kim 1982; Hull and Smith 1982; Dill 1983; Lugones and Spelman 1983; and hooks 1984. For work published after this essay, see, among others, Allen 1986; Spelman 1988; Asian Women United 1989; hooks 1989, 1990, 1992; Anzaldúa 1990; Hill Collins 1990; DuBois and Ruiz 1990; Williams 1991; and Sandoval 1991.

15. For early work, see Rapp 1979; Rosaldo 1980; Atkinson 1982; and the early essays in Spivak 1988 and 1990. For work published after this essay, see, among others, Behar 1990; Mohanty 1988; the later essays in Spivak 1988 and 1990; Kondo 1990; Mohanty, Russo, and Torres 1991; Mani 1992; and many of the essays in Gluck and Patai 1991 and in Behar and Gordon forthcoming.

16. The assumptions of much feminist criticism about literature and culture are quite parallel to the assumptions of the new Marxist cultural theory. See, for example, Bennett 1979; Jameson 1987; Ryan 1982; and Eagleton 1983.

17. On this contribution of feminism, see Kuhn 1982: "One of the major theoretical contributions of the women's movement has been its insistence on the significance of cultural factors, in particular in the form of socially dominant representations of women and the ideological character of such representations, both in constituting the category 'woman' and in delimiting and defining what has been called the 'sex/gender system'" (4). See also Howard 1983: "Long before Marxists began citing Gramsci on hegemony and construction of consent, feminists recognized the political importance of cultural analysis" (5). In fact, the black liberation movement preceded the women's movement in this regard. The motive behind the simple and effective slogan "Black is Beautiful" was to change the way black people are *seen* by the dominant culture and, consequently, the way they *see*, that is, construct, themselves.

18. For a more current definition, see Hennessy 1993, 14.

19. Most of this draws on the work of Louis Althusser (1971). See also Barrett 1980; Howard 1983; and Kuhn 1982.

20. See, for example, the scholarship of those who have contributed to The Feminist Press's reprint series and its Women Working Series, including

Mary J. Buhle, Florence Howe, Nancy Jo Hoffman, Elaine Hedges, and Tillie Olsen.

21. As a contemporary reader of this essay pointed out, it employs a broad notion of dialectical criticism that in Marxism "depends on a concept of contradiction internal to a system and argues that such contradiction can only be read symptomatically since contradiction works by making its agonistic logic disappear." This is a just observation, but defining dialectical and contradiction in this more rigorous way would have made the terms inapplicable to many forms of the criticism we wished to include as "materialist-feminist." Our political objective in 1984 was to intervene in mainstream feminist criticism, to push it in different directions by describing a materialist-feminist work that was not strictly Marxian. Our sense of what could count as materialist-feminist work, especially in the United States, and our strategy vis-à-vis mainstream feminist criticisms impelled us to less strictly Marxist understandings of some traditional Marxist concepts. Were we to write this essay now, our strategies and analysis would be different on many levels.

22. See Belsey 1979; and Barrett 1980. Both draw from the work of Macherey (1978) and from the work of Eagleton (1978). For a helpful summary, see Bennett 1979, 106–12.

23. See also Bennett 1979, 136–37; and the essays in Tompkins 1980.

24. Some materialist-feminist positions on the canon are more uncompromising in their insistence on the relativity of aesthetic standards. See, for example, Barrett (1980, 105), who suggests that the preoccupation with aesthetic value has been detrimental to feminist criticism in that it has reproduced "the assumption that aesthetic judgment is independent of social and historical context." Vicinus (1974, 1) argues that "our definitions of literature and our canons of taste are class bound; we currently exclude street literature, songs, hymns, dialect, and oral storytelling, but they were the most regular forms used by the working class."

25. See Howard 1983: "It is, in its mild way, a political undertaking just to advocate viewing works of high culture as part of a wider field of signifying practices, rather than as unique creative achievements" (25).

26. Olsen 1978 is an excellent example of an analysis that treats the "circumstances" of men's as well as women's lives historically and sympathetically.

27. The essays in Gayle 1971 provide the clearest articulation of black cultural nationalism in criticism. The influence of this tendency survives in some of the essays and interviews in Bell, Parker, and Guy-Sheftall 1979. The conclusion of Dance 1979 exemplifies this universalizing tendency of cultural nationalism:

As we look back over the history of the Black American mother, we see that she emerges as a strong Black bridge that we all crossed over on, a figure of courage, strength, and endurance unmatched in the annals of world history. She is unquestionably a Madonna, both in the context of being a savior and in terms of giving birth and sustenance to positive growth and advancement among her people. It is she who has given birth to a new race; it is she who has played a major role in bringing a race from slavery and submission to manhood and assertiveness. (131)

28. For example, Allen (1975) offers an important interpretation of American Indian values and myths, one related to Allen's perspective as a cultural feminist, without suggesting any essential differences between pre-Columbian tribal life and contemporary Native American experiences; Ordoñez (1982, 19) suggests that texts by Toni Morrison, Estela Portillo, Maxine Hong-Kingston, and E. M. Broner explore "a particular female and ethnic socio-historical identity," but Ordoñez focuses exclusively on the "text itself" as "both the means and embodiment of modifying and reshaping female history, myths, and ultimately personal and collective identity."

29. In a paper delivered at a women's conference, for example, Barbara Smith remarked:

The question has been raised here whether this should be an activist association or an academic one. In many ways, this is an immoral question, an immoral and false dichotomy. The answer lies in the emphasis and the kinds of work that will lift oppression off of not only women, but all oppressed people—poor and working-class people, people of color in this country, and in the colonized third world. If lifting this oppression is not a priority to you, then it's problematic whether you are a part of the actual feminist movement" (Hull and Smith 1982, xxi).

30. See, for example, Vicinus 1974; Lauter 1980; and the essays on letters and diaries in Hoffman and Rosenfelt 1982.

31. Christian (1980, 240) speaks of the need to recognize variations among black communities and to avoid "a homogenized picture of Black culture."

History as Usual?
Feminism and the
New Historicism

(1987)

To write about new historicism is to encounter a problem of definition and of self-definition as well. What do we mean and what are we to mean by this term? The critical assumptions and techniques currently identified with new historicism inform a variety of critical practices, but new historicism, as articulated by those who identify themselves as "new historicists" or cultural materialists or materialist-feminists, produces readings of literature and history that are as marked by difference as by sameness.[1] Are new historicists to be identified as a new school and new historicism itself as a unique, and hot, commodity, fast becoming the "newest academic orthodoxy" and promising to secure for those who can produce it the power to define a new inner circle of acceptable critical practice? (Montrose 1986, 7). Or is new historicism to be defined as a set of widely held, loosely postmodernist assumptions and strategies that may be given very different articulation depending on the politics of the practitioners? Both possibilities for the term are in the air.[2]

Many of the postmodernist assumptions[3] currently identified with new historicism, of course, are intensely familiar. The new historicism, we are told, generally assumes that there is no transhistorical or universal human essence and that human subjectivity is constructed by cultural codes that position and limit all of us in various and divided ways. It assumes that there is no "objectivity," that we experience the "world" in language, and that all our representations of the world, our readings of texts and of the past, are informed by our own historical positions, by the values and politics that are rooted in them. It assumes that representation "makes things happen" by "shaping human consciousness" and that various forms of representation ought to be read in relation to one another and in relation to other social practices such as "events." All are assumptions that inform and have informed a number of critical practices for many years.[4]

The constructions of history attributed to new historicism are also familiar from other contexts. There is the notion that history is best told as a story of power relations and struggle, a story that is contradictory, heterogeneous, and fragmented. There is the (more debated) notion that hegemonic power is part but not all of the story, that history is a tale of many voices and forms of power, of power exercised by the weak and the marginal as well as by the dominant and strong. Even the technique of "cross-cultural montage,"[5] or the juxtaposition of literary, nonliterary, and social texts, is not unknown. In the afternoon, indeed, when I am no longer writing this essay, I sit at my well-laden desk, patiently working through a series of connections between essays on political economy, parliamentary debate, women's manuals, medical writing, novels, and the formation of the modern state. It's enough to make me think I'm a new historicist too.

But self-definition in this case is contingent upon the larger process of defining what new historicism itself is to mean. And in the histories of new historicism that I have read so far, whether new historicism is defined as a school or more loosely as a set of assumptions and techniques given different articulation depending on the politics of the practitioners, my own entry into these same assumptions and techniques has only partially been mapped, my own articulation of them barely hinted at. New historicism, we are variously told, comes out of the New Left, out of cultural materialism, the crisis of 1968, and the postmodernist response to that crisis, out of poststructuralism as part of that response, and most particularly out of the historiography of Foucault.[6] New historicism is also to be read as a reaction to the formalism of structuralism and poststructuralism and as a response to the perception that American educational institutions and culture, in particular, with their focus on technological and preprofessional training, are rapidly forgetting history. New historicism, finally, has also emerged out of fear on the part of literary critics that they are being further marginalized within their culture (Montrose 1986, 11). Since this fear is particularly well grounded for literary critics in the United States, where the study of literature has been "trivialized," according to some, by the conservative institutionalization of the latest reigning orthodoxy, deconstruction, the upshot in this country at least has been a nagging sense of "professional, institutional, and political impotence" (Felperin 1985, 219; Montrose 1986, 11).

Some parts of these histories, of course, do tell the story of my own trajectory into the assumptions and strategies attributed to new historicism. The New Left and cultural materialism, in particular, are central to my own construction of my heritage, both intellectual and political. But barely alluded to in most of the histories of new historicism so far is what was in fact the mother root—the women's movement and the feminist theory and feminist scholarship that grew from it. I am struck by the relative invisibility of feminist theory and scholarship in these histories of origin, in part because I spend the afternoons revising histories of the nineteenth-century British middle class, writing British middle-class women into history in new ways, writing the history of the ways in which these women, along with men, have constructed culture too. I spend the afternoons, that is, working against the remnants of my own immersion in middle-class nineteenth-century cultural codes and, in particular, that remnant of my immersion in an ideological division of the world into "public" and "private," into a world of men and a world of women, into a world in which labor was seen as labor and a world in which real labor was in most respects invisible, into a world that was equated with history and a world that lay just beyond history's margins.

But I am also struck by the relative invisibility of feminist theory and feminist labor because histories of "the new historicism" are beginning to remind me of more recent accounts of the past, chronicles describing the advent of "theory," say, or of postmodernist thinking or, more particularly, of deconstructive thought. Even the most current and retrospective histories of deconstruction, for example, histories that are really reflections on what deconstruction has meant and what it can mean in the future, are given to representing feminist theory as the simple receptor of seminal influence. One recent book on deconstruction, for example, describes feminist criticism as if it had never generated a good idea of its own. "Fluctuating between a para-marxist materialism, a post-freudian metaphysics of the female, and a semiological critique of cultural patriarchy," feminist criticism, it asserts, "has yet to generate a theory or a practice comparable to those of its models in intellectual coherence or explanatory power" (Felperin 1985, 209).

Feminist histories of deconstruction are, of course, more generous than that, but even there feminist theory may be represented as a womb containing the "seeds" of (usually white, male-authored) deconstructive thought. Since what we are often told in these histories, however, is that deconstruction is essential or crucial to feminists because it enables them to think ideas that were already being thought before the advent of poststructuralist theory (how the categories of nature and culture are artificial, for example, how there is a gap between biology and gender), I am left with my suspicion that those seeds were really ova all along.[7]

Feminists, therefore, the very women who spent their afternoons writing women into history, have sometimes participated in this erasure of their own intellectual traditions, have been too ready at times to accept the position of the marginalized "other," especially when so fashionably presented as in the past few years.[8] But as Jane Marcus has observed, "She who writes history makes history"—and, I would add, she whose activities are visible as history has a kind of power that she whose contributions are placed at the margins of history does not. Changing "history," I am convinced, depends on having that first kind of power; it comes from speaking somewhere other than from the margins, although speaking from the margins has its uses too.[9]

For feminists, of course, the point is not only to make ourselves heard, to make others see us as in history; the point is to see ourselves in history too, to give value to our own work, our own theory, our own heritage, and so to give value to ourselves.[10] Self-confidence, after all, not only feels good; it is also a form of power. But writing feminist theory and scholarship into the histories of critical movements or traditions can have other agendas too. In this case, writing feminist work into the history of new historicism, as I intend very briefly to do, may mean participating in the definition of what new historicism is going to mean—not, I hope, a new orthodoxy but, rather, a set of assumptions and strategies that may be articulated differently by those with different politics. At least the visibility of feminist literary and historical practice will constitute another argument for defining new historicism in this broad way. A second goal in writing feminist scholarship and theory into the history of new historicism is to participate in raising consciousness about the potential social effects of different articulations of new historicism—in this culture at this particular moment.[11] A third goal is not just to suggest that feminist articulations exist but also to argue that feminist articulations of the assumptions and techniques associated with new historicism can produce histories that are different in ways that should prompt all of us to think beyond some current understandings of history and social change, understandings that often inform less feminist versions of new historicism.

Feminists, to begin this revision of the histories of new historicism, were around in the late 1960s too, as some historians of postmodernist thinking have noted. Like French philosophers, moreover, whose "disillusion" with totalizing theories is often cited, feminists had their own breaks with global theories, at least with those that were male centered (Eagleton 1983, 149).[12] Disillusion, however, is not the word I would choose to characterize the emotional quality of that break. For white women like myself anger is more like it, anger at having been taken in—and yet also exhilaration, a sense of political possibilities. For many of us it felt like a moment of empowerment, not of impotence. Dominant and totalizing theories were not objectively true; they were informed by male bias. Our identities had been culturally constructed, and we were not alone.

I begin in this way, of course, because it reminds us of how certain "postmodern" insights *seemed* (in those early days at least) to come straight out of critical reflection on our own experience,[13] out of the contradictions we felt between the different ways we were represented even to ourselves, out of what we had learned to see as the inequities in our situations. The conditions in which these new constructions of our lives could emerge had been prepared for in many ways—by the struggles and critical discourses of civil rights and of the New Left, to name two. But it was the grounding of critical insight in constructions of our own personal experience that made critiques of objectivity and analyses of the construction of the subject so passionately a matter of concern; it was our (constructed) subjectivity after all! It was our passion that put them first on the theoretical agenda. It was the processes of intimate, personal change, moreover, in ourselves first and then in others, the need to believe in the possibility of further change, a very personal commitment to bringing change about, that made and has made many feminist articulations of these postmodern ideas different from other more fashionable articulations, different and more useful, more redolent of "explanatory power," at least to those engaged in struggles to change the world. But more of that later.

There can be no question, I think, that the women's movement, along with the civil rights movement and the rise of the New Left— and I shall speak now from a mainly American context—were centrally important to putting a critique of "objectivity," an assertion of the political nature of ideas, theory, representation, an investigation of the cultural construction of subjectivity, of the relations between the personal and the "political," on the theoretical agenda. Terry Eagleton, one of the few male theorists to write the women's movement into the history of postmodernist thought and poststructuralist theory in particular, suggests that the movement from structuralism to poststructuralism was in part a response to the "political demands" of the women's movement for a theory that would put representation and the construction of subjectivity at its heart (1983, 149). Unfortunately this still makes it sound as if women may want theory but men produce it or else bring the theoretical bacon home. And one is left, all over again, to ask why feminist theory has been so hard to see, especially for men, and even for men in sympathy with feminist politics. Why, in particular, one is prompted to inquire, has feminist theorizing of concepts such as the construction of subjectivity or sexuality received relatively little attention outside of feminist communities while the same concepts as theorized by elite white men have been duly and widely received with a sense of discovery and great seriousness?

I suspect one answer is that most men "doing theory" did not read the earliest theory to emerge from the women's movement and that many white men, doing theory even now, do not read feminist theory, history, or criticism to anything like the degree to which they read theory and history and criticism by men themselves.[14] (Here is another example of how the discourse of the less powerful does not escape the consequences of its own production.) Another answer I suspect is that feminist theory, and history and criticism, are informed by politics, by political visions that are still not easily received, that are uncomfortable, and that therefore lack "explanatory power." I also suspect that much of the earliest feminist theory and even some later theory had a situated quality, maintained a sense of connection to (discursively constructed) feeling and personal life, was marked by an absence of jargon (that was part of its effort to build political community), which made it sound like something different from what men were doing when they were doing theory. Like housework, women's theoretical labor seemed part of life and therefore not like "real," that is male, theoretical labor at all.[15]

At the same time, of course, feminist intervention in the way we perceive knowledge, the subject, representation, social relations, has been profound and on some level impossible to ignore, even if not universally dignified as "theory." One multiply articulated move in relation to that intervention has been to appropriate it as white and male-authored and in the process to dilute and/or change its politics. This has sometimes been true even of those men whose sympathy with feminist politics one also believes in.[16]

Whatever the reasons, however, I do not think feminist theory has lacked visibility because it has not been "good," because it has not brought world-changing insights to the fore. (What is theory, after all, "good" for?)[17] And feminist theorizing of the kind that paved the way for various other postmodern critiques has been part of the women's movement from the beginning.[18] *Sisterhood Is Powerful* (Morgan 1970), in fact, in its critique of androcentric discourse, reads like a compendium of the postmodernist assumptions currently attributed to new historicism in its new historicist and cultural materialist varieties—no universal humanity; subjectivity culturally constructed; bias and politics in our readings of literature, our readings of history; representation and social relations interacting; representation, in particular, having material effects, producing our very bodies. In its juxtaposition of cultural texts, moreover, its reading of the cultural codes that inform academic disciplines, advertising, sex manuals, popular culture, diaries, political manifestoes, literature, political movements and events, and feminism itself (in the critiques here of white feminists by feminists of color), *Sisterhood* also sounds like a blueprint for the methodology attributed to and recommended as new to those who would do new historicism. (I hardly need to point out to anyone who was doing feminist work in the early 1970s that this blueprint also reads like a syllabus for early versions of Introduction to Women's Studies 101).

Of course, the critique that white feminists made of dominant, androcentric theories, that what passed for "necessary, universal and ahistorical truths" were "contingent, partial, and historically situated, was not immediately applied to their own discourse (Fraser and Nicholson 1988).[19] As many historians of feminist theory have noted, white feminists in particular often generated large social theories that claimed to identify key causes and central features of a sexism that operated across cultural lines. But if these theories tended to be falsely universal and essentialist, they were not purely so, as Linda Nicholson and Nancy Fraser have noted. White, middle-class, heterosexual feminist theoreticians lived from the beginning with "the political pressure to acknowledge difference among women," a pressure very frequently brought to bear by poor and working-class women, by lesbians and by feminists of color in particular (Fraser and Nicholson 1988, 26).[20] As women's studies was institutionalized in the 1980s, moreover, the growing fund of feminist scholarship meant that feminists could "regard their enterprise more collectively, more like a puzzle whose various pieces are being filled in by many different people and less like "a construction to be completed by a single grand theoretical stroke" (28). The trend in much mainstream white feminist theorizing from the 1980s on has been away from grand theory toward an emphasis upon the historically specific. In the late 1980s, indeed, unified notions of "theory," "feminism," "women," and "gender" are being thoroughly critiqued and rearticulated as multiple and internally different. The core terms of feminism are now in flux.[21]

My point, of course, is not that early feminists created postmodernist thinking, even their own brand of it, singlehandedly, that they didn't learn from Marxism and later from cultural materialism and male-authored poststructuralist theory. My point, in part, is that feminists and particularly feminists of color, contributed in a crucial way to perspectives that have been largely appropriated and popularized as an implicitly white, male-authored postmodernism or as postmodernism without footnotes.[22] My point is also that feminist theorizing produced different versions of postmodern assumptions, versions that significantly alter what *postmodernism* should mean. These are versions that allow for human agency and social change and that, therefore, I would argue, are not just strategic for persons hoping to make the world a better place but also have greater explanatory power. Because commitment to a political agenda has informed feminist theorizing generally, feminist challenges to the notion of objectivity have not usually led to relativism, to the assumption that, since "truth" is inaccessible, anyone's truth is as good as any other. Many feminist theorists, in fact, are at work on defining a "feminist version of objectivity," "situated and embodied knowledges," as Donna Haraway puts it, which recognize the provisionality and multiplicity of local knowledge but which maintain that it is possible to give truer accounts of a "real" world and to translate knowledges among very different communities (1988, 583, 580).[23]

The point of such theorizing, moreover, is not always theory as usual, is not always making it big on the intellectual exchange, although feminists these days are scarcely immune to careerist motives. Basically, the point is also collective and political, is making sense of, facilitating, and justifying what we want to do, which is, in part, to forge "webs of connection, called solidarity in politics and shared conversation in epistemology" (Haraway 1988, 584). The point, that is, has not always been to facilitate power moves in a game of rhetoric but, rather, to smooth the way for learning "to see faithfully from another's point of view" (583). By the same token, feminist insistence that the subject is constructed has not generally led to the belief that subjects are culturally determined or that human agency in changing the world is for the most part illusory. The emphasis has been upon defining a self that has continuities but that is at the same time multiple, contradictory, and in process—in process, moreover, not for the sake of being in process but for the sake of the connections and unexpected openings such a conception of self makes possible.

Feminist politics and feminist theories, then, along with the black liberation movement and its discourses and the New Left have helped generate postmodern assumptions about objectivity, the construction of the subject, and the cultural power of representation currently identified with new historicisms, but they have articulated those assumptions in ways that are significantly different from what have become the more dominant, the more fashionable, the less politicized articulations. (In this respect feminist theory and, as I will suggest, feminist literary and historical work are closest to cultural materialism within the spectrum of practices currently identified with new historicism.)

Feminist historians, of course, helped to generate, as they later drew upon, feminist postmodern assumptions in their development of feminist history. The earliest women's history, for example, sought to challenge traditional, masculinist, objective history by making women, as well as men, visible—by writing women, as well as men, into a history that in most other respects was informed by traditional, thus masculinist, categories and historical periods and that reflected masculinist values. Early on, however, many historians of women, although they drew heavily upon the work of social historians before them, saw that writing women into history might well mean that traditional definitions of history would have to change.[24] One way in which feminist history, in conjunction with social history, began to change what history was going to mean lay in making the construction of subjectivity, representation, role prescription, ideas, values, and psychology a point of focus. The difference between feminist versions of this emphasis and social historical versions or cultural materialist versions (which came later) was that subjectivity was gendered as well as raced and classed and that women as well as men were at the heart of historical study.[25] In feminist history, moreover, sexuality and reproduction, both constructed, both seen as sites of power and struggle, were central to the subjectivity of both men and women.

Like social historians, for the most part, feminist historians operated out of a commitment to social change. Thus, they were alert to the ways in which hegemonic ideologies and oppressive social relations might operate unevenly across an entire culture. One early focus in feminist history, for example, was on the gap between role prescription and women's actual behavior, which might register "role anxiety" or "role resistance" (Smith-Rosenberg 1975b, 189). Feminist history also explored the multiplicity of women's roles and identities and the intersections and contradictions between the roles and identities imposed by race, sex, and class.[26] The tensions and contradictions between these roles and identities implied that hegemonic ideologies were far from being unified or static and suggested that anxiety, resistance, and power struggles in general might have many local sites.[27]

Power, indeed, was a term that feminists in many fields, literary criticism included, were reconceptualizing in the early 1970s. Power as dominance was opened up to include power as ability, for example. Venerable insights about the dependency of the powerful upon the weak were revived, and resistance was defined more subtly than before—as silence, refusal to participate, power in disguise.[28]

This work on power developed alongside the work of Foucault, whose historiography was to have a later influence on feminist work.[29] But while feminists have drawn upon Foucault, they have also been insistent, for the most part, upon identifying those who have power and asserting the agency of those who have less. These differences, of course, are in keeping with the different ways many feminists have theorized postmodern versions of the subject and of knowledge.

Defining women's power as the power of resistance, however, keeps women in a purely reactive role while assigning the construction of culture, as usual, to men. An important challenge to this finally male-centered view of history and culture has come out of the important work on "women's culture." Although the domestic sphere, in particular, might be seen as a place in which women are subordinate and minister to children and to men, it has also been explored as a place in which women enjoyed considerable status and power, in which they bonded to other women, entered into homo-erotic relationships, defined and participated in exclusively female rituals, maintained a sense of community and love, articulated different values from those of men, criticized dominant values, maintained communities of resistance to racist and economic oppression, and/or prepared themselves for entry into the "public sphere" as volunteers and as activists seeking social change.[30] Different groups of women, it has been suggested, may have participated in and helped construct dominant or shared cultural forms while maintaining a culture of their own, just as women may have shared versions of history and social relations with their men while operating inside of their own oppositional representations of the world.[31] As these once invisible persons, relations, institutions, ideologies, and cultures have become visible, have become part of history, their relation to the already visible, the larger economic and political structures usually assigned to men, have been and are being explored.[32] This exploration has often involved a species of cross-cultural montage in which (once) untraditional sources, women's letters and diaries, wills, women's manuals, women's novels, even séances, are juxtaposed with more traditional and public texts—parliamentary debate, sociological writing, medical literature, news reports, and medical journals.[33] Some of this work has maintained that gender relations and gender struggle have been as significant as struggles over class and race and/or that the values and powers of some women along with some women's representations of subjectivity and the world have had as great, if not greater, force than that of men in more dominant positions in constructing culture.[34]

What has emerged in feminist history, then, are versions of history that overlap with those currently attributed to new historicism in their focus on the cultural power of representation, on the construction of subjectivity, on local sites of power and power struggle, in the use of cultural montage (both in work by literary critics and by those more than self-trained as historians.) But the most consistent difference still lies in the degree to which gender relations, gender struggle, women, and women's activities and power are seen as in history, are seen as having significant or causative relation to the political and economic realms traditionally associated with men.[35] This difference, as I will later suggest in more detail, makes for other differences in what history looks like, makes for differences in what is included as history in the first place, differences in what constitutes a historical period. It makes for differences in the degree to which hegemonic power is imagined as monolithic and anonymous or as composed of many voices. It makes for differences in the degree to which hegemonic ideology and power are seen as stable and impervious to change and the degree to which they are imagined to be internally divided, unstable, in constant need of construction and revision, creating the conditions that make social change and the agency of the weak possible.

It has taken me awhile to get to feminist literary criticism in these notes toward the revision of the histories of new historicism because feminist literary critics, whatever other communities they have belonged to, have generally written out of the multiple, various, and interdisciplinary communities of feminist and ethnic studies scholarship, journals, conferences, or enclaves within conferences. It is largely because of their relation to these communities, moreover, communities that were generated by the larger configurations of the women's movement and movements for national liberation, that feminist literary critics have most often been interdisciplinary and interested in questions of history in at least three ways: (1) Feminist definitions of literature in England and America have drawn on assumptions, partially generated by women's and ethnic studies and by Marxist, post-Marxist, and poststructuralist theory, about the political power of cultural representation and have usually situated literature in relation to "history," in relation to some construction of men and women's lives. Works of literature, like other forms of representation, that is, such as literary canons and criticism itself, are imagined to be the products of specific historical situations, are imagined to act upon specific cultures in return and to affect power relations, to be political. In this sense feminist critics have always been centrally interested in questions of history and can hardly be included among those whose sense of history may be said to have been "renewed." (2) The questions that feminist critics bring to texts have to do at least with gender and gender relations—and, increasingly, with the coconstruction of gender, race, sexual identity, and class—and are informed by theories about gender, race, sexuality, and class in all their multiple significance for subjectivity, social relations, and the rest of history. These theories, which come out of many fields—history, anthropology, sociology, psychology, linguistics—are cross-disciplinary. (3) Some strands of feminist literary criticism have been characterized by readings of literary texts placed in relation to a construction of social relations in a specific culture, a construction often pieced together from secondary sources and always partial but not always self-consciously explored for the lines of its partiality. And/or they have been characterized by readings of literary texts placed in relation to readings of nonliterary and social texts—specific events, social developments, and so on.[36]

That more feminist literary criticism has not been historical in this third sense has to do with several features of the American literary critical scene: it has to do with the formalist training that many of us received (as opposed to our self-training, which has been interdisciplinary); it has to do with our membership, or our desire for membership, in communities that are more formalist and that have had more status and power; it has to do with the difficulty of "doing" literary criticism and history and theory, which—let us be honest—is a bloody lot of work; and it has to do with the difficulty of practicing that kind of literary criticism in a critical climate that has rewarded very different kinds of endeavor. (If the potential popularity of new historicism does anything for feminist literary and historical criticism, it will be, I hope, to further sanction the kind of criticism that many feminist critics have been doing all along.)

Although most feminist understandings of literature imply the kind of literary and historical work that I have just described, the feminist critics who have tended most to practice it are those whose commitment to questions of history has been doubly forged by ties to Marxism, socialism, cultural materialism, or the Left or leftist currents in struggles for racial or national liberation. I refer (in "Toward a Materialist-Feminist Criticism") to these ties and elements as defining elements of a materialist-feminist criticism, but the multiplicity of political ties I have just listed suggests the necessary plurality of reference that this term must bear, just as the multiple terms for leftist politics suggest both the various and tension-filled ways in which feminists have defined their relation to the Left and the various ways in which male leftists have renegotiated their own relation to traditional Marxism over the last fifteen years. If there ever were a time, politically speaking, for embracing a feminist version of subjectivity, with its provisional and multiple identities and political positions, this is it.

Although materialist-feminist criticism has drawn heavily from Marxist and cultural materialist theory and criticism, it may still be differentiated from the latter, in both its American and British forms, by the degree to which it takes gender, often coconstructed with race, class, and sexual and national identities, as organizing categories in history. This is still true, despite the fact that many cultural materialists are more attuned to issues of gender and race in their work than they used to be. Materialist feminism, I would argue, is not quite to be subsumed under the title cultural materialism, as Dollimore suggests, nor is it to be subsumed under his more general category materialist criticism. As with the women's movement, the separate— but also plural, multiple, open—identity of feminist and materialist-feminist criticism still has political usefulness and significance.[37]

The practice of something like materialist-feminist criticism, which begins at least with Kate Millett's *Sexual Politics* (1970), has been overdetermined (and the critics overworked) by the flood of theory—poststructuralist, cultural materialist, feminist, antiracist (the categories are not discrete)—that has emerged in the last fifteen years. This ingestion of theory and history and sociology and anthropology has meant that materialist-feminist practice has changed and grown more self-conscious, more theoretical. Its interest in history has been refined. Perhaps its weariness of formalist orthodoxy has also deepened along with the weariness of those whose interest in history can more properly be said to have been "renewed." Its sense of its task has grown more taxing as well, and so has its resentment, I would add, of the relative invisibility of its labors. A reflection that surfaces rather frequently during these days of retrospection and taking stock, during these days between the seeming decline of one orthodoxy and the potential rise of the next, is that feminist scholars and theorists read one another and male theorists, while "they" do not by and large read "us." "We" have two jobs, and "they" have one. Women as usual! No wonder we're interested in history!

As part of my effort to make feminist literary and historical work more visible and in an effort to investigate the potentially transformative effect of feminist politics and analysis on some of the points of focus, critical assumptions, and techniques currently identified as new historicist, I want briefly to consider three complex and often brilliant works on white, nineteenth-century, British, middle-class culture, the culture on which I also write, which share many of the assumptions and employ many of the practices attributed to new historicism. Each is particularly marked, for example, by a focus on the cultural force of representation and by an interest in the intersection of literary, written but nonliterary, and social texts. Each also employs the strategy of cross-cultural montage by which literary texts are read in relation to parliamentary debates, women's manuals, medical writing, legal codes, and, more occasionally, events or other nonwritten "material developments." Despite their shared assumptions and techniques, however, each book produces history differently. The differences, I will suggest, have much to do with their different relation to traditions of feminist scholarship and feminist politics. The three texts are Catherine Gallagher's *The Industrial Reformation of English Fiction: Social Discourse and Narrative Form, 1832–1867* (1985), Nancy Armstrong's *Desire and Domestic Fiction: A Political History of the Novel* (1987), and Mary Poovey's *Uneven Developments: The Ideological Work of Gender in Mid-Victorian England* (1988).

Uneven Developments is most explicitly identified with materialist-feminist politics and theory. *Desire and Domestic Fiction* is identified with feminist and Marxist politics and with politically informed criticism generally—Armstrong is less comfortable than Poovey with the strategy of situating herself in one group more than in another. *The Industrial Reformation of English Fiction* does not *explicitly* situate itself in any politics, although its definition of terms and its conception of history suggest its indebtedness to cultural materialist theory and to Foucault.[38] Given the different ways these texts are placed in traditions of theory and politics—and there is always a gap between the political heritage of a text and the politics of an author, site of discourse, though she may be—there are predictable differences in the degree to which gender and gender relations play a role in history. There are related differences in the degree to which gender is seen in relation not only to class but also to race and imperialist ventures and the degree to which a focus on multiple axes of analysis helps produce histories that break with and raise further questions about familiar historical paradigms and categories.

In one important way, at least, each of these books breaks with the ideological division of the world into "public" and "domestic," man and woman, class and gender, and so works within a central insight of feminist theory, that public and domestic are not separate but intersecting. Each book, that is, examines the way in which a mode of structuring gender relations informed the discourse in which white, middle-class, British women and men imagined the relations of class. This investigation, of course, is only part of Gallagher's study, the larger focus of which is a series of paradoxes (of which the public-private division is only one) that centrally informed the "Condition of England" debate. In Armstrong and Poovey the division of the world into public/private, culture/nature, man/woman, mind/body is explored across a wider range of middle-class debates and institutions and is discovered to be a crucial, and in Armstrong, the primary, organizing principle of middle-class ideology and culture as a whole. In this important way, by placing gender along with class at the heart of nineteenth-century, British, middle-class culture, Armstrong and Poovey radically break with the Marxist and cultural materialist models of history from which they also draw.

In all three texts, as one might suspect, the centrality or marginality of gender as an organizing category in history informs what counts as history in the first place, informs the choice of discourse and of event. Gallagher, for example, writes of discourse traditionally seen, and seen here, as having to do with class, the Condition of England question and parliamentary debate over reform. She also focuses on texts that she looks at in their relation to class issues—novels, reports, parliamentary speeches, antislavery writing, women's manuals. Although a way of structuring gender (the division of the world into domestic and social) enters into discourse over class, gender, and race relations, the intersection of class, race, and gender are not really points of focus in this book.[39] Armstrong concentrates on texts that are centrally informed by a focus on gender—manuals for and often by women and novels that Armstrong sees as an essentially feminine genre in the nineteenth century. She then draws on sociological writing and parliamentary debate over the Condition of England question to suggest how a fully elaborated discourse on gender began to structure debates traditionally seen and seen here as having to do with class. Neither race relations nor imperialism are discussed. Poovey, finally, focuses on a system of differences in the form of binary oppositions—legal subject/nonsubject, property owner/commodity, etc.—which were based on the "natural" differences between women and men. She then examines this system as it informed five controversies in the 1840s and 1850s and suggests the complex and shifting ways in which this system of differences was deployed and the multiple ways in which constructions of gender intersected with constructions of class and also race, imperialism, and national identity.

Both Poovey and Armstrong, then, deal centrally with gender, but their strategies for placing gender in history are rather different. Armstrong's strategy is to suggest the way in which texts informed by discourse on gender acted upon representations of class, modern institutions, and class relations. Armstrong also suggests how centrally, how dominantly, a way of structuring gender was a feminine affair, feminine in the sense of being authored by women, or by men writing in feminized genres, and feminine in the sense that the way middle-class women's subjectivity and sexuality were constructed became a model for the way in which men's subjectivity and sexuality were constructed later on. Thus, the first modern individual, modern because her value lay in personal qualities rather than in rank, was a female—a radical break with traditional histories of the "bourgeois subject." Desire for this ideal female, moreover, unified the middle class before the middle class officially existed. The moral authority attributed to this figure, the authority of the heart, became the authority of the middle class as a whole, while the officially feminine and apolitical power that was attributed to her, the power of moral surveillance, became the mode by which modern institutions were to operate and the mode by which the problem of the working class, newly redefined as domestic and as sexual, was to be resolved.

Although Armstrong does not specifically situate herself in the traditions of feminist history, she certainly pursues two of its central projects, the exploration of women's cultural power and the investigation of the connection between what have been seen as separate spheres—public and domestic. Thus, Armstrong tries to "defamiliarize the division of discourse that makes it so difficult to see the relationship between the finer nuances of women's feelings and a capitalist economy run mainly by men," and she insists that "those cultural functions which we automatically attribute to and embody for women—those, for example, of mother, nurse, teacher, social worker and general overseer of service institutions—have been just as instrumental in bringing the new middle classes into power and maintaining their dominance as all the economic takeoffs and political breakthroughs we automatically attribute to men" (Armstrong 1987, 26).

This is an extremely significant challenge to traditional political history, one that should open up our investigations of the British nineteenth-century past, and yet the challenge is uneven. For Armstrong chooses to focus on the way that representations of gender informed representations of class, shaped class relations, and structured an otherwise male-dominated public sphere. But she chooses not to explore the way in which representations of gender also shaped gender relations and women's as well as men's lives. And she chooses not to consider the way in which representations of class structured gender relations as well or the ways in which class and gender relations intersected with the construction of race and imperialist ventures. One effect of these choices is that the book seems to privilege the traditional, political, class-centered history that it also self-consciously and very powerfully challenges.

Poovey has a different strategy for widening our sense of what social relations are to count as history. The strategy is to examine controversies in which gender is prominently at work, controversies that, by and large, have been invisible in traditional political history—debate over the use of chloroform in childbirth; the debate over the Divorce and Married Women's Property bills; debate over governesses, the entry of women into the labor market, and women's sexual aggression; debates over the professionalization of literary writing and the development of nursing as a profession for women. Poovey then explores the ways in which systems of difference based on sex were deployed within these controversies to structure both class and gender relations and sometimes race relations and colonial policy. One effect of this strategy is to place discourse over gender less centrally at the service of class relations, to give gender relations a more autonomous historical significance, to suggest the global stakes of both British class and gender relations, and in this way to suggest a more thoroughgoing redefinition of what relations count as history.

The division in these works over the degree to which class and gender relations finally count as history is tied to another split over the implied definition of significant "events." In the works that most privilege class, events (especially those that stimulate controversy) and what one used to call "material conditions," without quotation marks, remain fairly white, British, and male centered. This correlation, I would argue, between a focus on class and a focus on male-centered material developments, suggests the persistence of a tendency still familiar in much cultural materialist work, a tendency to define class in terms of white men's economic and social relations with one another, a tendency to define class consciousness in terms of the same men's values and interests, and a tendency to associate the development of class identity with events in which men played the central role or in which women's participation has not been fully explored.[40]

Thus, in *The Industrial Reformation of English Fiction* events or social developments are largely male and/or are those that have been traditionally seen, and are seen here, in terms of white British men— antislavery and proslavery agitation (represented here by men), the Ten Hours movement, Chartism, factory bills, and parliamentary reform. The labor of working-class women and children also enters in but is seen largely as a class issue, and in this instance, I think, class has not been redefined to reflect women's values, interests, and social relations. In *Desire and Domestic Fiction* as well, although Armstrong's consciousness about the masculine nature of traditional political history is very high, and although she does redefine middle-class consciousness so as to make middle-class feminine values and feminine modes of representing subjectivity and sexuality not only central but dominant, events are still largely masculine, or their traditional association with men is not explicitly questioned. Thus, Armstrong deals with the introduction of machines, working-class protest, the development of Chartism, factory reform bills, and the development of a national curriculum. There is no thrust beyond these national concerns, moreover, to more global considerations, such as, for example, the discourses of British imperialism.

In Poovey, however, there is a more thoroughgoing effort to widen our assumptions about what events or social developments count in history. Many of the events or material developments in this text have to do with women and women's activities: women's entry into the labor force is a point of focus, as are feminist organization and agitation over property reform and the development of female professions (governessing and nursing) and of female institutions (women's colleges and the Governesses' Benevolent Institution). The parliamentary bills that Poovey investigates also have to do with women and more generally with gender. *Uneven Developments,* moreover, also makes reference to more global connections such as the realization of England's imperial ambitions, a traditionally class-focused and masculine development, as it is usually read, but one that this book reads in relation not only to class but also to gender and in relation not only to men but also to women's activities, in this case the development of nursing as a female profession. The goal, therefore, is not to propose a completely alternative history to the class-centered or nationally centered histories of the past but, instead, to suggest the lines along which we will have to rethink what, in fact, significant events are and how historical periods might be newly delimited if multiple axes of analysis—gender, race, and colonialism as well as class—are to be written into our histories.

The most politically charged differences in the histories produced by these three texts have to do with the ways in which, and the degrees to which, social change is imagined to be possible and the degree to which the conditions for social change are imagined to be a function of contradictions in discourse itself or of human agents struggling for power or liberation. In works so focused on the cultural power of representation, these distinctions are largely expressed in the way that representation itself is represented. Although the differences I shall discuss are undoubtedly overdetermined by complexities I can't hope to account for here, they may also be related, I would argue, to the following political considerations: the degree to which each author situates herself as author of her text within feminism, seen as a vital political movement, and the degree to which she thereby expresses a political predisposition to see social change and human agency as possible; the degree to which not only class but gender and other axes of analysis are made central to history; and the consistency with which each text takes other kinds of material conditions into account in its analysis of representation.[41]

The Industrial Reformation of English Fiction, for example, which challenges the usefulness of the term *bourgeois ideology*, with its implication of a unified class position, is scrupulous in laying out the many different and overlapping strands of discourse and intellectual tradition that informed the Condition of England debate. These strands of discourse, moveover, have their origin in groups taking political positions—over slavery, over the plight of the working class. But the book's strategy is to focus on a set of central paradoxes–freedom/determination, public/private—that variously informed each strand and that then had impact upon the form of the English novel. Thus, the initial focus is on a multiplicity of voices and positions, but the voices tend to blend together and to lose political affiliation as the recurring and fairly homologous sets of paradoxes are examined. Ultimately, the emphasis of the book falls, to a large degree, on logical and internal contradiction within representation, rather than on, say, even local struggles between interested groups to control representation itself. Although the debate over political representation "impinged" on the "theory and practice of literary representation," change, in the construction of representation and culture, emerges to a large degree from logical contradictions in representation itself and from a generalized need for new principles of cohesion (Gallagher 1985, xiii). Change does not emerge for the most part from human agents acting out of specific, discursively organized historical positions and with historically determined politics.

Gallagher's complex analysis of representation is always impressive, but the book's focus on the formal properties of representation, its lack of continuing attention to the social position of the various speakers, works against a consideration of what might be read as politically charged differences in the way that different speakers articulate what would otherwise seem to be the same set of ideas. Representation, therefore, although it is beset by internal logical paradox, appears more cohesive, more stable, more resistant to change than it otherwise might. This muting of what might be read as politically charged nuance is also tied to the absence of gender relations as a point of focus in this work. This second connection is, for me, most dramatically evidenced in Gallagher's discussion of two ways of thinking about the division between public and domestic, a way of structuring the world that informed much of the debate over the working class. With her usual thoroughness Gallagher lays out two traditions, that of domestic ideology and that of social paternalism. Domestic ideology, she mentions in a footnote, was an essentially female tradition and was developed in manuals by women for other women. In contrast to the discourse of social paternalism, domestic ideology does not see the family as a metaphor for social relations and therefore does not look for the replication of familial hierarchy in the public sphere. Rather, in domestic ideology family and society are contiguous, are related but different.

What Gallagher outlines here are two ways of seeing the world that might be read as having significant political implications. Upper- and middle-class men look for the extension of familial hierarchy into the public sphere, and middle-class women do not. One narrative, moreover, that of social paternalism, is briefly imagined to be informed by a gendered position: elite men sought to control women's independence as well as the independence of the working class in imagining the world as a patriarchal family with themselves at the head. But the other narrative, women's narrative, is given no politics to speak of, although the political nature of this feminine representation of the relation between public and domestic trembles just below the surface. Gender politics, for example, seem particularly striking in some of the women's factory novels that Gallagher explores, novels that are informed by fantasies of women rescuing factory children and setting up female-headed households in Rhenish castles, novels informed by fantasies in which well-meaning men are largely impotent while men in power are often villains. What Gallagher's text points to but does not investigate, in part because gender relations and the different social positioning of subjects in ideology are not consistent points of focus, are deep-seated and potentially destabilizing tensions within middle-class ways of imagining the world.

In Armstrong change comes very centrally from struggle, largely between classes and over control of representation: "In the model of culture I am proposing, culture appears as a struggle among various political factions to possess its most valued signs and symbols" (Armstrong 1987, 23). The middle-class, for example, comes to power when it wins "the intellectual war to determine the definition of culture itself" (162). The effects of representation, of course, are not neatly defined by class interests but are more complex and less predictable than this would suggest, and yet middle-class ideology in this book is a fairly unified and therefore fairly stable affair. There is, for example, little sense of tension between men in subgroups of the middle class and little sense that the different social and economic situations of middle-class women and men might have affected their relation to middle-class ideology differently. Here is where greater attention to other "material conditions" might once again have altered the representation of representation itself.

Armstrong, of course, has deliberately chosen not to deal with the power relations of gender and with women's oppression, wishing instead to focus on "the contrary political affiliations for which any individual provides the site," in this case the affiliations of class (Armstrong 1987, 24). This is an important emphasis, and it has not been pursued much in literary critical work. But one effect of this single focus is to reaffirm some traditional equations, the equation of "political resistance," for example, with matters of class (252). Until late in the book, with the introduction of Dora and Woolf, women have class politics, but they scarcely have any politics of gender. Cultural struggle and politics itself, therefore, remain interclass issues. Middle-class ideology is implicitly challenged from without, by upper-class and working-class modes of representing the world, but it is internally fairly stable, beset neither by tensions between middle-class men differently positioned in the social formation nor by tensions between middle-class women or between women and men.

Poovey's conception of middle-class ideology, of its relative stability and vulnerability to change, is significantly different from Armstrong's and from Gallagher's, although she draws on insights from both. Her focus, I have suggested, is upon a system of difference based on the "natural" divisions of sex and articulated as a series of polar oppositions that imply and order one another and that centrally inform Victorian middle-class ideology and institutions. Since the oppositions depend on the subordination of one term, they are internally unstable, and it is in part because of this internal instability that middle-class ideology "was both contested and always under construction; because it was always in the making it was always open to revision, dispute, the emergence of oppositional formulations" (Poovey 1988b, 4). But this system of middle-class ideas and institutions was also "developed unevenly," hence the title of the work. It was uneven in the sense that it was "experienced differently by individuals who were positioned differently within the social formation" (by sex, class, race, for example), and it was uneven in the sense that it was "articulated differently by the different institutions, discourses, and practices that it both constituted and was constituted by" (4).

It is in large part, I would argue, that Poovey more consistently takes material conditions other than public written representation into consideration that she imagines women positioned differently inside middle-class ideology than men, that she also imagines some men positioned differently from other men and some women positioned differently from other women. Thus, the conditions for social change, as constructed by this book, are not merely a function of internal ideological contradiction but of social positioning and human agency as well. That agency, moreover, is informed not just by the concerns of class but also by the concerns of gender and sometimes race. Hence, dominant ideologies are multiply fractured by contradictions and tensions, many of them internal to the middle class and many of them experienced within the most intimate and most psychically charged relations of middle-class culture—those of family and home. In some ways, of course, Poovey's construction of middle-class culture belongs to an earlier historical model than Armstrong's, a model according to which men construct a culture and women inhabit it but do not feel entirely at home. Women protest, of course, as individuals such as Caroline Norton, or as organized feminist groups, but women do not construct dominant culture in the way that Armstrong suggests, and even their protest is severely limited. Opposition, indeed, is more of a theoretical possibility in *Uneven Developments* than a concretely realized phenomenon. This is especially true when Poovey focuses on debates to which women had no access, the debate over chloroform, childbirth, and women's sexuality, for example, as it was carried on in medical journals. But even in debates to which women did have access, in which women did intervene, such as the debate over the Divorce Bill and the Married Women's Property Act, Poovey's emphasis falls not on the voice of organized feminist protest but, instead, on the lonely, individual, and ultimately conservative struggles of Caroline Norton.

In both cases a shift in focus might considerably alter the impression of sometimes unrelenting male domination. Women, for example, wrote very differently from medical men about childbirth and mothering in letters and diaries, as well as in novels, and later in the century women allied with the movement to rescind the Contagious Diseases acts and with social purity crusades sustained public discourse over sexuality that was overtly critical of discourse identified with men. Still, if women's protest remains more of a theoretical possibility than a concretely realized phenomenon, *Uneven Developments* does keep us in touch with a sense of the economic and social bases for female agency and discontent. It impresses upon us, for example, the extreme inequities of women's social position vis-à-vis men of their own class and women's frequent and necessary deviations from the positions they were assigned (many middle-class women also had to earn a wage). Finally, of course, it also reminds us that women's organized protest did exist. Indeed, Poovey's is the only work to include feminist discourse and feminist institutions.

Many questions remain to be asked and explored. My purpose here, for the most part, has been to suggest how a literary and historical practice that is consistently feminist and materialist, attuned to gender in its intersections with class, national identity, and race, tends to produce definitions of representation and of history that are more complex than those that are less consistently both. My purpose has also been to suggest that a feminist and materialist literary and historical practice tends to produce history in a way that allows us better to account for social change and human agency. To persons engaged in progressive politics that they still feel to be vital, such models of history, I would argue, are at once more useful and have greater explanatory power than those that tend to deny both the possibility of change and agency. And nonfeminist new historicism, in its noncultural materialist modes, has been widely criticized for its tendency to insist upon the totalizing power of hegemonic ideologies, ideologies implicitly informed by elite male values.[42]

In its emphasis upon the different ways that gendered subjects enter into ideology, however, materialist-feminist work suggests an important direction for new historicist practice, no matter what its politics. For if we wish to be serious about our assertion that representation "makes things happen," we will need to explore the way that discursive meanings circulate throughout a culture. It is here that we all have something to learn from feminist historians. Historians such as Judith Walkowitz, for example, who also works in a species of cross-cultural montage, do not simply juxtapose isolated written and social texts in order to suggest the homologous operations of dominant ideology throughout an entire culture. Walkowitz not only attempts to construct the different ways in which groups differently placed in the social formation articulate or reproduce ideologies; she also attempts to construct the complex "cultural grid" through which overlapping and conflicting representations passed. That grid, moreover, has much to do with such material (though still constructed) matters as access to social space, a very different access for men and women of the same class and for persons of different classes (Walkowitz 1992).

For those doing critical work on gender there is still much to know about the ways in which subgroups of women and men entered into dominant ideologies. Indeed, the distance between Poovey's construction of middle-class women's participation in mid-Victorian culture and Armstrong's construction of the same, the first emphasizing the mainly oppositional role of middle-class women, the second emphasizing the dominance of middle-class feminine values and power, suggests one immediate line of inquiry. How might we proceed to investigate these alternative constructions of the past? One strategy, of course, is simply to submit more discourse by subgroups of women and men, discourse that is, of course, also already gendered, classed, and raced, to analysis and examination, to expand what is in history and what is seen as having significant relation. We might follow Poovey's example and the example of several feminist historians by juxtaposing the discourse of subgroups of men and women on the same social topics or in the same organizations and movements.[43] We might investigate too what men and women of different subgroups appropriated from one another. As an index to how widespread the cultural tension or unity between the genders may have been, we might pursue another line of questioning laid out over a decade ago in the agenda of feminist history. That is, we might explore the gap between prescriptive and public representations of gender, class, and race and the way that gender, class, and race relations were constructed by individuals in their daily lives.[44] Most important, we must investigate the differences within gender, the coconstruction of gender with racial, national, and sexual identities, as well as with class, and we must bring a more global perspective to bear on any social formation that we investigate. There is crucial work as well to be done in relation to those traditionally understood "material conditions," which so many of us declare at the moment to be "beyond the scope of this book."[45] This work may lie in the future: there is so much to do in making a classed and raced gender even visible. And perhaps feminists will have to enlarge their collectivity to do it. I can see it now—a materialist-feminist literary and historical critic working with a feminist historian and, in a brave move beyond the dyadic bond, with an ethnic studies scholar, a postcolonial critic, and a cultural materialist too, and with others as well.[46] Perhaps their labels by now may be wearing thin; perhaps they are invisible. Perhaps all five (or six) now work inside a set of assumptions about literature and history that are centrally informed by critical gender, antiracist, postcolonial, and materialist politics and concerns. Perhaps in this sense their new history is no longer new. And perhaps in this sense it is no longer history as usual.

NOTES

I want to thank Judith Stacey, Judith Walkowitz, and Lesley Rabine for their helpful comments on this piece.

1. For an account of "cultural materialism," see Dollimore 1985. For an account of materialist-feminist criticism, see Newton and Rosenfelt 1986.

2. Montrose (1986, 6) refers to new historicism both as a potential orthodoxy and more broadly as a "new historical orientation among critics who are heterogeneous in their practice." For other broad definitions of new historicism, see Goldberg 1982, Howard 1986, and Dollimore 1985. For critics who see new historicism more narrowly, as a school or as a potential orthodoxy, see Pechter 1987, LaCapra 1986, and Gallagher 1986.

3. I am using *postmodernist* in the way that it is now often employed—to refer to a set of generalized assumptions about knowledge, language, and subjectivity (listed in my text), which may be articulated very differently by "postmodernists" (a term that usually includes Jean-François Lyotard, Michel Foucault, Richard Rorty), French and American deconstructionists (the most often cited being Jacques Derrida), and cultural materialists, feminists, and ethnic studies scholars of various stripes. These categories, of course, are also

used in a fluid way. For a recent summary of postmodernist assumptions, see Flax 1987.

4. Some obvious cases here are cultural materialism and many strands of white feminist, feminist of color, and ethnic studies criticism.

5. The term is LaCapra's (1986); see also Goldberg 1982 on the "homologies" in new historical work; and LaCapra on what he calls "facile associationism."

6. Gallagher (1986), for example, mentions the New Left, poststructuralism, and Foucault; Dollimore (1985) emphasizes the role of cultural materialism; and Howard (1986) stresses the postmodern tendencies of new historical work. Many critics also specifically mention the influence of Foucault.

7. Feminists are often split. Thus, the works I cite also mount powerful critiques of deconstruction, suggesting (in Rabine's case) how feminist theory developed ideas that are similar to, and which developed alongside, deconstructive versions of the same concepts or suggesting (in Poovey's case) how feminism will ultimately rewrite deconstruction altogether and leave it behind. See Rabine 1988 and Poovey 1988. See also Meese 1986 for a nuanced argument about the advantages for feminism of adapting deconstructive strategies. Finally, see Ryan 1982, 194–221, for a politically acute account of some parallel lines of thought in socialist feminism and deconstruction.

8. See Modleski 1986, 121–38.

9. Meese (1986), for example, recommends a complex strategy of refusing the insider's role while simultaneously trying "to win that authority in an institution we ceaselessly attempt to undermine and unsettle" (148).

10. See Christian 1987 on the importance for feminist, black, and third-world critics of embracing their "own antecedents" (55).

11. See Graff 1983, 153.

12. The critique of sexism in the early 1970s was what linked most white feminists and feminists of color, but from the beginning feminists of color maintained this critique in relation to a critique of racism and economic exploitation. Although a number of white feminists also maintained critiques of racism and economic exploitation, gender critique, often based on a fairly undifferentiated (therefore white and middle-class) notion of gender, was more central to their politics. My use of the word *feminist* is meant to signal a politics of opposition to sexism in the 1970s, but one that was articulated very differently by different groups of women. See hooks 1989, 23, for a revised definition of feminism as a movement to end sexist oppression but one that employs the paradigms of sex, race, and class.

13. Since this line has been taken out of context and radically misconstrued, I should make it clear that I am alluding here to how many of us *constructed* our politics in the 1970s. I am not arguing that politics actually come out of unconstructed experience—who would make such an argument these days?—but that many of us constructed our politics as a direct reflex of our experience in the early women's movement. This construction, however problematic it may seem now, had empowering and galvanizing effects for white feminists and feminists of color in the early 1970s.

For further reflections on the legitimate role of "experience" in feminist theory generally and feminist theories of knowledge, see de Lauretis 1986, 11; Harding 1987, 20–29; Nelson 1987, 166; Ryan 1982, 199, on Rowbotham; Hartsock 1985, chap. 10; Modleski 1986, 134–35; Eagleton 1983, 215; Collins 1990; hooks 1992; Williams 1991. See also Elizabeth Meese's citation of Mae Henderson 1989, xxv.

14. The ethnographic work that I have been conducting over the past two years at cultural studies, multicultural, and disciplinary conferences has suggested a difference to me between many white, leftist men on the one hand and many male African-American and Chicano scholars on the other. In papers delivered at conferences, at least, the latter two groups cite feminist work, especially work by feminists of color, far more often than white, leftist men, and they incorporate gender and sexuality (in organic relation to race and class) to a far greater degree in their analyses.

15. Feminists of color have criticized white feminists and other scholars for similar limitations, for failing to grasp the theoretical dimensions of work by women of color, which has, to a far greater degree than the work of white feminists, maintained a situated quality. See hooks 1989, 35–36; and Anzaldúa 1990, xxv–xxvi. Many feminists, of course, white feminists and feminists of color, have proved adept at appropriating and sometimes generating jargon, often in an attempt to get heard. See the following for some reflections on the role of jargon in overly narrow definitions of theory, past and present: Piercy 1970, 427–28; and Christian 1987. See also Howard 1988. For reflections on the way feminist theory has been ignored, see Meese 1986, 137; Christian 1987; Gallop 1987, 115; and Kaplan 1986a, 58.

16. For reflections on the way feminist theory has been appropriated by men sympathetic to feminism, see Spivak 1983, 361–66; Nelson 1987, 165; and Showalter 1987, 116–35. For reflections on the way that feminist theory has been travestied or appropriated without footnotes, see de Lauretis 1986, 11; Russo 1986, 225; Showalter 1987, 116–35; and Braidotti 1987, 233–41. Finally, for a reflection on the way feminist critics have been attacked both for having no "real" theory and for trying to define one and so recapitulating the phallocentric economy, see Meese 1986, 136–37.

17. For feminist accounts of the role of theory as practice, as "ideas that help us and disappear," as a guide to decision making, and as a strategy for defense, see Ryan 1982, 210 (on Rowbotham); Meese 1986, x; and Anzaldúa 1990, xxv–xvi.

18. For an account of parallel developments in feminism and postmodernism, see Fraser and Nicholson 1988. For further reflections on feminism and postmodernism, see Harding 1986; Haraway 1983; and Jardine 1985.

19. See also Kaplan 1986a, 59, on the duality of early feminist critiques of "objectivity."

20. See the following for early critiques of the white and heterosexist focus of much mainstream feminist theory: hooks 1984; Lugones and Spelman 1983; and Rich 1980.

21. Among the more recent works critiquing feminist categories, all of

which were published after this piece first appeared, see Riley 1988; Malson, O'Barr, Westphal-Wihl, and Wyer 1989; Fuss 1989; Alarcon 1990; Butler 1990; hooks 1990; and the essays in Butler and Scott 1992.

22. Mohanty (1990) notes, for example, that the political analyses of third world feminists prefigured the recent feminist turn to postmodernism, which suggests the fragmentation of unitary assumptions. Flax (1992) also notes the overlap of work by feminists of color and postmodernism, although, in suggesting that white feminist critiques of postmodernism may express guilt, anxiety, and anger at women of color for disturbing the comfort of "sisterhood," she fails to note the very different ways in which many feminists of color and many white poststructuralist feminists articulate postmodernism, especially in relation to identity, experience, and political agency. Many white feminists find themselves allied with the former while critical of the latter. Flax also fails to take into account the ways in which feminists of color have critiqued articulations of postmodernism by white feminists.

23. There is disagreement, of course, over the degree to which feminists should embrace "feminist objectivity" or the idea of a "feminist standpoint." Harding and Haraway recommend a "feminist objectivity," or "successor science," that is also postmodern in its recognition of its local and situated nature. Flax (1987), who situates feminism more firmly in mainstream postmodernism, is critical of that project. For a review of some important work on this area, see Longino 1985; Fausto-Sterling 1986; and Harding 1986. For important and more recent work on black feminist thought and standpoint theory, see Hill Collins 1990.

24. See, for example, Lerner 1975.

25. For an early account of feminist history, see Smith-Rosenberg 1975b. For a recent account of the beginnings of feminist history, the role of social historians in its construction, and of the projects that currently engage feminist historians, see Gordon 1986, 20–30. For a critique of the Annales school over its failure to deal centrally with women or gender, see Stuard 1981 and Faure 1981. For a similar critique of past work on slavery, see White 1990 (1983).

26. See, for example, Davis 1971; Glenn 1980; Jones 1982; Lebsock 1982; and White 1983. For more recent work, see de Alva 1990 and Dubois and Ruiz 1990.

27. Power was the theme of the first issue of *SIGNS*. See Janeway 1975 and Watson 1975.

28. See, for example, Glenn 1980 and Jones 1982.

29. For work antedating Foucault, see Walkowitz and Walkowitz 1974, 192–225; for feminist work influenced by but revising Foucault, see Walkowitz and Walkowitz 1974; Walkowitz 1980, 1986; and Smith-Rosenberg 1985.

30. See, for example, Davis 1971 on the role of enslaved women as that of "custodian of a house of resistance"; and the work of White 1983 on female life under slavery. See also Stack 1970 on black women; and, on white, middle-class women, see Smith-Rosenberg 1975a.

31. For the idea of a separate women's culture, see Lerner 1975, 13. For

an influential essay on the different meaning of historical periods for women and men, see Kelly-Godal 1976. See White 1990 (1983) for a working out of the idea that "the female slave world allowed women the opportunity to rank and order themselves and obtain a sense of self which was quite apart from the men of their race and even the men of the master class" (27).

32. See Jensen 1990 (1977) on the past failure to systematically study the contribution of Native American women to the agricultural economy of tribes in the eastern half of the United States.

33. For some examples of "cross-cultural montage" in nineteenth-century work, see Walkowitz 1992 and Gonzalez 1988.

34. See, for example, Ryan 1981; Davidoff and Hall 1987; Poovey 1988; and Armstrong 1987.

35. Taken as a whole, this emphasis on gender and especially on women is what has most consistently set feminist history off from new historicism and from much male-authored history informed by Marxist and/or antiracist perspectives. As I have suggested, however, the divisions between history that maintains a critical perspective on gender and history that reads gender in organic relation to race, national identity, sexuality, and class cut across the category "feminist history" and throw the term into some question. *Radical multiculturalism, cultural studies,* and *materialist criticism* have been proposed as terms for scholarship that includes critical work on gender, race, class, and national and sexual identity, although in practice critical gender critique sometimes fails to make an appearance in essays delivered under these signs. I myself have used *materialist-feminist* to suggest a practice that, among other things, reads gender as coconstructed with these and other categories.

36. One of the earliest essays to call for a feminist criticism that was historical in each of these three modes is Robinson's "Dwelling in Decencies." See Robinson 1978. Millett (1970) practices a similar criticism. See also Showalter 1975; Christian 1980; Carby 1987; Smith 1987.

37. For a fuller account of the relation between materialist-feminist and other feminist criticisms, see Kaplan 1986a and Newton and Rosenfelt 1986.

38. Gallagher (1986) does place herself politically, in "Critics of Power."

39. Race and imperialism did not enter into most white women's writing on nineteenth-century British culture (including my own) until the last few years. I reflect on some of the reasons for this in the preface to this volume. See Hall 1992 on this topic.

40. In nineteenth-century British history, class has traditionally been defined in relation to events in which women played no or little part or in relation to developments in which women's participation was invisible. For a critique and revision of male-centered definitions of class, see Hall 1981, 164–75. See also Alexander 1984.

41. Poovey's work, like Gallagher's and Armstrong's, has been influenced by Foucault in its concern with discourse as domains of meaning with internal logics and sets of rules. But her appropriation of Foucault has been different. Armstrong and Poovey both emphasize how the action of individual

agents has impact on discourse, but Poovey's conception of dominant discourse as heterogeneous and unstable is one that emphasizes the possibilities for social change. One might call Poovey's emphasis Derridean, which of course it is, but the feminist and materialist elements of her politics and analysis seem, to me at least, more profoundly shaping. For an exploration of a similar model of history in the work of male historians and theorists, see Toews 1987.

42. See, for example, Goldberg 1982; Pechter 1987; and Waller 1987.

43. Taylor (1983), for example, examines the discourse of Owenite men and women over, among other things, the free love debate. Walkowitz (1980) juxtaposes male and female discourse over the Contagious Diseases acts; and (1992) over sexuality, class and gender, and "Jack the Ripper." Mani (1992) juxtaposes eyewitness accounts of widow burning with widow testimonials. Chabram-Dernersesian (1992) contrasts different forms of Chicano movement discourse.

44. Feminist ethnography often focuses upon this gap. See Ong 1987; Behar 1990; Kondo 1990; and Stacey 1990.

45. The words are Poovey's, but the strategy is also that of Gallagher and Armstrong and, implicitly, of many others.

46. These categories are extremely problematic, especially in the West, in which "radical multiculturalism," as an intellectual and political enterprise focused on studying subordinated forms of difference, cuts across the formations historically identified as women's and ethnic studies, post-Marxist scholarship, and gay and lesbian studies.

Family Fortunes:
History and Literature in
Materialist-Feminist Work

(1988)

That literary critics meditate publicly upon landmark works of history such as Leonore Davidoff and Catherine Hall's *Family Fortunes: Men and Women of the English Middle Class, 1780–1850* may be seen as emblematic of the current shift in relations between historical and literary studies, a shift in which *Family Fortunes* itself may be located. In literary critical circles this shift is evidenced in talk of a "turn to history" or a "renewed interest in history" and in the rise to prominence of "new historicism" as a literary critical mode (Howard 1986, 14; Montrose 1986, 8, 11).[1] In history circles the shift is evidenced by talk of a "linguistic turn" or a "new interest in linguistic theories" and by the rise of a "new history of meaning" (Toews 1987, 879, 881).[2] The new historicism and the new history, moreover, are variously rooted in a common set of "postmodern" assumptions about knowledge, human identity, and the real.[3] Both tendencies are associated with the view that the real is apprehended only in "language," language being understood for the most part as systems of meaning rather than as words or words alone (Scott 1987, 6).[4] Languages, or systems of meaning, are seen as constructed, historically specific, and political and are expressed, according to the same set of assumptions, not only in words but also in social institutions and practices.

Human beings (often referred to in literary criticism as "the subjects") are also immersed in symbolic systems through which they are identified and in which they apprehend the world. More precisely, human beings are immersed in multiple sublanguages, or discourses,[5] which operate as parts of symbolic systems as a whole. According to the same set of assumptions, historical documents, like literary texts, are immersed in discourse too. Both may make reference to the real (though the referential nature of historical documents is mainly asserted by historians), but both have a "worklike" function, heavily conditioned by the various sublanguages by which they are informed. Both literary text and historical document construct the real to which they also respond.[6] Thus, practitioners of new historicism and new history both, while they may disagree over the extent to which discourse constitutes the real or is constructed by it and over the degree to which discourse may be altered by individuals bent on remaking their world, place systems of meaning at the heart of their investigations.

The critical assumptions and practices that inform new historicism and the new history are often read both as a product of poststructuralist, and other postmodern, theories, with their emphasis upon language, or systems of meaning, and as a reaction against the formalist bent of much poststructuralist practice, with its focus upon contextually isolated texts. For it is the project of new historicism and the new history to read written and social texts, constructions of "experience" and the material world, in relation to each other. Similar assumptions and practices, however, have had a long and relatively autonomous history in feminist work. Indeed, despite the fact that discussion of new historicism and new history is often carried on as if their assumptions and practices had been produced by men (feminist theorists, if they are mentioned at all, are often assumed to be the dependent heirs of male intellectual capital), feminist labor has had much to do with the development of this literary-historical enterprise.[7] As I have argued in "History as Usual" in more detail, the postmodernist assumptions that inform new history and new historicism were partly generated by the theoretical breaks of the civil rights movement and of the early second wave of the women's movement, by antiracist and feminist critiques of "objectivity," by antiracist and feminist assertions of the political and historically specific nature of knowledge itself, by antiracist and feminist analyses of the cultural construction of identities, and by critiques of white, heterosexual, feminist theorizing for essentialism and for racial and sexual biases.

Since the late 1960s, moreover, feminist work has implicitly emphasized the role of "ideas," or symbolic systems, in the construction not only of identities but also of social institutions and social relations as a whole. It has done so not only in response to poststructuralism but also because the subordination of women, who have always been at least half of humankind, has seemed ideological to a large degree.

Thus, although feminists have been influenced by and have reacted against poststructuralist theory and practice, the focus on systems of meaning that currently inform nonfeminist new historicism and new history has had other, politicized origins in feminist work. I shall suggest at the end of this essay how the political commitments of feminist new history and new historicism tend to set them apart from nonfeminist or less feminist versions of something similar.

In feminist scholarship, finally, the divisions between different disciplines, including literature and history, have always been relatively porous. The shared project of investigating gender, in its co-construction with race, ethnicity, sexuality, and class, as they operate throughout a whole culture, the shared assumptions about the centrality of symbolic systems in the construction of identity and social institutions, and above all the shared political project of changing the world have all tended to bring feminist scholars together across disciplinary lines. The current accelerated convergence of literature and history in feminist work participates, of course, in that complex response to poststructuralism (with its focus on language, or systems of meaning), which is often cited as a major force in the development of new historicism and the new history generally.But to some extent the current meeting of feminist literature and history is also the fruit of a long process, the product of patient self-training in the other's skills.

The convergence of literary and historical studies in feminist investigations of the past is strikingly evident in Davidoff and Hall's *Family Fortunes* (1987). Based on two detailed case studies of urban Birmingham and rural East Anglia, *Family Fortunes* is a history of "the ideologies, institutions, and practices of the English middle class from the end of the eighteenth to mid nineteenth centuries" (13). The product of a collaboration between a historian and a sociologist and explicitly rooted in the women's movement, feminist history, and literary criticism and theory, it is a fine example of feminist interdisciplinary labor.

But *Family Fortunes* also employs Marxist concepts, and in its fusion of feminist and Marxist theory it continues a twofold project familiar to materialist-feminists in both literature and history—that of revising radical and liberal feminist models of history and that of revising traditional (and less traditional) Marxist models as well. The first project is perhaps of more interest to me, as a literary critic in the

United States, than to Davidoff and Hall, since the concept of unchanging patriarchy or male domination, although it has been a
popular model of history in feminist criticism here, has not had much
play in British feminist historical work. The second project, revising
Marxist history, seems more central to the authors of this book, writing, as they do, out of a British context, in which Marxism has been
a culturally viable political position. I shall focus, therefore, on this
second project.

On the most basic level, *Family Fortunes* significantly revises traditional Marxist (and all masculinist) histories by placing gender, and
women as well as men, at the heart of its investigation and by
redefining in this way what class and class consciousness can mean
and what "real history" consists of. In so doing, of course, it draws
upon the work of earlier feminist histories such as Mary Ryan's *Cradle
of the Middle Class* (1981). *Class* in traditional Marxist texts (but also
in some more recent poststructuralist Marxist work) is implicitly
defined as men's relations to production and their related cultural
forms, that is, as men's interests, values, and relationships. Its important moments of development, moreover, are seen as those having to do with events or organizations in which, for the most part,
only men participated or in which women's participation has been
trivialized or has gone unnoticed. *Class,* so defined, is essentially
masculine, and yet women have been implicitly covered by that
definition (in continuation of the principle, I suppose, that women
are best represented by their fathers or their husbands). Gender, in
these texts, if it is mentioned at all, is conceived of as gender *roles* and
mainly women's roles at that. Thus, gender is implicitly identified as
feminine, while men remain gender neutral.[8]

In laying bare the "beliefs and activities of middle-class women,
the "silent" majority of the British middle class it studies, *Family
Fortunes*, like Ryan's work on the nineteenth-century, white, American middle class, revises what we can mean by class and class consciousness (Davidoff and Hall 1987, 18). *Class* is now defined as the
relation of men and women both to the mode of production, distribu-
tion, and exchange and as the related cultural forms—that is, as the
interests, values, and relationships of women as well as men. Middle-class consciousness, therefore, is less centrally defined in this
book as essentially masculine, as a belief in liberal individualism,
competition, and freedom of opportunity, than as a way of organiz-

ing perceptions of the world that English middle-class men and women really did share—the division of the world into public and private, masculine and feminine, rational and emotional, intellectual and moral. The primary fissures in class consciousness, moreover, have less to do with divisions between men in subgroups of the middle class, have less to do with divisions between male professional and male entrepreneurial interests, than with culturally imposed divisions between women and men.

While the conceptual division of the world into public and domestic, masculine and feminine, united these men and women, it also assigned them different values, traits, and roles and thus divided them as well. To be English and middle class meant something different for women than it did for men: it meant different as well as shared languages, different as well as shared symbols. The self-activating entrepreneur was not the "ideal citizen" for the bulk of the middle class, not even for the middle class that was associated with trade (Perkin 1986, 221). Since being middle class meant an ethic of self-advancement for men but an ethic of self-denial for women, the self-sacrificing domestic woman was equally (and perhaps more dominantly) a representative of middle-class virtues. *Family Fortunes*, then, suggests that a system of meaning[9] that informed middle-class consciousness in early-nineteenth-century England was most fundamentally organized by a division of the world by gender. But it does not install gender as the motor of history, in a feminist appropriation of the traditional and monocausal Marxist model. In its investigation of the way that middle-class women and men organized their perceptions of the world, *Family Fortunes* suggests that the division of the world into public and domestic was an expression not only of gender as an organizing principle but of class and religion too (not of race or nationalism, however, although Davidoff and Hall have both written on these categories in relation to white, middle-class British culture).[10] The operation of these determinants, moreover, was not stable. Gender as well as class was continually "forged, contested, reworked and reaffirmed" (Davidoff and Hall 1987, 29). Multiplicity and fluidity, therefore, are defining features of the book's explanatory system, a system in which changing configurations of gender, class, and religion are intricately interwoven and in which the ideological or symbolic informs and acts upon, but is also shaped by, daily behaviors and social and economic relations.

The peculiar emphasis given to the ideological and (later) the physical division of the world into public and domestic in early-nineteenth-century Britain, for example, is thus read in many ways. It is read, for example, as an expression of middle-class men's investment in traditional gender hierarchy, as a response to the fear that the more fluid forms of capital might permit women fuller entry into the marketplace, and as their attempt to control women in the face of that seeming threat. It is read as an attempt to reconcile secular goals with religious ones, to accommodate the pursuit of profit with that emphasis on inner moral life that religious belief had made central to the middle-class code. It is also read as an effort to reconcile capitalist ideology, a belief in the free market, with the maintenance of traditional social ties, ties now relegated to a world set apart from what increasingly appeared to be male economic affairs. But since home as a locus of morality and social ties was important to establishing a reputation for respectability and commercial responsibility (an important asset given the instability of many family firms), the division of the world into public and domestic is also read as a means of legitimating the capitalist ethic of self-interest.

In proposing that bourgeois ideology was principally organized by a division of the world into public and domestic and in demonstrating how this division served the needs of gender and religion as well as of class, *Family Fortunes* breaks with traditional economistic and political histories. In so doing, of course, it breaks with models of history that are deeply patriarchal.[11] The particular originality of *Family Fortunes'* contribution, however, is that it works in a British context in which there has been comparatively little work on middle-class women, and that it significantly revises past histories of bourgeois men. Economistic and political histories, for example, characteristically define "real history" as the economic and political and implicitly identify both of those realms with men, relegating women to the margins of what real history is about. In assuming that men are moved by needs or motivations that are also economic and political, such history also implicitly suggests that men carry out their affairs—their real, historically significant affairs—in a state of psychological independence from their relations to women and the home. *Family Fortunes* breaks with the patriarchal exclusions of this history in several ways but most originally by establishing the domestic as a central point of investigation for writing the history of white, middle-class English *men*. Indeed, it argues that many of these men were as motivated by religious and domestic values as by entrepreneurial and economic ones, and it further argues that religious and domestic values shaped economic development.

Thus, in *Family Fortunes* nineteenth-century English male middle-class identity is marked as much by the importance of providing for dependent women and children as it is by the appearance of being an autonomous economic agent pursuing profit. This identification of oneself as provider, of course, served many kinds of interests: it reenforced gender hierarchy, and, in transforming a self-interested pursuit of profit into a demonstration of disinterested love, it also helped to reconcile religious and secular goals and to establish the moral and cultural authority that middle-class men and women both wished to claim in relation to men and women of other classes and in relation to colonized nations as well. This multiply determined self-identification, moreover, shaped capitalist development in many different ways. The search for safe forms of provision, for example, often led men to curtail the pursuit of profit while religious investment in domestic living also led them to early retirement from business affairs. In contrast, the need to enforce women's economic dependence helped promote increased reliance on trusts as a capitalist form of inheritance; these were a boon to male relatives who administered those trusts while using women's capital to engage in their own enterprise. Finally, the new desires generated by the construction of home as a haven separate from the world meant new patterns of consumption that shaped and expanded the market and thus contributed to a middle-class prosperity based on the provision of goods and services.

In *Family Fortunes*, therefore, capitalist development, traditionally assigned to the public world of men, is shaped by domestic and religious values and is organized by gender as well as by class. "The public world of men," however, is a concept that disappears before our eyes since *Family Fortunes* also challenges the view that middle-class economic affairs were essentially masculine. Indeed, one of its most important contributions is its demonstration of the degree to which the officially autonomous entrepreneur was embedded in and dependent on women and a network of family and kin and the degree to which women participated in family enterprise on a large scale, constituting a species of "hidden investment." There are, for example, the less direct and more familiar contributions that women made in running households, producing heirs and personnel for the firm, displaying rank, establishing the respectability and morality attached to the family firm, and forging personal contacts. And there are the more direct and less visible ways, such as supplying capital and directly participating in the conduct of business affairs. Thus, while laying out the conceptual and material significance of that division of the world into public and domestic for men and women of the nineteenth-century middle class, *Family Fortunes* undermines our own lingering investment in this way of dividing and organizing the world.

Although a significant weakness of *Family Fortunes* is that it does not situate white middle-class men and women in relation to men and women of the working class or in relation to British imperialist ventures, its strength, and it is an impressive strength, lies in this massively documented analysis of the way that a system of meaning organized by class and gender informed the material lives of ordinary men and women of the middle class. Over and over again *Family Fortunes* teases out an intricate web of class, gender, and religion as it informed and was acted upon by individuals, economic processes, social institutions, and daily domestic life. Indeed, the careful detail and Dickensian breadth with which this investigation is carried out can make reading *Family Fortunes* an overwhelming experience. (Like Victorian novels, this is a book to be consumed on the installment plan.) But the theoretical and political challenge of *Family Fortunes* is also exacting, to masculinist history in particular. For when gender is conceived of as an organizing principle rather than merely as a set of roles, when it is seen as central to a system of meaning that informs behavior, economic processes and social institutions, then there is no "gender-free zone." Even debate between men and institutions and movements in which men only participated are informed by a way of organizing the world in which gender at least is as central as class. It is in this theoretical and political challenge that *Family Fortunes* most intersects with some recent materialist-feminist literary critical work on the nineteenth century.

Although *Family Fortunes* is finally separated from this materialist-feminist literary and historical work by methodological differences that are also political, there are many ways in which this study and recent feminist literary and historical work converge. Like *Family Fortunes*, most principally, the feminist literary critical work that I am going to discuss also focuses on a white middle-class system of meaning and employs feminist and Marxist concepts in a way that challenges masculinist history in particular. (The challenge to radical and liberal feminist history as it has informed much feminist criticism in the United States is also present but receives less emphasis for reasons that I will suggest later on.) The same feminist literary and historical work also focuses on the intersection of class and gender, public and domestic, and, while exploring the significance of these concepts for the nineteenth-century middle class, undermines our own investment in them. The work I am going to discuss, finally, also emphasizes the hidden dependency of the English middle-class masculine upon the English middle-class feminine and the centrality of cultural definitions of the middle-class feminine in constructing what has been seen as a male public world—the world of masculine discourse and social institutions, the world of economics, law, medicine, government, national education, sociology, and imperial conquest.

Mary Poovey's recent work on the nineteenth-century middle class, *Uneven Developments* (1988), elaborates the kind of ideological logic less complexly outlined in *Family Fortunes*. As I suggest in more detail in "History as Usual," the thrust of Poovey's work as a whole is to suggest how a division of the world into masculine and feminine, a division seen as "natural," underwrote a whole series of oppositions (public/domestic, property owner/commodity) that structured Victorian ideology, as it was expressed in ideas, written texts, social practices, and institutions. In each opposition the identity of the first term depended upon the construction of the second and subordinate one. Thus, men could be autonomous because nonmen, women, were defined as dependent.

In some of her most interesting work Poovey investigates the way in which "skirmishes between religious and secular institutions for the authority to legislate social behavior," and also men's more individual struggles with one another, not only reaffirmed these oppositions but were often carried on as a battle to define women and women's sexuality. Because middle-class men's self-identification depended on the way women were represented—an idealized representation of women, in fact, was integral to bourgeois economic and social power—men's conflicting interests prompted them to articulate received ideology about women with different and often contradictory emphases. Poovey's work, that is, suggests how gender division as the primary organizing principle of a white, middle-class system of meaning intersected with class, was articulated in different and conflicting ways, had multiple effects, and was inherently unstable at the same time that it informed all levels of the culture, not excepting male political struggle. One of Poovey's examples is the debate over chloroform and the struggle over the professional organization of medicine that was inscribed in it. One might make a similar case for the debate over the Factory Act of 1844, in which conflicting definitions of working-class women and of their situation in factory labor functioned as a form of struggle between upper-class reformers and the representatives of entrepreneurial interests over how to conceive of and organize social relations as a whole.

Nancy Armstrong's *Desire and Domestic Fiction* (1987) also focuses on the intersection of class and gender, though not race, in a nineteenth-century middle-class system of meaning, and her argument, although quite different from Poovey's and Davidoff and Hall's, still enforces a central tendency in their work: the demonstration of complex intersection between public and domestic, masculine and feminine, and the hidden dependencies of the former upon the latter. Armstrong's thesis, in brief, is that what have passed until now as English, nineteenth-century, middle-class (and implicitly male) values and procedures were, in fact, feminine. The bourgeois individual, she suggests, the individual identified by internal worth and qualities of mind rather than by rank, was female before it was male. It was women's moral authority, moreover, that became the moral authority of the middle class as a whole, just as it was women's domestic work—moral surveillance, the ordering of internal space—that became the model by which modern institutions were to operate. This feminine power, moreover, was all the more powerful for being seen as apolitical and not power at all. Indeed, this officially apolitical power, along with a construction of women's sexuality and of sexuality itself, as natural and independent of politics provided a set of terms in which the problem of the working class could be explained and depoliticized. The problem of the working class, that is, was reconceived as moral and sexual. What was required was not anything recognized as political control but, rather, domestic surveillance and moral reeducation.

The juxtaposition of *Family Fortunes* with *Uneven Developments* and *Desire and Domestic Fiction* tends to throw certain features of each into relief; most particularly, the juxtaposition tends to deepen our sense of the contradictions that each presents in middle-class life. When one reads Davidoff and Hall's analysis of middle-class men's material dependence on their women, in relation to Poovey's analysis of the logical dependence of middle-class masculine upon middle-class feminine identity, in relation to what Armstrong argues was the essentially feminine nature of English middle-class values and social institutions, the autonomy that was so central a feature of male middle-class self-identification begins to seem rather fragile, or at least contradictory. These contradictions, moreover, seem even more pronounced if one reads them in relation to another central feature of male middle-class life, as hinted at by Davidoff and Hall: men's dependency as infants on the mother or mother substitute. For *Family Fortunes* reminds us that sons "had the task of breaking way from an intense and dependent relationship with their mother (or substitute female caretaker)" (Davidoff and Hall 1987, 356). This imperative to separate from the mother must have had particular resonance in a culture that so glorified white, middle-class women for their maternal and domestic power.

It is not surprising, then, given the tensions between middle-class men's identification of themselves as autonomous agents and their real dependencies on the feminine, on women and kin, that middle-class men appear to have articulated the relation between public and domestic more conservatively than did many women. In their analysis of John Claudius Loudons's *The Suburban Gardener and Villa Companion*, for example, Davidoff and Hall suggest that Loudon imaginatively contains women by drawing attention to their bodies, by emphasizing the purely local nature of their influence, and by undercutting their important role as moral guides in praising their role as arbiters of taste. This effort to curtail women's power not just in the public domain but also in the home informs a good deal of male middle-class writing on the domestic in the 1830s and 1840s. Anxious affirmation of autonomy and separation, moreover, seems to inform men's obsessive concern with female sexuality as well. (In all these books textual efforts to contain middle-class women's sexuality are seen as displaced efforts to control women's economic and social desires, but surely they are also efforts to control the mother's body and the mother's physically expressed power.) The same anxiety may inform fantasies of escape into the feminized brotherhoods that are everywhere in Dickens and Kingsley and that, as Davidoff and Hall remind us, were concretely realized in the Oxford movement. Indeed, the same anxiety seems to have informed fantasies of escape into brotherhoods that were educational, scientific, or imperialistic in a rigorously masculine mode.

Reading these works together, indeed, is like witnessing the concerted violation of an old taboo. For there has been much less resistance (among men and women both) to seeing class, race, or economic development as a force in constructing gender than to seeing gender or sexuality as a force in constructing race or class. (This may be one reason that the critique of radical feminist history is relatively muted in these studies.) We are used to thinking that it is men, or things associated with men, that act upon the world. There has been far greater resistance to the notion that politics, public institutions, and economic development have been significantly informed by gender, gender relations, the family, and in particular men's psychological and emotional investments in, and anxieties over, women. This has seemed almost a dirty secret of history. But it was not, I think, equally a secret to women as to men.

Family Fortunes, then, overlaps with materialist-feminist literary critical work in ways that deepen our sense of both the cultural force and significance of white, middle-class English women and the white, middle-class feminine and the multiple tensions that this force may have generated within a system of meaning that officially assigned men not only superior power but autonomy as well. And yet there are also significant differences between works that still read like history and like literary criticism, differences related to disciplinary training and to the greater impact of poststructuralism upon the latter. Although this materialist-feminist criticism, for example, also relates systems of meaning to (always constructed) economic and social relations in interesting and provocative ways, its emphasis is upon the complex logics of those meanings in themselves. There is far less work on the way in which systems of meanings inform, construct, and are constructed by economic and social relations. In *Desire and*

Domestic Fiction, indeed, representation, cultural hegemony, and systems of meaning are more powerful than economic changes (Armstrong 1987, 23). This is a reading, of course, that gives the white, middle-class feminine—if not white, middle-class women—a great deal of power since in Armstrong's rendition of nineteenth-century systems of representation or semiotics, representation is dominantly informed by middle-class feminine values. (Since representation itself has often been assigned the role of the feminine in Marxist histories, that is the role of the secondary, while the social and economic have been constructed as male and as having the primary, masculine role, Armstrong, in her elevation of representation, may be said to empower the feminine twice over.)[12] The primary focus in these examples of materialist-feminist literary criticism, moreover, is still on systems of meaning as they inform written or spoken texts rather than as they inhere in social practices and institutions. The best work of these critics, moreover, is marked by their literary critical training—by their sometimes mind-boggling ability to construct intricate patterns among repeated and varied images and narrative paradigms and to perform intricate analyses of textual "dream work," the text's displacements, condensations, repressions, and symbolic actions (Poovey 1988). *Family Fortunes,* in contrast, although it emphasizes the shaping role of ideology, or systems of meaning, gives social and economic relations and institutions, as well as daily behaviors (all discursively constructed), a far more active role and is less strict in its modes of reference to the real. Poovey and Armstrong, for example, would never claim, especially in a theoretical preface, that they were going to "reconstitute the world as provincial middle-class people saw it," although, like many of us, they might go on to describe the real as if they did have fairly direct access to it after all.

Although *Family Fortunes* does important work on systems of meaning as they inhere in written texts, its work on literature is far less intricate. (At times, indeed, *Family Fortunes* cites literature for its referential value alone.) The focus of *Family Fortunes* is not upon a relatively select number of texts that reward close reading with their intricate and "worklike" functions but, rather, upon the thousand and one texts or documents that do not always so reward fine scrutiny (and that would soon exhaust us if we began to think they did), the "train tables" and census data, so to speak, out of which historians have classically forged their accounts of economic and social life.

Many familiar divisions, then, remain, and there are many ways in which one might explore their significance. What I wish to focus on here, however, are some of the ways in which each emphasis relates to one of the important projects in feminist scholarship generally, a project in which all of these books participate to some degree—that of writing women, as well as men, into history and into the construction of culture. What I want to suggest, in a rather speculative way, is that the attention to economic and social relations and to daily behaviors in a work such as *Family Fortunes,* although it does in some ways emphasize the multiple ways in which white, middle-class women were oppressed, also gives these women a more active role in the construction of middle-class culture than in works that focus on public written representation, even works so attuned to the nonliterary as *Uneven Developments* and *Desire and Domestic Fiction.* For the world of public written or spoken texts, especially if it includes more than the literary, as new historicists are pledged to do, if it includes the medical, the legal, the sociological, is still a world in which middle-class men have more voice than women and more authoritative voice at that. This is true even if, like Armstrong, one reads middle-class systems of meaning as essentially feminine, for such readings may give the middle-class *feminine* power while leaving middle-class *women* silent and invisible. It is also true if, like Poovey, one reads male discourse as dependent upon a construction of the feminine, for it is still men who do the constructing. It is true, finally, even if one focuses primarily on female writers, for most women did not write in the public sphere, and it is true in studies of female literary traditions, such as my own, in which oppositional female voices may appear to be those of isolated, if strong-minded, individuals. It is in daily life with the undeniable, and anxiety-provoking, authority of the mother, the household manager, the participant in family enterprise, the volunteer, that the majority of white, middle-class, English women "spoke," that they enforced but also set up tensions within and acted upon the system of meaning that informed Victorian middle-class culture at every level. For systems of meaning are constructed and acted upon at many levels in a culture and not just at one. To focus on written representation and on representation in the public sphere is still in many ways to leave most women out of history, to significantly eclipse their participation in the construction of culture, which even more than the family firm, was not the work of autonomous self-activating men but a family enterprise.

In its focus on the interaction of systems of meaning and daily behaviors *Family Fortunes* raises questions that must give not only historically minded, materialist-feminist critics but also new historicists generally some pause. What bearing did public written representation, with its intricate dream work and contradictions, have on the way that ordinary men and women conceived of themselves and lived their lives? How was meaning transmitted from one layer of culture to another? And what force did public written discourse finally have? It is a question of great significance to those whose work is motivated by feminist politics. But these are also questions of significance for new historicists whose work is not as informed by such commitments. In contrast to the work I have just discussed, nonfeminist, or less feminist, new historical work has often focused not just on public written discourse but also on the discourses of elite men, discourses dominated by the interest of political institutions such as the monarchy. It has often portrayed the latter as fluid but at the same time as persistently resistant to the interventions of human agency and as representative of the way an entire culture was constructed. How might these readings of culture change if the focus were extended, if, say, the material world of the domestic were included?

It is instructive in this regard to consider two essays that were published side by side, Stephen Greenblatt's new historicist "Fiction and Friction" (1987) and Natalie Davis's new historical "Boundaries and the Self in Sixteenth-Century France" (1987). The two essays, to begin, are linked by most of the postmodern assumptions that I have already mentioned and most particularly by the view that the real is apprehended in languages, or systems of meaning, that are historically specific and political and that are expressed not only in words, including literary texts and historical documents, but also in social institutions and practices. In this case both essays investigate the ways in which cultural codes set the conditions for representing European gendered individuality in English and French Renaissance culture. There are some dramatic splits, however, in the way this cultural investigation is carried out, differences that relate to the critics' discipline of origin. Greenblatt's essay, for example, despite its ostensible return to history, bears the imprint of a rather formalist literary critical heritage. The focus of the essay, for example, is on the close reading of cultural codes, in all their complex logics and displacements, as they inhere primarily in public written discourse and theatrical production. The essay, moreover, tends to privilege public written discourse and theatrical production, first, by implicitly offering them as the primary sites on which the terms for representing European gendered individuals in Renaissance culture as a whole were produced and, second, by demonstrating a relative lack of interest, familiar in formalist literary criticism, in exploring potential gaps between the complex cultural codes produced in written discourse and daily relations and behaviors. Indeed, the only account that the essay gives of daily relations and behaviors is limited to that of a single case history chosen to illustrate the principle that even persons very marginally related to dominant cultural codes, such as hermaphrodites, move toward reconciling themselves with cultural norms.

Davis's essay, in contrast, does far less close reading of the intricacy of cultural codes and focuses instead on the way that cultural codes inhere in a much wider range of sites: in written discourse, including medical writing and literature but also memoirs, wills, and notarial documents, and in institutions, norms of behavior, and individual behaviors among the upper classes in sixteenth-century France. (Davis's construction of the latter, of course, draws on a wide range of written documents and inferences from them.) Davis's essay, moreover, gives less privilege to public written representation as the site on which cultural codes were produced and more to social institutions and practices. She focuses, that is, on how individuals construct their identity in relation to the social groups to which they belong rather than on how they construct their identity in relation to written texts. Finally she demonstrates a social historian's interest in exploring the gap between cultural codes as they inhere in public written discourse and in the norms of institutions, daily relations, and behaviors. Her essay, in contrast to Greenblatt's, emphasizes the different ways in which individuals receive but also revise cultural codes, often turning those codes to their own individual uses.

The first, more traditionally literary, set of emphases, I would suggest, is once again less conducive to feminist exploration of women's participation in the construction of dominant culture than is the second. For to see culture constructed in theatrical production or public written discourse—especially when public written discourse is expanded, and rightly so, to include a wide range of nonliterary writing as well—is unnecessarily to marginalize even elite women and other more subordinated groups in the very model of culture that is being entertained. For the construction of culture here is equated with something that even white, middle-class women managed far less often than elite men in any period of time—the production of public written discourse. The marginality of even elite women within this model of culture, of course, becomes particularly extreme when, as in this case, all the discourse chosen for inclusion is by men and when the one episode offered as an illumination of individual behavior focuses on the experience of a hermaphrodite who passes through being female to becoming male. This choice of sources, of course, might be accounted for on the grounds that the essay proposes to investigate a set of patriarchal codes in all their dominance, but the absence of any discourse by women or any dissenting nonhomologous discourse by men assumes in a way what the essay sets out to prove, that patriarchal codes were universally dominant, and enforces what the model of culture already implies, that elite men create culture. Both impressions might be interrogated if different sources were also explored.

Davis, of course, does look at written representation by subgroups of women too, and that seems mainly a reflex of feminist politics and intent, but her focus on institutions, relations, and behaviors as a site for the construction of culture, for the articulation or revision of cultural codes, her assumption that culture is constructed at many levels and not just on the level of public written representation alone, seems as much rooted in social historical training and values as in feminist politics. A social historical focus on the family, in particular, has been fruitful for feminist exploration, although here it must be stressed that feminist historians such as Davis have investigated the family as nonfeminist social historians have not—as a site not only for men's but also for women's power and authority as mothers, as household managers, as participants in family enterprise, as a place from which the majority of women spoke, in which they enforced but also set up tensions within, acted upon, and created the systems of meaning that informed their culture at every level.[13]

It is to such relations and behaviors that we must also look if we are to explore the cultural agency of various subgroups of women, and it is in the context of such daily relations and behaviors that we should read public written discourse by subgroups of women and men. Greenblatt's primarily written, literary, and male-authored authorities, for example, are explored for the way in which they reproduce what Greenblatt sees as a dominant understanding in Renaissance culture as a whole—that, although the existence of two sexes may be a necessary fiction, there is in reality one gender alone. But would those sources read differently to us in the context of larger understandings of daily relations and behaviors, say the relations of childbirth and child rearing in elite households, or in the context of analyses that emphasize, as Davis's do, the ways in which different subgroups of women turned cultural codes to their own uses?

It may be with some sense of this distance between the ideological sharpness of written texts and the more cloudy way ideology is expressed in the intricacies of material lives that Davidoff and Hall do not dwell for pages upon their theory but, instead, embed it in their concrete construction of the past. To one whose sensibilities have been altered by the explosion of theory in literary criticism, in particular, over the past few years, *Family Fortunes* might seem at first to be less engaged with theory than it should be. But this is an illusion of the moment. What *Family Fortunes* accomplishes, indeed, is what many new historicists and practitioners of new history as well are just setting out to do, many in response to the "carnival" of abstraction that has colonized our intellectual scene (Russo 1986). That is, they have begun to "recognize the resistance that particularity offers to the grandiosity of abstraction" by testing theory in practice and by beginning to reexamine the relation between discourse and other forms of the material (Miller 1991, xiii).

NOTES

1. See also Goldberg 1982; and Dollimore 1985.
2. See also La Capra 1983; Scott 1987; and Stansell 1987.
3. On my use of postmodernism, see "History as Usual."
4. Other terms such as *symbolic economy*, *ideology*, and *representation* are also used with some rough equivalence.

5. Discourse is often defined as systems of statements governed by rules that determine what can be said and how it can be said. See Toews 1987, 890. As with most of these critical terms and assumptions, however, definitions are shaped by the different agendas of those who use them.

6. See Toews 1987, 885 (summary of La Capra).

7. Representative essays are Dollimore 1985 and Montrose 1985 on new historicism and La Capra 1983 and Toews 1987 and on the "new history of meaning."

8. Representative texts are Neale 1972; Thompson 1983, 143–64; and Perkin 1986. For further discussion of the same idea, see Hall 1981; Alexander 1984; and Davidoff and Hall 1987.

9. Davidoff and Hall (1987) use different but again roughly equivalent terms such as *ideology, symbolic representation,* and *view of the world.*

10. See Davidoff 1979 and Hall 1992.

11. See Armstrong 1987 for a critique of the way political history has shaped literary critical accounts of the past (chap. 1). See Scott 1987; and Stansell 1987 for similar critiques of labor history.

12. See Stansell 1987 on this point.

13. For similar emphases in work on black women in slavery, see Davis 1971; and White 1990 (1983).

Historicisms New and Old: "Charles Dickens" Meets Marxism, Feminism, and West Coast Foucault

(1989)

"Historicism" is sometimes associated with the position that all ideas and beliefs are historically situated or relevant to the age and that an adequate understanding of the nature of anything and an assessment of its value are to be gained by considering it in terms of the place it occupied and the role it played within a process of historical development.[1] If one takes this emphasis, however, upon the historically situated nature of all thinking to be one core assumption of the historicisms that my title names, it might seem clear that Foucauldian "new historicism," like most current versions of Marxist and feminist criticism as well, have moved some distance from that older historicism—scientific Marxist theory and literary critical practice. For in contrast to the latter, most current forms of Foucauldian and feminist new historicism, and Marxist criticism too, have embraced some version of the idea that history as well as literature is constructed and that there is no scientific or even privileged access to the past.

In practice, however, this line of division is less clear-cut than it may seem. For despite the obligatory paragraph or introduction emphasizing the constructed nature of our knowledge of the past, in the applied analyses of the texts, the Foucauldian "new historicist," poststructuralist Marxist, and feminist critic, understandably eager to get on with the literary and/or historical work at hand, are liable to refer to their models of history as if they afforded fairly reliable access to the past after all. Our work, our desire, that is, often prompts us to be less skeptical about our knowledge than our theories would seem to require.

The more consistent lines of division between the historicisms that my title names have to do with the way in which history and power are conceived and with the degree to which progressive agency in history is made to seem possible. These divisions, to be sure, have something to do with the theories of knowledge that these historicisms share, for the idea that literature, history, and experience itself are apprehended in culturally constructed languages or symbolic systems is sometimes extended to the view that human beings are imprisoned within discourse. And the rejection of scientific knowledge of the past is sometimes accompanied by a rejection of totalizing knowledge or even large-scale models of domination and subordination. But here again the degree to which skeptical theoretical positions are consistently embraced, beyond or even within the introductory paragraph, has much to do with what work the critic hopes to accomplish. And the latter has much to do with the political commitments, the needs and desires, of the critic.

In the pages that follow I want very briefly to consider some of the ways in which an exemplary piece of Foucauldian new historicism is like two exemplary versions of one old historicism, traditional and poststructuralist Marxist work, and some of the ways in which it differs, and I wish to explore in more detail how both the similarities and the dissimilarities enter into the relation of Foucauldian new historicism to what might be called that "other" historicism, feminist politics and analysis.

It might seem odd, at first, that I have chosen to illustrate the relations between traditional Marxist, new historicist, and feminist criticism by analyzing some readings of Charles Dickens, and indeed the choice, as with most historical actions, is in part the result of chance. But "Dickens," as it turns out (whether conceived of as an author or a set of texts) has been significant for historically oriented criticisms in several ways. Dickens has been significant for traditional Marxist criticism in that his texts deal explicitly with social issues and in that he writes at a period in which, according to Lukács, the forces for making change were particularly clear.[2] He has been important to poststructuralist Marxists for similar reasons and as a site on which to revise more traditional Marxist readings. Dickens may prove significant for Foucauldian new historicism too but for opposing reasons since the attraction here appears to be to those novels, such as *Bleak House*, which might be seen as suggesting that social institutions such as the legal system operate outside of individual human agency and so are impervious to change. The 1980s, finally, have seen a new surge of feminist writing on Dickens, a development that, I shall argue, marks an interesting and politically significant turn in some feminist thinking about the role of subgroups of women and of various forms of the feminine in culture.

In a very traditional Marxist, such as Arnold Kettle, who explicitly roots himself in Marxist politics, and whose analysis of *Oliver Twist* was published in 1951, pervasive and identifiable relations of domination and subordination are assumed, and so is progressive agency or resistance. Agency is to be found within the novel's world, in the operations of the novel upon us, and in the critic who facilitates the novel's progressive work. In more current forms of Marxist criticism as well, although poststructuralist critiques of totalizing knowledge have left their trace and although dominant forms of power and their interests are more variously defined and agency more tenuously asserted, the lines of continuation are often clear. Thus, David Simpson's reading of *Bleak House*, published in 1982, alludes if not to the poor and the bourgeoisie then to "vested interests," an "exclusive clique," and an excluded class. Agency, moreover, is retained within the characters and within the author too, and by implication within the critic himself, who valorizes Dickens, and it is Dickens who is valorized rather than the text, for being the site of "moral intention," "coherent protest," and "radically creative" strategies (Simpson 1982, 52, 63, 65). In the more popular forms of new historicism, however, which tend, interestingly enough, to be those that do not explicitly root themselves in a political movement, this line of continuation appears to end. D. A. Miller's reading of *Oliver Twist*, for example, first published in 1981, and his reading of *Bleak House*, first published in 1983 (and republished in 1988), although they do less close reading of historical events or nonliterary texts than most of the literary critical work popularly identified as "new historicist," suggest nonetheless many of the assumptions and emphases that inform the Foucauldian new historicism, which practices a more thoroughgoing cross-cultural montage (Miller 1981, 1983).

Drawing upon Foucault's notion of a new type of power whose very diffusion precludes its being located in an attackable center, Miller's essay has little truck with broad-based relations of domination and subordination or with groups in power whose interests may be defined. In Miller's reading of *Bleak House*, in particular, "power organized under the name of Chancery" is faceless and anonymous, its interests other than those of creating business for itself, and therefore perpetuating its existence, impossible to gauge (1983, 60). This power, moreover, can never really be resisted. What seems outside Chancery's power, what seems to limit or contain it—the family, the detectives, the police—not only functions to make "the power organized under the name of Chancery" seem bearable but is also ultimately within that power, doing the work of what it seems to limit.

The role of the text, moreover, is not to spark resistance through a representation of the way that discipline permeates the novel's and perhaps the reader's world but, rather, to train us to endure it and thus to defend the status quo. In *Bleak House*, for example, this defense of the status quo inheres in the way that the novel keeps us off guard by suggesting that Chancery is and is not everywhere and that the family is and is not outside its power, by the way the novel keeps urging us in effect to work at maintaining an outside to Chancery even though that outside may be an illusion. The role of the literary critic is similar, as suggested by Miller's self-fashioning of his name.

Miller, for example, is vague about the degree to which the novel's representations of power actually correspond to anything outside the novel and about the degree to which the novel's ideological operations correspond to ideological operations more broadly produced and distributed. Miller too, that is, seems to train us in not knowing whether we are inside or outside the world of power that *Bleak House* may or may not be said to re-present. Thus, seemingly outside the disciplinary system that he so dexterously describes, in this model of the world in which every outside turns out to be an inside, the critic acts as part of the policing system too. Indeed, the critic as revolutionary, in Arnold Kettle, appears to have given way to the critic as district attorney for the prosecution, that is, to D. A. Miller.

It is in this distance between Foucauldian new historicism and traditional and contemporary Marxism, I would suggest, that Foucauldian new historicism is most distant from feminism too while in many ways appearing more involved than traditional Marxism with issues of gender. Kettle, of course, in contrast to a poststructuralist Marxist such as Simpson, does not deal with gender, the family, or women's cultural agency, and one would hardly expect that of a male Marxist critic writing in 1951. It is not, to be sure, that Marxism had nothing to say about gender in the 1950s but that it conceived of the inequities of gender as the products of private property and class division and saw the family, in so many words, as a "dependent variable" of a mode of production chiefly driven on by men.[3] Gender divisions, therefore, were something to be resolved in the working out of class struggle, a struggle implicitly led by males.

In traditional Marxism, moreover, human identity is always primarily shaped by class. In Kettle's reading of Dickens, therefore, it is not surprising to find that some of the central concerns of feminist analysis, the construction of gendered identity and of familial or intimate "personal relationships," are implicitly identified with the domestic and the feminine and therefore with what is marginal in history. Dickens, for example, in focusing on class struggle, is said to raise issues that make the "whole world of Jane Austen tremble" (Kettle 1960 [1951], 125). *Oliver Twist*, in contrast to *Emma*, is said to deal with what can be called "Life," not with "the day-to-day problems of human behavior" while Dickens's "nauseating" sentiments about mothers are said to interfere with his portrayal of real relations (127).

Yet even Kettle's 1950s model of history, which focuses after all upon broad-based relations of domination and subordination, and which identifies male domination and female subordination as a secondary set of oppressive relationships at least, seems in some ways more conducive to feminist revision than Miller's Foucauldian model, with its faceless "power" and that power's evenhanded involvement and subjection of us all. For models of history, to be useful, must allow us to carry on our work, and many feminists begin with the assumption of systematic subordination when they try to construct theoretical explanations for how social relations operate. Even feminists deeply influenced by poststructuralist distrust of totalizing knowledge characteristically see broad-based relations of domination and subordination as a necessary postulate and prelude to most forms of feminist political labor. One form of this labor, of course, might be to complicate and interrogate the necessary postulate.[4]

In Miller's Foucauldian and often brilliant reading of *Bleak House*, however, although familial and intimate relations are often a point of focus, broad-based relations of domination and subordination, such as those of gender, disappear. All are within power and are victimized by power in turn. Since the ideological operations of power are carried on homologously throughout nineteenth-century culture, moreover, gender and class appear to make little difference even in the degree to which men and women perpetuate disciplinary power or in the effects of the power they perpetuate. Thus, "the family will sometimes be shown as only a slight modification of Chancery's bureaucracy (comfortably domesticated with the Jellybys) or of the police (one of whose different voices can be heard in Mrs. Pardiggle, 'the moral policeman' who regiments her own family in the same spirit she takes others 'into custody')" (Miller 1983, 107). Gender as a subject of overt analysis has been elided, although on the level of critical practice certain habits of thought that owe their existence to traditional gender systems may be seen to lurk.

Despite the fact, for example, that male and female characters are generally construed as acting homologously in their relationship to power, it is women's power that is said to be a reflection or extension of the "power organized under the name of Chancery," which is to say power-organized-under-the-name-of-a-public-institution-run-by-men. By the same token, although Miller's reading tends implicitly to assume that the metaphors that characterize the activities of elite, male-run institutions (stagnation, for example) are those that characterize the activities of female characters as well, it sees the most dramatic developments in the novel, those having to do with the detection of Lady Dedlock's secret and the capture of Hortense, as having been produced by a desire that a public institution run by men calls into being. For in Miller's deft reading Dickens's representation of Chancery, in all its formlessness and indecipherability, prompts Dickens to produce, and the reader to long for, some representation of power that is limited and comprehensible. Since these forms of power are introduced into the novel primarily in the characters of Tulkinghorn, the lawyer, and police inspector Buckett, the most distinctly active, though ambivalently productive, forces in the novel remain implicitly (though never explicitly) masculine. Since Dickens's representation of power in *Bleak House* is assumed to reproduce the operations of power in nineteenth-century culture at large, "real history," as in Kettle, is still mainly a masculine affair.

In our feminist reading of the text (and I draw here on several feminist readings between 1973 and 1983, with extensions and revisions of my own),[5] the text's representation of gender difference, as one would expect, is a central point of focus. Indeed, the text tends to be read as a site on which threats to traditional gender difference are reproduced and then recontained. The power of some women such as Jellyby, Pardiggle, and Snagsby, for example, is seen as being differently represented from "power organized under the name of Chancery" in that these women's power tends uniformly to undercut the privilege, status, and comfort of males. Each of these women is indicted by the text for having exercised surveillance and control in the service of an unbecoming enhancement of her own ego, and in each case this misdirection of surveillance and control produces disorder in the household—drunken servants, dirty rooms, unruly children, and, most important, henpecked men. Mr. Jellyby, for example, is so miserably submerged in "the more shining qualities of his wife" that he appears throughout the novel leaning his head against the wall, while the meek and poetical Mr. Snagsby is said to be not only one bone and flesh with Mrs. Snagsby but one voice as well, "that voice appearing to proceed from Mrs. Snagsby alone" (Dickens 1960 [1852], 119, 32).

Women's social experience as a whole, moreover, is often seen as being constructed somewhat differently from that of men's. Lady Dedlock's flight, for example, and the sight of Hortense walking "shoeless through the wet grass," have been read as part of a larger pattern in the novel whereby women are linked to reckless, independent movement outdoors.[6] The significance of this physical movement, which is produced as negative when it works against male interest or fails to sustain an appearance of male control, is enlarged by the numbers of female characters who have moved out of the domestic sphere to maintain some role in the public sphere as well— Esther, in her charitable work; Mrs. Bagnet, who operates a musical instrument shop; and Caddy, who takes over Prince's school and makes it pay. Movement, of both sorts, is also formally embodied in the split narrative, which gives Esther over half the story. For in contrast to the covertly masculine voice of the omniscient narrator with its focus on the grim side of things (on death, decay, the absence of change), with its reduction of people to types and its detached and disembodied use of present tense, Esther's overtly feminine narration is embodied, connected, and is inclined to emphasize life, the future, change, and the possibility of happiness.[7]

In our feminist reading, of course, the link that the novel forges between women and movement is primarily contrasted rather than made homologous with the images of stagnation and decay that are frequently assigned to Chancery and Parliament, that is, to public-institutions-run-by-men. This split, moreover, is read as a reworking, a re-presentation, of historical developments about which Dickens may have felt some threat—the newly perceived dominance of female writers in the fiction market, for example, and the emergence of organized feminist activity in the late 1840s and early 1850s.[8] Thus, in our feminist reading it is not Chancery alone, Dickens's representation of power organized in a male public sphere, but his representation of the rebellious energies of women that also drive on the narrative's development. For our feminist reading emphasizes the fact that the most significant police action in the novel ends in the arrest of a murderess, Hortense, while the central detective story works to uncover a *woman's* sexual secrets and desires.[9]

The pursuit of Lady Dedlock, moreover, is given significance beyond itself, for Lady Dedlock's desire, her desire for her lover and for upper-class status, is seen as representing multiple kinds of female desire, both social and sexual, in this novel and as resonating with the disorder of that first desiring woman, Eve. As the illegitimate daughter of these failed mothers, even the self-sacrificing and desire-suppressing Esther is somehow tainted. The outer limits of women's autonomous desire, and of its potential threat to social order, are represented, of course, in the French foreigner, Hortense, whose murder of Tulkinghorn, it is suggested, may be linked to her homoerotic jealousy of her mistress. As still another of Lady Dedlock's alter egos, Hortense represents the socially disruptive nature of "women's" desire at its most extreme and is duly associated with "some woman from the streets of Paris in the Reign of Terror."

In our feminist reading of the text, therefore, the most dramatic developments in the novel emblematically enact the curtailment not just of Chancery's formlessness and indecipherability, as Miller suggests, but also the chaotic threat of women's autonomous desire. Miller's Foucauldian reading, in contrast, phases out broad-based relations of domination and subordination and elides what some feminists see as the text's representation of, investment in, and anxiety over gender difference and women's agency (while also maintaining, we should note, some fairly traditional, polarizing, and gender-bound equations of history with men). But there are other differences as well in the way that history is being conceived. For in adding an analysis of gender difference and women's agency to the text, our feminist reading does more than put women in, offering a "ladies' auxiliary" set of concerns. It also changes the way in which we might understand Dickens's representation of the male-run public world on which Miller implicitly focuses, and it complicates the way in which we might understand Miller's own representation of power.

Miller argues persuasively, for example, that Dickens has constructed Chancery within a dual discourse, first working toward containing that power and then doubling back to imply that the power of Chancery cannot be contained after all and is in fact everywhere. Such contradictions, Miller implies, re-produce or re-present the way that nineteenth-century bureaucracies in fact presented themselves or were received, and these same contradictions functioned as a means by which bureaucracies perpetuated their control. It is here, of course, in its tendency to naturalize a representation of dominant forms of power as inescapable, that Miller's essay most intersects with the Foucauldian forms of new historicism that have so far received most comment.[10] But where Miller sees in Dickens's representation of Chancery a re-production of power as it operated in nineteenth-century culture as a whole, our feminist reading might see a set of investments having to do with gender. Both Miller's reading and the feminist one I shall present, for example, see the middle-class family as an institution constructed in relation to the public sphere. The middle-class family, that is, was to offer refuge from the hostilities of the public sphere and, thus, on some levels it was to make that sphere bearable and so facilitate business as usual. In Miller, however, the middle-class family, as represented by Dickens and, seemingly, as constructed in nineteenth-century British culture as a whole, remains—ideologically speaking and despite a complex set of displacements—a dependent variable of a male-run public world. The internal dynamics of the family are therefore muted, and Miller, although he sometimes refers to the family as Esther's and though he alludes to women's work, makes little note of the gender arrangements and gender inequalities by means of which this construction of the family was secured. Miller, indeed, frequently implies that men and women's relations within the home are not only homologous but inexplicably harmonious as well, and the only familial conflicts that his reading officially registers are the largely masculine struggles represented by an allusion to Monk's "oedipal and sibling rivalry" in *Twist*.

Our feminist reading, in contrast, brings Dickens's representation of gender conflict within the middle-class family to the fore, and in so doing it might render the ideological dynamic between representations of the family and representations of a male public world more complex. That is, it sees Dickens's representation of a male-run public world as also dependent upon his representation of the middle-class family. The construction of the middle-class family as refuge depended on a division of gender identities and roles, which excluded middle-class women from the public sphere and defined them as different from men because they lacked or contained autonomous desire.[11] This division, moreover, was inherently unstable, for, if dominant versions of separate spheres ideology functioned to rationalize the inequity of denying autonomous desire to women while liberally granting it to men, they also inevitably offered women a dual discourse, offered them a set of self-interested (masculine) rather than self-sacrificing (feminine) terms in which to imagine their identity and their lives.

A version of the discourse of self-interest is employed by Mrs. Jellyby, Mrs. Pardiggle, and Mrs. Snagsby in conducting missions, pursuing business, and practicing detection without a license. It is this set of terms that Lady Dedlock refuses to relinquish when she walks herself to death and chooses to expire on the steps outside her lover's grave and that Hortense retains when she submits to Buckett with the line "I pity you, and I despise you" (692). In *Bleak House* and in representations of history, our feminist reading suggests, middle-class women resist the containment of their desires, destabilize the construction of the bourgeois family, and disrupt the ideological economy by which the hostilities of a male-run public sphere might seem to be compensated for and also licensed. All of this, our reading suggests, shapes Dickens's representation of Chancery and the dynamics of a male-run public world.

That Dickens, for example, imagines females evading custody, persistently resisting house arrest, suggests of course why Chancery might be represented as what *cannot* be contained—because Dickens sees women failing to provide refuge for men by refusing to suppress their autonomous desires. But the persistence of female desire also suggests why for Dickens Chancery *ought not* to be contained either, why for Dickens Chancery might be most compellingly produced as a form of power that cannot be resisted. For if some manifestations of "power organized under the name of Chancery" are represented as oppressing males too, other manifestations of that power might be seen as representing the power of elite men, a power secured through property and a power exercised and signified by custodial care and control of dependent women.

This custodial power of elite men over women, for example, is ostentatiously, though unsatisfactorily, represented in Sir Leicester, who is repeatedly associated with Chancery and with Parliament, all three being representatives of the principle that property is inherited through the male line. If Chancery, as the text repeatedly suggests, works to sustain a status quo that keeps Lord Dedlock at the top, the latter returns the favor, duly believing that to sanction any complaints in regard to Chancery would be to encourage "some person in the lower classes to rise up somewhere—like Wat Tyler" (Dickens 1960 [1852], 12). Dedlock's status in the world, however, is also defined and secured by his position as head of house and as custodial caretaker of his wife. It is this feature of Dedlock's position above all that Tulkinghorn, who also works for and is sustained by Chancery, means to reestablish or protect in his exposure of the ways in which Lady Dedlock has violated the rules of masculine possession. A parallel investment in custodial care, moreover, appears in other figures who drive on Chancery's power and whose goal in life is to keep themselves in business so they may, in the case of Vohles, support a father and three daughters and, in the case of Guppy, secure a home and install Esther in it. The lord chancellor himself acts as a father figure to Richard and Ada.

It is significant, moreover, that Dickens's satire of Chancery and of Sir Leicester is mitigated by the sympathy with which he portrays them in the role of providers. Sir Leicester's "gallantry" to his lady is "the one little touch of romantic fancy in him," and the lord chancellor as father figure is "both courtly and kind" (Dickens 1960 [1852], 9, 29). Still, neither is particularly satisfying in this role. The lord chancellor is "a poor substitute for the love and pride of parents," and Sir Leicester appears to have purchased his lady's hand without having secured her heart (29). This dissatisfying paternalism is further delegitimated through the association of both with Tulkinghorn, whose investment in Sir Leicester's power is fueled by a distasteful misogyny: "There are women enough in the world," he is fond of saying. "They are at the bottom of all that goes wrong in it." That misogyny is punished, of course, although it is also justified by the act of murder that Hortense commits and the implied secret of her homoerotic passion. Then Tulkinghorn's misogyny is formally disavowed, along with its own homosocial intensity, as Tulkinghorn's dry bachelorlike pursuit is taken over by the familial Mr. Buckett: "What is public life without private ties?" (628).

But if the text formally disavows the dissatisfying paternalism of Sir Leicester and Chancery, it is only to revise and possess it more firmly in the paternal Jaryndyce. Mr. Jaryndyce, of course, is officially a victim of Chancery, and Bleak House, as Jaryndyce has restored it, is deliberately contrasted to that institution. It is a house linked with light rather than fog, flowers rather than mud, and views rather than enclosure. Jaryndyce himself, moreover, though old, is distinguished from Chancery and Sir Leicester both by being linked with change and motion and with robustness rather than stagnation and blight. Jaryndyce and his house, indeed, with their delightful irregularities, suggest nothing so much as nature that has been left to take its course rather than nature enclosed, by the upper class, or nature polluted. And yet Bleak House, like Mr. Jaryndyce, is "old fashioned," like Tulkinghorn and Lord Dedlock, like Chancery itself. And Jaryndyce effectively reworks one of Chancery's powers. In his multiple and self-sacrificing provisions for Esther, he is the tradition of paternalism at its most natural and benign, a tradition handed on by Jaryndyce to Alan Woodcourt, along with Esther and a cottage—so much property through the male line.

Dickens's investment in this masculine inheritance, I would suggest, goes a long way toward complicating our understanding of the contradictory way in which he has imagined Chancery's power, suggesting on the one hand that Chancery is being contained and then doubling back to imply that the power of Chancery cannot be contained after all and is in fact everywhere. The thrust of Miller's argument, as I have suggested, is to imply that such contradictions reproduce the way that nineteenth-century bureaucracies in fact presented themselves or were received, but the same contradictions might also be read as one effect of Dickens's investment in the male custodial power that Chancery drives on or represents. For the operation of even so oppressive an institution as Chancery, like the class and race power of some men over others, is made bearable to a degree if it supports less powerful men's control and ownership of women. If men must be slaves, as Dorothy Dinnerstein has put it, they can at least be rich ones (1977, 191). Our feminist reading, therefore, sees in Dickens's representation of Chancery as that which cannot be contained, a sign of his ambivalent investment in its power, an investment that has much to do with gender.

The investment of many male postmodernist philosophers, including Foucault, in theories that argue for the totalizing force of discourse or disciplinary power is open to a parallel interrogation. This investment, for example, has very often been seen as a response, especially in men once on the Left or in men otherwise invested in social change, to the political disillusions of the 1970s—the dissipation of revolutionary fervor after 1968, the invasion of Czechoslovakia, the failures of Maoism, the disasters of Cambodia, the coming to power of the New Right, the failures of Marxist history to predict historical development.[12] Some critics of Foucauldian new historicism, moreover, suggest that its practitioners continue to invest in totalizing constructions of power as a way of participating in the dominant forms of power that they have also critiqued, as a way of compensating for a sense of political helplessness and disempowerment.[13]

This same investment, I would like to suggest, should also be read in relation to another significant feature of the 1970s and 1980s landscape: the emergence of the women's movement in its second wave and the entry into the academy of a feminist scholarship that was also politically at the cutting edge. Ironically enough, of course, many erstwhile leftist academic men did not respond to the feminist movement as the one bright feature irradiating the postmodern gloom but, if anything, as further cause for throwing politics into question. For if male leftist intellectuals in the 1970s had begun to feel that they were not the solution after all, within feminism they were the problem too. If they experienced increasing impotence in relation to the structures of capitalism, they were now being pushed to relinquish phallic power. If they were obliged to watch the dissolution of a vital movement that had in some respects been theirs, they were now forced to witness the beginning of a revolutionary "party" to which many were hostile and to which, in many ways, they were cordially not invited.

Indeed, Rosa Braidotti has suggested that envy of feminism has been as much a part of the picture as guilt or a sense of threat:

> Lacking the historical experience of oppression on the basis of sex [white, male, middle-class intellectuals] paradoxically lack a minus. Lacking the lack, they cannot participate in the great ferment of ideas that is shaking up Western culture. It must be very painful indeed to have no option other than being the empirical referent of the historical oppressor of women and being asked to account for his atrocities. (Braidotti 1987, 235)

What better time to speculate about how knowledge is interpretation, the truth value of which is low on our list of priorities, and how oppressive discourse scripts and recontains the very resistances that it provokes.[14] For to invest in the inescapability of dominant forms of power, to insist that men and women are in it equally together, is to deny the efficacy of feminism as well as to render feminist analyses obsolete. As in Dickens, this emphasis upon the inescapability of dominant forms of power could function as a form of compensation and of retained control.

The desire for control at the very least seems a force to be reckoned with in many masculinist applications of Foucault's work, and here once more is a lesson in how politics, needs, and desire inflect theory. Much Foucauldian work, in its aversion to constructing broad-based relations of dominance and subordination, in its reluctance to identify interests and specific groups that those interests oppress, appropriates Foucault in his rejection of totalizing knowledge and specifically scientific Marxist theory, yet, like Foucault himself, much Foucauldian-based work recuperates totalizing knowledge in different form. A certain lust for homology, increasingly familiar in Foucauldian new historicist work, often performs this totalizing labor—by flattening out some forms of difference, such as those between women and men or between men of different classes or races, by repetitively locating the same declassed and degendered power dynamic or ideological operation throughout a text or culture, and by implying that an officially degendered but implicitly male and elite power always, in a sense, wins.

Feminists, of course, have also appropriated Foucault as a means of extending, complicating, and sometimes legitimating forms of feminist analysis that converged with or preceded those of Foucault himself. Feminist critiques of masculine elitism in Western knowledge, feminist theorizing about the social construction of sexuality and the body, and feminist definitions of power as less hegemonic, less unified, more multiple, more local, more resisted than traditionally understood—all of these preceded Foucault, although feminist scholars later drew upon his theories (Diamond and Quinby 1988). Feminist appropriations of Foucault, however, have largely deviated from those of nonfeminist men, and again the difference has much to do with needs, desires, and politics. Despite the fact that many feminists have been deeply influenced by skeptical poststructuralist philosophy, and despite the political setbacks of the last few years, many feminist critics still operate not only out of a belief in gender, race, and class oppression but also out of a belief and investment in change. Thus, they tend to retain a sense that those with power may be identified and their interests to some extent gauged, and they tend to retain a sense that progressive human agency is possible, no matter how qualified by the shaping force of dominant ideology.

Belief in the possibility of identifying power, belief in the possibility of progressive agency and change are, of course, preconditions for most feminist and oppositional politics and have been preconditions for many of the scholarly projects that grew from them. One such project, beginning in the early 1970s, is that of writing women into history. In literary criticism this project was first carried on as an attempt to recover the voices of female writers conceived of as writing from the margins or as forming a female subculture. More recently, however, emphasis has shifted to defining the roles of women in all their specificities and differences and to constructing their differing participation in shaping culture itself. Many feminists now work on Dickens and on other discourse by men as a means of demonstrating not just how male writers have symbolically limited and contained women through representation but also as a means of reading the logic by which men's fears and anxieties about women and women's agency—as mothers, as participants in family enterprises, as volunteers—structured the whole of what we have thought of as male capitalist ideology and a masculine public world.[15]

Such readings of culture, I have tried to suggest, are helpful to us in understanding the varying impact of subgroups of women on social relations as a whole and, beyond that, the nature of dominant masculinist ideologies themselves—in Dickens, in the nineteenth century generally, and also in the masculinist histories and literary critical fashions of the present moment. At the same time, feminist readings, in adding an analysis of women's agency, gender relations, and gender and often racial, class, and sexual conflict to their constructions of both the domestic and the interrelated public sphere, will tend to construct dominant ideology as less monolithic than many Foucauldian new historicist readings have done. In adding another layer of tensions to the historical picture, they tend to see dominant ideology not just as more complexly oppressive but as more internally unstable as well.

This tendency to see dominant ideology as unstable, a tendency deeply rooted in the political commitments of the present and the past, may have impact upon the way white feminists respond to the dismantling of their own dominance over theoretical discourse within the U.S. women's movement. For many years, of course, white women's subjectivities, even their reconstructed feminist subjectivities, have been under fire as racist along with their proprietary attitude toward "feminist theory."[16] Now, like white males at the end of the 1960s, white middle-class feminists are more clearly seen as "part of the problem too."

As white middle-class feminists begin to take these criticisms seriously, moreover, as they begin not only to talk and think but also to act, to insist that women of color be hired in women's studies programs, to work at integrating race and ethnicity into their own analyses of gender, they are being called upon to give up privilege within institutions, within women's studies programs, and within the field of feminist theory too. Some white feminists, indeed, anticipate the decentering both of themselves and of gender as a category of analysis. Perhaps "women's studies" may give way to something more like the "study of diversity," and expertise on "diversity" has not been the province of privileged white women. What has been and is going to be white, middle-class women's response?

Elizabeth Spelman (1988) has written about the ways that privilege finds ever deeper places to hide, about the ways in which tolerance, for example, or postmodern emphases upon the relativity of all knowledge, may shore up the privilege they were meant to challenge: if I cannot control the production of truth, then there is no truth at all; everyone is as wrong as I.[17] Will privileged white women take up the theoretical dodges employed by white Western men? Recent critiques of "woman" and theorizing about multiple subjectivities and multiple truths have not generally been accompanied by an embrace of the relativism of knowledge as a whole[18] or a rash of white feminists declaring that racist discourse scripts the very resistance that it provokes. Will it prove the case, then, as Wini Breines (1989) has argued in a recent essay, that privileged white feminists harbor fewer illusions of grandeur than white men? It is too early to say. We are still a long way from the structural changes in women's faculty and curriculum and in feminist theorizing that we are beginning to imagine. Even if white feminists should prove more humble and less given to illusion than their white Western male peers, it is clear that we have illusions of our own to let go of and greater humility to learn. As we analyze the theoretical dodges and self-indulgences of our white male colleagues, we need to reflect, in a continuing way, on the danger of falling into our own.

NOTES

I want to thank Judith Stacey, Martha Vicinus, Judith Walkowitz, and Lesley Rabine for their helpful comments on this piece.

1. For a short history of the term, see "Historicism" in *The Encyclopedia of Philosophy* (Edwards 1972). Critics disagree about the relation between Foucauldian new historicism and poststructuralist Marxist criticism. Pechter (1987, 292), for example, sees "new historicism" as "at its core or at its cutting edge—a kind of Marxist criticism." And Dollimore (1985, 7, 15) lists *new historicism* along with *cultural materialism* under the rubric of "materialist criticism," which he then characterizes as "oppositional." Lentricchia (1988), in contrast, suggests the distance between Marxist perspectives and Foucauldian new historicism and Foucault.

2. See Jameson's account (1971, 204–5).

3. For an analysis of Engels on gender and the family, see Elshtain 1981, 258–62. See also Nicholson 1986, 192–97. On the construction of subjectivity in Marxism, see Smith 1988, 3–23.

4. See on both points Fraser and Nicholson 1988; Diamond and Quinby 1988, 3–19.

5. Although a concern with gender is a central feature of feminist readings, I do not mean to suggest that all feminist readings of *Bleak House,* or of any other text, are alike. Feminist critics, however, do tend to read and build upon one another's work, and there are in fact a group of feminist essays on *Bleak House* that significantly overlap with one another. I shall draw here on the following essays with extensions and revisions of my own: Moers 1973; Kennedy 1979; Senf 1973; and Blain 1985.

6. The following paragraph summarizes much of Moers's (1973) argument.

7. See Senf 1973, for the most detailed analysis of this dual and gendered narrative.

8. See Moers 1973, for a more detailed account.

9. Blain (1985), who sees Lady Dedlock as a scapegoat for the sins, and especially the suppressed sexual violence, of a patriarchal society, elaborates on the representative quality of Lady Dedlock in this novel.

10. The emphasis that Stephen Greenblatt's work, in particular, gives to the power of dominant institutions and the impossibility of progressive change has been the subject of several critiques. See Goldberg 1982, 533; Pechter 1987, 300; Neeley 1988, 15; Boose 1987, 739–41, and Waller 1987, 19.

11. See, for example, Poovey's (1988) analysis of separate spheres ideology in her chapter on *David Copperfield.*

12. See, for example, Eagleton 1983 , 142–44; Jay 1984, 510–37; Felperin 1985, 213–15; Dews 1987, 148, 162, 165; and Simpson 1988, 726–39.

13. See Neeley 1988 and Boose 1987. I have been asked how the following argument can apply to gay men such as Foucault and Miller. My answer is that homosexuality and gay politics do not magically protect one from masculinist investments and desires, just as feminism does not magically protect one from being racist. Much as we may wish for a rainbow coalition, coalition building is not without tension and contradiction.

14. Mascia-Lees, Sharpe, and Cohen (1989) suggest that in the postmodern period (essentially white Western male) theorists stave off their anxiety over "the tremendous loss of mastery in traditionally dominant groups" by "questioning the basis of the truths that they are losing the privilege to define" (14–15).

15. See Poovey 1988b and Armstrong 1987.

16. See, for example, hooks 1984; and Lugones and Spelman 1983.

17. See also Lazreg 1988 on the ways in which academic feminists sometimes exercise discursive power over third-world women through their use of poststructuralist philosophy.

18. See, for example, de Lauretis 1986; Haraway 1988; and Harding 1989.

Sex and Political Economy
in the *Edinburgh Review*

(1990)

Cultural Revolution

The 1830s in Great Britain were marked by struggles to increase the political and social power of middle-class men, by pressures from radicals and feminists to extend political and social authority more widely, by the social dislocations and increasing militancy of the working class, and by the gradual refashioning of "society" to include, under conditions of carefully negotiated control, male laborers and the poor. Not surprisingly, this decade is often characterized as a time of transition, deeply informed by a sense of history, a heightened consciousness that the past was distinctly different from the present and that the future was liable to be marked by greater difference yet.[1] Public written representations of society and social relations, whether structured as novels, as narratives of the past, or as accounts of the principles of historical development, offered a sense of control over time and change while extending to those who could interpret the flux a superior cultural authority.[2] Writing history, indeed, in which self-interested norms and values implicitly governed "disinterested" accounts of the "laws" by which society as a whole progressed, was an important means by which struggles for cultural authority took place.

It was through struggles for cultural authority, in part, that "some values, norms, and qualities (appropriate to the life situation of some social groups) were elevated to become value, normality, quality of life itself" and that "a revolution in government" took place (Corrigan and Sayer 1985, 123).[3] Although this "revolution" signaled no simple triumph of the "middle class," essentially bourgeois and capitalist groups of men were incorporated into the English ruling class, forming an alliance with older aristocracy. At the same time there was "a concerted attempt to disentangle 'the state' from inter-

97

ests, from clientage, from its previously more overt class and patriarchal register," so that the "state" came to represent "a neutral, natural, obvious set of institutionalized routine practices" that successfully laid "claim to the legitimate monopoly of national means of
administration" (Corrigan 1980, 123).[4] The construction of an effi-
cient, centralized, and depoliticized state, in turn, supplied necessary
conditions for the justification of English imperialism (194).

Much has been made in accounts of British state or "cultural"
revolution of the role played by professional middle-class men. Half
in the market and half out of it, ambiguously related to the status of
gentleman as well, their indeterminate social identity made them
well placed to promote values and forms of social authority seemingly unbound to rank or wealth—the value of expertise, for example, and most particularly the value of "disinterested" social
knowledge. On the one hand, of course, professional ideals intersected with the entrepreneurial. The emphasis placed upon expertise, for example, overlapped with entrepreneurial celebrations of
competition based on talent so that, in the process of offering their
own values as the quality of life itself, male professionals may have
shored up entrepreneurial values by displacing them onto higher
ground.[5] But on the other hand, by emphasizing the disinterested
nature of their expertise and by proposing that expertise as a basis
for state operations as well, professionals helped construct the state
as a neutral set of routine practices seemingly divorced from the
interests of class (Corrigan and Sayer 1985, 123; Perkin 1968, 429,
261; Weiner 1981, 8–30). At the same time, of course, male professionals helped secure their own cultural capital as "experts."

As with many accounts of the middle class, in which *middle class*
is largely masculine, *cultural* or *state revolution* is often conceived of
as a "struggle over signs," conducted for the most part by sets of
men.[6] And yet middle-class women, particularly women of letters,
entered into these struggles too, forming their own "counter publics"
(Fraser 1990). Women of letters articulated their own versions of the
laws of historical development, offered their own values as "value"
and the "quality of life itself," and in this way struggled for cultural
space and social authority. Their more marginal position in relation
to the market and the professional "public" world made them even
better placed than professional men to enact the role of social
"crank,"[7] to offer social analyses and critiques of the very market or

social relations on which their class position to some degree hinged. Like their male peers, women of letters promoted values seemingly unlinked to rank or wealth—the value of moral rather than intellectual expertise, the value of cooperation in opposition to the value of competition, whether of money or of merit—while also extolling the values of capitalist enterprise and of an imperialist state.[8] The roles traditionally assigned to genteel women in religious discourse, moreover, those of moral teacher and guide, tinged their social commentaries with a rectitude that the social commentaries of most male professionals lacked.[9] Like men of letters, women of letters might also lay claim, and competing claim, to the role of expert.

Cultural revolution, therefore, like the creation of the modern state, involved a struggle over signs that was conducted by middle-class women as well as by middle-class men and that involved the negotiation of gender as well as class relations. Gender relations, moreover, were not only an issue *between* women and men; they were an issue *among* women of different social positions and political persuasions, and they were an issue *among* men differently positioned in the social formation as well. Although men have sometimes been constructed as gender neutral in past accounts of the "making of the modern state," this cultural revolution was accompanied by the renegotiation of male hierarchies based as much on conflicting masculinities as on conflicting class ideals.[10] Since hegemonic masculinities characteristically offer successful strategies for maintaining the subordination of women,[11] the legitimating processes by which some groups of men secured new forms of authority in relation to other males involved establishing distance from and authority in relation to women as well. These negotiations over gender, moreover, were characteristic of men involved in what would appear to have been the most masculine of discursive worlds, that of the principal writers for the *Edinburgh Review*.

Political Economy and the *Edinburgh Review*

The *Edinburgh Review* was the first of the great political quarterlies and the most successful. In the 1830s, for example, it had a circulation of 12,000–14,000 (in contrast to the *Quarterly's* 10,000, *Blackwood's* 8,000, and the *Westminster Review's* 2,000–3,000) and in addition may have had four to five readers for every copy (Heyck 1982, 33). The

Review was founded in 1802 by a group of young intellectuals whose backgrounds were mainly urban, professional, and middle class. Francis Jeffrey was the son of a deputy clerk in the Court of Sessions and was himself a lawyer. Francis Horner, also trained in the law, was the son of a merchant; Sydney Smith, who had taken orders in the Church of England, was the son of a London businessman; and Henry Brougham, another lawyer, was the child of an impoverished family of the gentry.

The ostensible purpose of the *Review* was "personal amusement" and "the gratification of some personal and national vanity," and in the latter regard the *Review* was certainly functional.[12] As young middle-class men, maintaining Whiggish politics in Tory-dominated Edinburgh, the founders of the *Review* felt themselves marginalized and impeded in pursuing professional careers. The *Review* proved an ideal vehicle for establishing social authority on other grounds. First of all, the *Review* reviewed and therefore claimed authority in relation to texts on a wide range of topics, from political economy to women's novels, scientific treatises to debates in Parliament, imperialist ventures to various kinds of reform, and collections of Greek poetry. The *Review*'s goal, according to Jeffrey, was to "to go deeply into *the Principles*" on which the judgment of a work rested and "to take large and Original views of all the important questions to which these works might relate."[13] Even the length of the essays—individual issues averaged ten to twelve pieces and 250 pages (roughly equivalent to 500 pages in manuscript form)—laid claim to interpretive authority, as did the unusual vigor with which reviewers characteristically expressed their ideas, while the *Review*'s policy of anonymous contributions gave a collective, institutional quality to the individual authorial voice.

In their identification with, and voluminous contribution to, the journal its principal writers found a means of exercising vigorous institutional authority over texts, and, in an age that saw the production of public written representation on an unprecedented scale, this was no insignificant avenue to social capital.[14] The *Review*, moreover, was instantly a success. Sales figures for the first year were 750 copies, and by 1814 the journal had a circulation of 13,000. Although half of the *Review* between 1802 and 1824 was written by Brougham, Jeffrey, and Smith, it also featured a wide range of more famous writers such as Walter Scott, William Wilberforce, Thomas Arnold, Thomas

Carlyle, and William Hazlitt, a testament to and a means of establishing its popularity. Readers of the *Review*, moreover, crossed class lines. Despite the fact that the *Review* is often characterized as a key institution of middle-class life, its implied audience was, to a significant degree, Whig aristocracy, including many figures among the governing elite.[15] The breadth of its audience, the range of classed individuals that it addressed, suggest that the reviewers' claims to social authority were far-reaching.

The most central and overt basis for the *Review*'s claims to interpretive authority lay in the expertise of its writers with relation to political economy. The latter itself was an aggregate of converging views rather than a single specific doctrine, but its characteristics might be described as follows: a reading of historical progress that sees the development of civilization as "characterized by the successive emergence of different modes of production"; an assumption that, "despite the greater degree of inequality of resources which it exemplified, modern commercial society is more compatible with the material welfare of the great majority and with political liberty than any other earlier form of social organization"; an assertion of the belief that market society was ruled by rational laws and was thus a possible object of scientific understanding; and that "any transformation of society for the better could only rest upon the knowledge of such laws and on the observation of the constraints which they indicated" (Fontana 1985, 8). Imperialist conquest, of course, was frequently justified by this coupling of material progress with progressive social transformation, and the *Review* was to become the major vehicle for this "scientific reading" of the laws of historical development in the early nineteenth century.

Many of the *Review*'s claims on behalf of political economy were set forth by John Ramsay McCulloch, the *Review*'s principal writer on political economy during the 1830s. McCulloch was the author of a volume on *The Principles of Political Economy* (1830) and of a commercial dictionary (1832), was the co-author of a statistical account of the British empire (1837), and, in general, was a great collector of statistical data who urged the formation of a Bureau of Statistics in London and regularly criticized the statistical inadequacy of British state policy. Since McCulloch went on to become a civil servant, taking the office of comptroller in the Office of the Stationery, he was doubly positioned, as a man of letters and as a governmental agent, to promote the "science" of political economy as a master theory of history and as a basis for state operations conceived of as natural, neutral, and divorced from class interests.[16]

The metatheoretical claims that the *Review* made on behalf of political economy, however, were launched in a context of cultural ambivalence toward expert knowledge in general and "scientific" knowledge in particular. The growth of a mass market for information, to take one example, and the multiplication of popular and elementary texts conveying knowledge in simple and accessible forms prompted intellectuals such as John Stuart Mill to characterize the 1830s as an era marked by the dogma of common sense and indifference to theory and expertise (Yeo 1984, 7). An essay published in the *Review* refers more darkly to the "vulgar horror with which theory is regarded" (Empson 1833, 8).

The distinction between common sense and informed judgments, moreover, was particularly difficult to make in the moral and social sciences. Writers on political economy, indeed, often refer to themselves as chemists or physicians and sometimes emphasize the abstract and a priori, as opposed to the practical and applied, nature of political economy in an attempt to claim the greater, though also tenuous, authority of natural science:

> We contend that the study is purely a science; our opponents, that it includes the practical adaptations of the science to existing circumstances. . . . The English writers adhere to a precise division of labour . . . upon the principle that the science can never be truly serviceable as a guide and controller to practice, unless it is studied in the first instance on hypothetical assumptions, and by the *a priori* method. (Merivale 1837, 77)

The relation of reviewers to their male audience (essays on political economy routinely position their readers as self-activating, implicitly male, individuals) was further complicated by the fact that their political and personal agendas involved them in conflicting or at least complex representations of their science. As liberals, for example, reviewers sought to establish the authority of political economy on the basis of its being a democratic, commonsensical knowledge, "the people's science," available to all—and therefore deserving of cultural dominance in a properly "open" society (Empson 1833, 8). At the same time they made equally determined attempts to establish political economy as a "recondite" knowledge that only experts like themselves could master (Jeffrey 1825, 6). Political economy was at once a knowledge "useful at all times, eminently useful among the people in times of distress and emergency," and a form of scientific theory so difficult and "abstruse" that only "those who have minds best prepared and most leisure to learn" could really understand it (Jeffrey 1825, 6; Coulson 1831, 338, 339).

Another source of difficulty in staking claim to social authority on the basis of this scientific reading of the world was that political economy was a relatively recent contender for the status of science. Coulson, for example, compares "the task of writing elementary works on a moral science of which the doctrines are not recognized" to

> administering a country imperfectly settled, where the characters of the legislator and the soldier are intimately blended and the reverend authority of a judge will not protect him without pistols at his holsters. The true church in political economy is still a church militant; and every teacher must act the part of a controversialist. (Coulson 1831, 339)

Dangerous and alien others are evoked here to consolidate the identification of political economy with the British state, to minimize internal differences among English citizens, and to identify opposition to political economy with treason to civilization. This transposition of political economy from a domestic setting, in which it evoked visions of self-interest and of competition between male English citizens, to an imperialist register, in which it evoked united effort against dangerous others, was an important strategy for securing the legitimacy of this new knowledge.

Political economy, moreover, was under attack in the 1830s, both in working-class and Tory journals, as an articulation of class and sectional interests. As somewhat marginalized middle-class men pursuing professional advance, the chief reviewers were understandably invested in a science that demonstrated the universal benefits of a society open to the pursuit of self-interest. But political economists such as McCulloch were also regularly accused of being "in the pay of capitalists" as well and therefore of not being objective or scientific at all (Thompson 1984, 22). Partially, though not solely, in response to these attacks, I would suggest, reviewers maintained an ambivalent relation to entrepreneurs and therefore to an important section of their reading audience. On the one hand, for example, the reviewers' insistence that commercial progress based on self-interest is a key to moral as well as to material well-being seems a strategy for joining forces with entrepreneurs. But on the other hand, this insistence on the moral outcome of material production suggests an effort to rise above the merely commercial. *Review* essays, indeed, are marked both by persistent celebrations of commercial progress and by persistent efforts to transcend the concerns of wealth and industry, which are continually linked to the body and to "sensuality" and therefore to what is less "exalted" than the "intellectual":

> It is by *this* process unquestionably that the body of any society ever becomes intelligent, moral, or refined and reflection and observation concur to show that their progress in these attainments is uniformly proportional to the increase of their wealth and industry; and that there is in fact no other training by which they can be exalted into intellectual beings, but that which is necessarily involved in their pursuit of those vulgar comforts and venal luxuries which may seem at first sight to terminate in selfishness and sensuality. (Jeffrey 1825, 5)

Commercial prosperity, moreover, is represented not only as supplying the necessary but less exalted preconditions for moral and intellectual improvement; it is represented as *dependent* upon an intellectual and theoretical project—the scientific understanding of, and reasoning from, the natural laws governing wealth, trade, and population. Thus, McCulloch writes in 1835 that

> it seems pretty certain that the best means of preserving our ascendancy in them [in a prosperity and power based on manufactures] will be most likely to be discovered by carefully investigating the causes that have brought them to their present high pitch of perfection in this country, and which have retarded their progress amongst our neighbors. (455)

In claiming social authority on the basis of theorizing material advance, reviewers placed themselves at the heart of "progress" while at the same time claiming a transcendent relation to material production and to entrepreneurs: political economy, though *"directly conversant only about wealth and industry*—though having for its *immediate* object but the bodily comforts and worldly enjoyments of men,*"* is at the same time "the best nurse of all elegance and refinement, the surest guarantee for justice, order and freedom, and the only safe basis for every species of moral and intellectual improvement" (Jeffrey 1825, 2). It was these delicate and multiple maneuvers with respect to its male readership that helped make the *Review*'s treatment of female discourse so central to its self-legitimating functions.

Sex and Political Economy

Although the *Review* devoted more essays to women during the 1830s than during the 1820s, a suggestion that women and women's writing were increasingly a matter of concern, it maintained a strict division between essays on "historically significant" topics such as political economy and its essays on female writers. Women, even working-class women for the most part, do not appear in essays on the former and are not officially addressed as readers. The audience for essays on women, however, is implicitly dual. While the female writer, and through her genteel women in general, are corrected, warned, exhorted, categorized, selectively praised, and defined as different from male writers, male readers are implicitly positioned as persons identifying with the reviewer. Since the thrust of *Review* essays on women was to justify placing limits on women's access to the public sphere, they offered a gender "knowledge" that most male readers could be assumed to see as objective, disinterested, and "true." *Review* essays on women, therefore, situated reviewers in a more authoritative position with respect to male readers than did essays on political economy and worked toward establishing the *Review*'s expertise and interpretive authority for male readers in other, more problematic spheres.

To some extent, of course, the *Review*'s essays on ostensibly neutral subjects such as Greek poetry and scientific inventions performed a similar function. But the *Review*'s essays on women also provided sites on which to establish the specifically masculine credentials of the *Review* and of its chief reviewers by: (1) constructing the *Review* generally as a powerful institution for maintaining genteel women's subordination through interpreting and limiting the significance of their entry into public discursive spheres, and (2) distinguishing women's limited authority as interpreters of history and social relations from the reviewer's own metatheoretical expertise (crucial in the case of women writing on natural science and on political economy).

Verification of masculinity as a form of distance from, superiority to, and control over women, and over other subordinated others, was of particular importance to liberal reviewers in the 1830s. Reviewers, for one thing, claimed social authority on the basis of mental abilities that were potentially more accessible to women (mental abilities, after all, might be honed in a sitting room) than the rank or money on which more entrenched forms of masculine social authority were based. And of what value is a form of masculine authority that women can share, particularly if that authority must contend with more established and less accessible forms of masculine power? Liberal constructions of the public sphere, moreover (including those of political economy as defined by the *Review*), opened up the public sphere, discursively speaking, to feminine appropriation as the overtly hierarchical and paternalistic ideologies of landed men did not.

Seventeenth-century liberalism, for example, while officially restricting women to the domestic sphere and implicitly omitting them from the category of rational individual and citizen, did not directly deny the rationality of middle-class women. Indeed, it offered terms for self-understanding (*rational individual*, for example,) which feminists such as Mary Wollstonecraft and Harriet Martineau effectively appropriated on women's behalf.[17] By the 1830s British feminists and radicals such as Mary Wollstonecraft, Walter Thompson and Anna Wheeler, W. J. Fox, and Mary Grimstone had challenged the exclusion of women from the categories of rational individual and citizen, sometimes drawing on religious discourse, in the case of Wollstonecraft, to argue that the doctrine of spiritual equality before the eyes of God provided a basis upon which to challenge the liberal division between women and rational man. By the 1830s, moreover, the rationality of women and the necessity of extending and improving their education was a well-established liberal position, although it was restricted in much liberal discourse to improving women's performance as wives, mothers, and/or guardians of the poor.[18] Bulwer-Lytton, for example, argues in an essay written for the *Review* that, "in the education women receive, we would enlarge their ideas to the comprehension of political integrity" but that "we are far from wishing that women, of what rank soever, should intermeddle with party politics" (Bulwer-Lytton 1831, 379).

Discourse on the education of women, moreover, became particularly significant in the context of debates over parliamentary reform, debates in which the *Review* played a leading role. The journal supported reform in the 1830s and was a major vehicle for propaganda on its behalf.[19] Its support, however, was based on expediency rather than rights. Reform for the middle ranks of men was justified because it promised them a degree of political influence proportional to the importance they had already acquired in the social and economic life of the country. Reform was not necessarily legitimate for the lower orders or for genteel women, who had not achieved the same social and economic standing.

Debate over reform, nonetheless, did raise questions, even for reviewers, about the degree to which democratization might be extended. It raised one question, for example, about the degree to which the continued education and material improvement of working-class men might be translated into a justification for further extending their political power. Reviewers supported education for the male working class but expressed anxiety at the idea that the consequences of such education might exceed their own political goals and interests. Jeffrey, for example, worries that the (male) lower orders are making "rapid and remarkable progress in political economy and all other branches of knowledge" and that, in so doing, they are acquiring the "distinction and visible predominance that attaches in public life to those who can counsel on it with authority":

Of all the derangements that can well take place in a civilized community, one of the most embarrassing and discredible would be that which arose from the working classes becoming more intelligent than their employers. It would end undoubtedly, as

it ought to end—in a mutual exchange of property and condition—but would not fail in the meantime, to give rise to great
and unseemly disorders. (1825, 11)

Debate on reform also raised the specter of political power for
women as well, an issue directly taken up by radicals such as Fox,
by feminists such as Martineau, and by Owenite socialists, who continued to advocate women's full participation in public life and to call
for a radical reorganization of familial relations.[20] The *Review*, however, generally drew the line here. Genteel women ought to be educated. Indeed, political economy itself might be recommended as a
subject for women on the basis of "its intimate connection with the
protection and comfort of the poor," but "the less women usually
meddle with any thing which can be called public life out of their
village, we are sure the better for all parties" (Empson 1833, 1).

Many intersecting discourses, then, helped to make genteel
women's education and potential entry into public political life a
matter of concern in the 1830s. The *Review*, moreover, directly participated in several, taking liberal positions—in relation to reform and
male working-class education—that might seem to implicate it in
further democratizing moves. It is in this context, the context of the
Review's own liberalism, that its essays on women must be read, for
it is not merely women's ambition or restiveness that reviewers encounter there and attempt to contain; it is the democratic tendencies
of their own liberal philosophies.

Men of Science

Reviewers eluded the implications of their own liberalism, to some
degree, by promoting a new and more exclusive category of cultural
authority to which to belong—the category "men of science." The
authority associated with men of science, of course, is more explicitly
masculine than the authority associated with rational individual (an
identity to which feminists and women of letters increasingly laid
claim). Women of letters may be comfortably acknowledged by the
Review to be rational persons making respectable contributions to
cultural knowledge, but they are not, we may agree, men of science.
As in some contemporary genealogies of theoretical fields, women's
knowledge is given its due, but its meanings are limited and the

nature of that knowledge is carefully distinguished from the superior knowledge attributed to the men writing the reviews. There is a second way, however, in which the category men of science is more exclusive than that of rational individual. Since the very identity men of science was being constructed through the growth of scientific societies, possession of it might, to some extent, be formally certified and controlled. Like other professional organizations, which proliferated in the 1830s and 1840s in Great Britain, scientific organizations such as the Royal Society, the Statistical Society, and the Political Economy Club, to which reviewers variously belonged, helped establish the social value of a specific form of expertise. Although scientific societies were not tied to a particular profession, in contrast to comparable organizations in other fields, they *were* restricted to those invested in and presumably capable of scientific knowledge, whether of the "facts" expressed by numbers, the laws governing wealth, or the operations of the physical world. Like other professional organizations, therefore, scientific societies helped establish the cultural authority of a particular expertise while also conferring the status of expert, men of science, upon their members.[21]

Although scientific societies included men belonging to various subgroups of the upper and middle classes, membership, to some degree, entailed being placed in a single category. Scientific societies, in this way, eroded vertical class distinctions between middle-class male professionals and male members of the upper class, improved the social standing of the former, and helped consolidate new cross-class alliances or brotherhoods. Working-class men were omitted from such brotherhoods but were frequently a target audience for the spread of scientific knowledge through mechanics institutes. Those who most distinctly defined the outside to these insiders' clubs were women.[22]

As with other professional organizations, scientific societies helped demarcate a newly burgeoning field as the sphere of gentlemen, enforcing in this way that emphasis on gender divisions that was so central a feature of industrial capitalist society. In contrast to the fields of medicine or law, however, the more amorphous field of scientific theory, entailing neither formal training nor official career structures, was less closed to women. Scientific brotherhoods, for all their exclusivity, did not prevent women such as Mary Somerville, Mrs. Marcet, and Harriet Martineau from publishing on natural and political sciences in the 1830s and entering thereby into a scientific public sphere, nor did they prevent them from enjoying immense popularity as well. It was in the context of the more porous boundaries marking the field of scientific theory that the *Review*, itself a form of brotherhood, played an important gate-keeping role.

As theorists and self-styled men of science, liberal reviewers had a stake in excluding women from the inner circles of scientific and theoretical expertise that less theoretical men did not, and yet their relegation of women to this outer circle was in some ways more tenuous than that of other reviewers writing on the same female authors. Reviewers for the Tory *Quarterly*, for example, were given to vigorously asserting biologically-based hierarchies between women and men: "Notwithstanding all the dreams of theorists there is a sex in minds" (Whelwell 1834, 65). They were also fond of exercising a species of discursive violence against women, by reminding readers, for example, of how eminent women of science had (unhappily) been burned and butchered or otherwise forcibly excluded from the public sphere by men (Whelwell 1834, 54–68; Scrope 1833, 136–52). Liberal reviewers were too immersed in discourse about the necessity for women's education, too wed to concepts of free choice and effort, as keys to success in the public sphere, for that.

Liberal reviewers, instead, sometimes based women's exclusion from authentic scientific expertise on a division of labor, freely chosen by women, in part, but also based on the association of women with the physical and the practical and the association of science with the theoretical, the abstract, and the disembodied. In a review of Mrs. Somerville's *On the Connexion of the Physical Sciences*, for example, the author is praised for her "popular treatise" on science but gently chastised, in this case, for having chosen a "limited and humble" sphere of practical activity over "pursuits more lofty in their aim" such as discovering new phenomena or tracing new relations (Brewster 1834, 155, 171). Harriet Martineau and Mrs. Marcet, however, are congratulated for having voluntarily "undertaken to preach the practical truths and blessings" of the science of political economy "rather than its mysteries and creed":

> Discoverers are seldom the best teachers. The moment, however, comes at last, when the revealers of hidden mysteries meet

with disciples who prove more successful missionaries than themselves. Political Economy, we rejoice to think, has apparently nearly waited its appointed time. The mysteries and abstractions have retired for a while into the inner sanctuary; whilst, among the ministers of the outer courts, and throughout even the surrounding multitude, there are symptoms of movement which bespeak the arrival of the missionary era. (Empson 1833, 2, 8)

Females, and less theoretical males, are represented here as practice-oriented "missionaries" and "disciples" and as physically active in the "outer court." The experts on political economy, "the revealers of hidden mysteries," are represented as inactive and theoretical, having "retired for awhile" with "the mysteries and abstractions" into "the inner sanctuary" (8).

The abstract and disembodied authority that reviewers constructed for themselves as men of science functioned, of course, as a discourse on masculinity as well. Political economy as a science that "regards Man in the abstract," as a science in which it is "essential to keep separate the theoretical from the practical," might logically require as its advocate the man of science who is bound,

like the juryman, to give true deliverance according to the evidence, and to allow neither sympathy with indigence, nor disgust at profusion and avarice; neither reverence for existing institutions, nor detestation of existing abuses . . . to deter him from stating what he believes to be the fact, or from drawing from those facts what appear to him to be the legitimate conclusions. (Merivale 1837, 83, 81, 82, 76, 77)

But this dispassionate and disembodied authority also served to separate reviewers from women, especially women writing in the same field, and it positioned reviewers as more authentically masculine in relation to competing subgroups of men. For the association of women with the physical and active, in essays on women, intersects with an association already established, in essays on political economy, between the physical, active life and entrepreneurs. (This association, of course, resonated with the negative valence of associations more widely entertained by middle- and upper-class people, associations between the active and the physical and nonwhite, or lower-class, others [Davidoff 1979, 79]). Indeed, the active, producing entrepreneur, whose masculine credentials were better established than those of reviewers, and less accessible to women as well, is frequently linked with the physical, the sensuous, and the body, all feminized sites in the pages of the *Review* (and classed and racialized sites in nineteenth-century British middle-class culture.) Physical, material, and practical qualities, present in earlier forms of elite masculinity, therefore, are displaced onto genteel women, while also being identified with competing subgroups of middle-class men, at the same time that political economists are defined as truly masculine, in newly cerebral, theoretical, and disembodied terms.[23]

The Power of Women

Although this construction of a theoretical and disembodied masculinity should be read in relation to the reviewers' concerns over status in the public sphere, it is inadequate to leave the matter there, as if these, or any, men lived in or for the "public" world alone, as if men had no stakes in, no concerns about, the domestic and familial. The familiarity of separate-spheres ideology should not obscure for us the porousness of public and domestic or the relative fluidity of boundary between constructions of the masculine and feminine, nor should it obscure for us the tensions and contradictions that traditional ways of drawing those boundaries have produced. *Review* essays on women, for example, may have focused on containing women and the impact of their written discourse to traditional domestic spheres, but this containment was itself accompanied by anxious reflection upon women's domestic power. Home, indeed, as constructed in the pages of the *Review,* is not a place about which many reviewers feel at ease but is, rather, another sphere in which boundaries must be drawn, fortified, and patrolled.

The novel, for example, is sometimes tentatively defined in the *Review* as a predominantly domestic and feminine genre. As items consumed in domestic space, novels, and women's novels in particular, are characterized by a focus on the "minutiae" of "domestic life" and are essentially on the margins of history. Women's novels may be in touch with those "varieties which chequer the surface of society," but they have nothing to do with that profound forward movement that is what real history is about (Lister 1830, 445–46). Thus, despite the fact that women's novels have value for their "improvement" of their reader's heart ("that office for which woman is by nature best calculated"), women's moral influence is strictly local in its field and its effects (447).

This confident containment of women's influence is, however, far from secure. For despite wish-fulfilling claims that women are "less ambitious" than men or that women's "personal ambition" is satisfied by "active benevolence in relieving the distressed," women's ambition appears to be lurking everywhere (Lister 1830, 446; Empson 1933, 1). Female novelists, for example, though focused on domestic life, have "stuffed the pages of an ordinary love tale with grave and weighty disquisitions," thereby "alluring" the masculine reader "to the well-cushioned sofa of the novel reader" but leaving him "seated in the uneasy chair of the scholastic disputant" (Lister 1830, 444). Women's ambition is also expressed through the "education they give their children and in advice they bestow on their husbands," resulting in that "senseless heartless system of ostentation which pervades society." Even motherly ambition on behalf of children may become the secret cause of "the tarnished character and venal vote of the husband" (Bulwer-Lytton 1831, 378).

Yet anxiety over domestic women is not restricted to strictures against unseemly feminine ambitions. Metaphors suggesting uneasiness and threat appear in descriptions of women at their least assuming and most domesticized. In a review of Anna Jameson's work on Shakespeare's heroines, for example, Jameson is praised for choosing "the department" in which her powers may be "most efficiently and conspicuously exercised," "philosophic *female* criticisms," "the female characters of Shakespeare." Female characters, the subject of Jameson's explorations, are then identified with the home itself:

> Study and observation may afford a sufficient glimmer of light to illuminate the common apartments and familiar passages, as it were, in the labyrinth of the female heart, but they desert us entirely, or only lead us astray, when we endeavour, by their fitful ray, to thread our way through the more mysterious recesses of the edifice;—its sacred retirements, its "chambers of

imagery," its wells of feeling, its vault of secrecy, suffering or crime. The torch that would guide us surely through these must be held by a female hand. (Anon. 1835, 180, 181, 183, 184)

The home, and by extension, women, as the place from which men freely come and go, the place in which "they read novels on a "well-cushioned sofa," becomes the labyrinth in which unfortunate men become entrapped and die (Lister 1831, 444). The sexual anxiety suggested by the figure of labyrinthine women seems obvious, and it is worth noting that the labyrinthine nature of women's sexual and reproductive organs was already being mapped by male medical experts, making a female guide unnecessary. But on another and related level the figure of the labyrinthine women also suggests that fear of being contained, a fear, in part, of being held by those who share the mother's sex.[24] Even the protective otherness of women, an otherness that grounds the construction of masculine identity in nineteenth-century texts, becomes a source of vague anxiety, for what is mysterious cannot be easily controlled. Indeed, the mind of man is a blind guide when "applied to the thoughts and actions of beings whose clay seems of another temper; and who are acted on by many secret and complex influences which we cannot see and with which we cannot sympathize" (Anon. 1834, 183).

What was to become the "woman question" in the early 1840s then, for the *Review* and for other male-run journals, certainly involved anxiety over women's entry into the public world of representation and political power, as it involved anxiety over the possibility that women might reject their confinement and their labor in the domestic sphere. (The most alarming feature of Martineau's *Illustrations*, according to the *Quarterly Review*, was her Malthusian criticism of working-class marriage and childbearing.) But the woman question also involved anxiety over the power that women wielded in the domestic life to which they were confined, a power, I would suggest, that was most forcefully expressed as mothers.

Leonore Davidoff and Catherine Hall (1987), in their study of nineteenth-century middle-class life, note that, "despite the emphasis on motherhood in the prescriptive material, the depiction of mother-son relationships is somewhat thin if overly idealized." They note, as well, the absence of the erotic overtones that frequently appear in allusions to father-daughter relations, reminding us that sons "had the task of breaking away from intense but *dependent* relationship with their mother (or substitute female caretaker)" (Davidoff and Hall 1987, 356). The relation between middle-class mothers and middle-class sons, moreover, may have become more intense in the early nineteenth century. The physical separation of homes from workplaces among the middle class isolated women in the family, probably intensified the relation between mother and children, mother and sons, and was accompanied by a shift from father to mother as primary parent.

Cultural assessments of the power of middle-class mothers, moreover, may have been exaggerated by some of the very ideological strategies by which genteel women's participation in the public realm was being contained. The fluidity of early capitalist relations and the expansion of capitalism and of capitalist-organized agriculture, according to Davidoff and Hall, produced a wealth that was gender neutral and that raised disturbing possibilities that women, as carriers of wealth, and as potential wage earners, might gain access to new forms of money and power. The specter of this possibility became the basis for a new demarcation and containment of women, a demarcation already present in preexistent ideas, laws, institutions and, most particularly, theology, and one that insured that the reorganization of the economy and labor would remain in male hands.[25] Widespread emphasis on the separation of spheres and the separation of the world into masculine and feminine was, of course, a major vehicle for this containment and control.

The ideology of separate spheres, however, may have had less functional effects as well, for its relegation of women to the home was accompanied by compensatory assertions about women's domestic power—"women have long reigned supreme over both the learning and the practice of domestic economy" that coincided with what appears to have been an actual increase in the centrality of genteel mothers within the home (Empson 1833, 1). If, as many feminist theorists have maintained, adult and especially white, middle-class masculine identities are grounded in an (always constructed) sense of separation from the mother, the "fantasized mother . . . terrifying in her power and wrath and overwhelmingly seductive in her promise of a recaptured 'oceanic' environment" and the mother as "nurturant ground of life itself and the 'other' against which modern individuated selves must assert their autonomy," then these shifts in and reconstructions of middle-class women's domestic power may well have produced cultural anxiety for genteel men (Di Stefano 1991, 14). Certainly, *Review* essays on women have as much to do with anxiety over women's power in the home as with the reviewer's concerns over women's ambition for status and power in the public world.

The tensions involved in domestic middle-class relations, however, including men's anxiety over women's domestic power, were not confined to discourse specifically on women but had impact, I believe, on all constructions of the so-called public world. If *Review* essays on women, for example, addressed some of the discursive tensions that attended the efforts of its main reviewers' to popularize political economy and to establish cultural authority vis-à-vis other men, essays on political economy might be seen as a species of dream work useful in working through anxieties and longings generated by (always constructed) relations in the middle-class home. Women, for example, and the intimate domestic relationships over which they presided, are not simply excluded, in some tidy dualism, from real history in the *Review*—real history being scientific accounts of the public world as inhabited by men. Relationships, roles, and functions associated with middle-class women are regularly employed in essays on political economy to humanize, soften, and enliven the reviewer's scientific reading of men's relations to men and the nature of industrial progress.

McCulloch's "Philosophy of Manufactures," for example, published in 1835, conceives of history in a way that appears to leave women out. For history is commercial progress conceived of as a giant "race," while the public world, in which history takes place, consists of implicitly male individuals pursuing their own self-interest: "In England the highest offices of the state have been accessible to every deserving individual, and every man has been allowed to exert his own energies in his own way" (McCulloch 1835, 459, 461). But the public world is divided in this essay into a domestic and a nondomestic front, one competitive and the other communal. Thus, the race for commercial progress is offered not as a struggle between English men in the domestic market but, rather, as a patriotic and unified struggle between England and other industrial capitalist nations in "the race of improvement," a struggle in which English men are domestically united "at home" (455). Shared and familiar understandings about the gendered division of the social world and about the relative harmony of domestic ties soften the essays' representation of Englishmen's class relations and are central here to the constitution of England as a nation-state, as that which transcends differences between citizens and that which is defined by what is threatening and outside.

McCulloch, however, does not imagine this national community in familial terms, as the full logic of separate spheres would dictate. Rather, male domestic relations are implicitly compared to the workings of a factory, which in itself is compared (in a quotation from Andrew Ure) to the operation of a giant machine. Each individual citizen, that is, an individual stripped of any embodied or material identity, asserts "his energies in his own way" and, in concert, "produce[s] results that must appear all but incredible to persons placed under less exciting circumstances" (McCulloch 1835, 461). Domestic society, like factories, appears to be "a vast automaton, composed of various mechanical and intellectual organs, acting in uninterrupted concert for the production of a common object, all of them being subordinated to a self-regulated moving force" (434). Domestic relations are appropriated, but they are also reimagined in disembodied, masculinized, and carefully atomized form.[26]

To employ familial metaphors for social relations, of course, would also have evoked older aristocratic views of the public sphere in which social relations are fixed and hierarchical and in which upper-class men are heads of house. This metaphorical structuration of the world was still very much alive in the pages of *Backwoods* and the *Quarterly* and in the discourse of factory reformers. As I suggest in "Ministers of the Interior," moreover, manual writers and also liberal and radical feminists constructed their own equally familial versions of social relations in which middle-class women, rather than upper-class men, took a leadership role. It is not surprising, then, that McCulloch avoids a familial or paternal model for social relations broadly conceived.

Paternalism, however, *is* evoked in the narrow and privatized sphere of the factory, a mirror image of the middle-class home. In a quote from Ure workers appear less like laborers than coddled dependents, idle nine hours of twelve, given to reading, well supplied with domestic comforts of tea water, doctoring, and dancing rooms (McCullock 1835, 465–66). Factories, moreover, like middle-class homes, are also "academies," in which children are imbued with moral instruction and with "regular, orderly, and industrious habits" (464). The buried metaphor by which English society has been compared to a factory, in which every part works on its own, gives way here to a view of social relations in which factories and English society are regulated and controlled by fatherly entrepreneurs.

The equation of home and factory, of course, reasserts male entrepreneurial dominion not only in the public but in the domestic sphere as well. Indeed, the equation ascribes to entrepreneurs those educating functions that women were supposed to carry on or else that women were supposed to facilitate in men. But just as the assertion of public dominance is muted by its metaphoric construction as domestic rule, so the assertion of domestic rule is displaced, coming as it does in an account of political economy rather than in an essay on women and women's sphere. Dominant understandings of domestic middle-class gender ties are evoked and reworked, therefore, to naturalize and soften McCulloch's representation of male class relations and the British state, but they are also reworked to reassert men's parental centrality within the home.

McCulloch's evocations of traditional middle-class familial relations suggest an investment in them and a corresponding sense of unease. The same is true of the essays' deployment of nature, mortality, and birth, qualities dominantly associated with women and with lower-class and racial others in middle-class nineteenth-century representation and qualities that the essay employs at times, ambivalently and with contradiction, to naturalize and assign life-giving functions to material and largely machine-based production. Early in his essay, for example, McCulloch suggests that nature, through the provision of natural physical and moral resources, is the real cause of industrial development. But this effort to create a unifying and legitimating myth, in which nature and not profit-making entrepreneurs bring about industrialization, stands in some tension with McCulloch's desire to present entrepreneurs and then political economists as the motor of history. Male human agency, for example, begins to erode the agency of nature early in the essay, when McCulloch represents man-made machines as at first rivaling and then displacing natural resources in importance; steam engines supplant water falls as a source of industrial power because "steam may be supplied with greater regularity, and being more under command than water, is therefore a more desireable agent" (McCulloch 1835, 457). Machines, moreover, are superior to horses, for horses are alive and inconveniently mortal: "What a multitude of valuable horses would have been worn out in doing the service of these machines and what a vast quantity of grain would they have consumed!" (458).

Implicit in this shift from natural resources to man-made machines is an ambivalent set of attitudes toward nature and mortality. Neither are fully "under command," and yet the shift from nature to machines, the shift to what can be easily controlled, to what is not mortal, represents an alignment with what is not alive. This is not an alignment that the essay will finally embrace. In a replay of the Frankenstein myth, therefore, what is dead must be made to live. As machines displace nature, they begin humanly to intervene in history, calling "into employment multitudes of miners, engineers, and ship-builders, and sailors," "causing" the construction of canals and railways, and otherwise taking on the role of the entrepreneur (McCulloch 1835, 458). Entrepreneurs are then praised for having produced these entrepreneurial machines in an "all but miraculous creation" (472). Entrepreneurs, that is, appear to give birth, by immaculate conception, to themselves and in the process endow machine-based industrial production with women's life-creating functions. This appropriation of birth, this fantasy of autonomous self-creation—especially interesting in a man whose wife bore him twelve children—suggests both a subterranean identification with and escape from mortality, from birthing bodies, from dependence on women and from proximity to classed and raced subordinates.[27]

The reference to "all but miraculous creation" also positions entrepreneurs as more Godlike than God, in their invention of machines that do more than nature to further material progress. Since the invention or creation of key machines was the work of "a few obscure mechanics," it seems at first that this central role is relatively open to men from below. But artisans prove less significant in this history than it would at first appear. In the hands of the lower-class inventor the spinning frame, "how ingenious soever, was of no use, and all traces of it seem to have been lost." The real credit belongs to Arkwright, who invented it "a second time," by showing "how it might be rendered the most prolific source of individual and "public" wealth" (McCulloch 1835, 471). It is the unembodied interpretation of material invention/life creation that makes it useful to the social world, just as it is the objective, disembodied political economist who, "in carefully investigating" the causes of progress, insures the continuation of that commercial race and imperialist ventures set in motion by more materially bound entrepreneurs.

The *Review*'s construction of a social authority based on theoretical, scientific expertise centrally involved a discourse on masculinity and gender, a discourse that must be read in relation to multiple interests and investments, not all of which have solely to do with power and status in the public sphere. If the construction of a cerebral, nonphysical masculinity is read as an attempt to establish the masculine credentials of chief reviewers by distinguishing reviewers from female competitors in the field and by implicitly laying claim to a superior form of masculinity with respect to entrepreneurs, if this distance from entrepreneurs is read as an attempt to suggest the reviewers' transcendence of class and personal interests and as an attempt to legitimate the objective, scientific nature of political economy, if this emphasis on disembodiment is read as an attempt to perpetuate genteel women's confinement to the domestic sphere, these same emphases must also be read as an attempt to deal with newly augmented anxieties in relation to women's power in the home. Despite their self-construction as objective, disembodied agents in the public sphere, reviewers, like most men, had familial longings and anxieties as well, and these longings and anxieties entered into their scientific accounts of history and social relations. Anxiety over the middle-class mother's and women's powerful embodiedness, indeed, may centrally explain that "dread of unruly forces" and of the "biological and economic processes on which life exists" that other writers have marked in the new class of professional intellectuals.[28] That same anxiety no doubt lay at the heart of Foucault's technologies of power and at the heart, perhaps, of his own equation of this degendered knowledge with the truth of the modern age.[29]

NOTES

1. Such characterizations, of course, began with the Victorians themselves. See, for example, Mill 1831: "The idea of comparing one's own age

with former ages, or with our notion of those which are yet to come, had occurred to philosophers; but it never before was itself the dominant idea of any age" (28). See also Houghton 1957, 1–23, 34–35; Knights 1978, 10–12; Heyck 1982, 122–23; Dale 1977, 1–4.

2. Knights 1978, 22. See also Heyck 1982, 28; and Klancher 1987, 5, on the "complex contention" over texts that marked the early nineteenth century.

3. See also Brantlinger 1977, 11–34. On the "crisis of hegemony" in the 1830s, see Richards, "State Formation and Class Struggle, 1832–48" in Corrigan and Sayer 1985, 75.

4. See Perkin 1968, 267, on the process by which social justification through service, expertise, selection by merit, efficiency, and progress became identified with the aims of government.

5. On the roles of professional middle-class men and especially men of letters in the construction of Victorian ideologies, see Heyck 1982, 24–46; Perkin 1968, 252–70, 428–37; Weiner 1981, 8–30; and Cooter 1984, 70.

6. See, for example, Perkin 1968; and, despite their consciousness of the exclusion, Klancher 1987; and Corrigan and Sayer 1985. For an account of middle-class formation in which gender and women are central, see Davidoff and Hall 1987.

7. Perkin (1968) applies this term to professional men on the grounds that their indeterminate class position enabled them to choose sides, often to come to the side of a class not their own (257).

8. As with men of letters, the alternative values proposed by women writers intersected with entrepreneurial (and professional) ideals. For the social and economic fortunes of many middle-class women were doubly bound to those of male relatives, in businesses and professions. Most middle-class women, that is, were supported by male relatives, and many also contributed to the economic and social position of their kin by sustaining, for example, the respectable family life out of which family businesses (and professional careers) were run. It is not surprising, then, that celebrations of moral expertise in women's writing often fade into celebrations of "industry" and work and that accounts of history as moral progress shore up equations of history with progress of a more material sort. In the process of offering sometimes legitimately alternative values, women of letters might well participate in the rationalization of entrepreneurial and professional values in which men of letters were also at times engaged.

9. See "Learning Not to Curse," in this volume.

10. These categories overlap in ways that are highly problematic. I am restricting the term *masculine identity* to refer mainly to strategies for maintaining difference from women and strategies for maintaining women's subordination to men. I am not proposing that this is all there is to masculine identity. For an account of the relation between masculine identity and the state, see Connell 1987, 155–57.

11. See Connell 1987, 183–88 for an analysis of hegemonic masculinities.

12. Francis Jeffrey to Francis Horner, 11 May 1803, cited in Fontana 1985, 3. For an account of the reviewers, see also Stewart 1985, 19–27.

13. Jeffrey 1966, 1:9.

14. See Heyck (1982) on the desire of the middle class for guidance, connection, and tradition (28). See also Klancher (1987) on the crucial role of periodicals in dividing audiences and in guiding them to compete for position in social and cultural space (4).

15. On the ties between the *Review* and the Whig party, see Fontana 1985, 7–8.

16. For an account of McCulloch's career, see O'Brien 1970. On the identification of science as a tool for constructing an ordered society, see Berman 1978, 109.

17. See Eisenstein 1981, 44–47; and Elshtain 1981, 121–27. For accounts of feminist appropriations of liberalism, see Eisenstein 1981, 89–113; and Rendall 1985.

18. See Rendall 1985, chap. 4 ("Educating Hearts and Minds"), for an analysis of the way that arguments for women's education moved beyond arguments for improving women as mothers and wives.

19. For an account of the *Review's* contributions to the debate over Reform, see Fontana 1985, 147–80.

20. For an account of Owenism and women, see Taylor 1983.

21. On the political economists as a scientific community, see O'Brien 1975, 11–16. On the way in which marginal men gained and propounded social identity through the institutions and groups of science culture, see Inkster 1983, 39–42. See also Cooter 1984, 70–71; Knights 1978, 128; Heyck 1982, 58–59; Davidoff and Hall 1987, 442–44.

22. See Davidoff and Hall 1987, 274, 310, 312, 425, on the exclusion of women from scientific culture.

23. See Davidoff 1990.

24. For extensive treatment of male ambivalence toward mothers, see Dinnerstein 1976; Chodorow 1978; O'Brien 1981; Hartsock 1985; Balbus 1982; and Di Stefano 1991.

25. See Davidoff and Hall 1987.

26. See DiStefano 1991, on the atomistic conception of individuals in political theorists such as Hobbes and Mill: "In the case of Hobbes and Mill, an atomistic conception of the individual prevails. This liberal individual inhabits a terrain populated by self-sprung persons whose discrete identities are autogenerated and self-contained. Inviolable egos such as these embody the modern masculine fantasy of secular omnipotence" (21). See also Hartsock 1985, 95–186.

27. In a reading of several political theorists (Hobbes, Marx, and Mill), DiStefano (1991) notes that

> political theories in which "the individual is constituted abstractly without ever getting born" . . . bear the·cognitive fruit of the wish to deny natural and maternal origins. Reevoking infantile omnipotence, that primal sense of self-sufficiency which we have all lost and only partially regained, second nature conceptions go on to express the adult and detectably modern masculine desire for a self-generation and a species generation that can be

self-consciously willed, created and controlled. Not insignificantly, the body, that physical locus of dependence on the (m)other, is eliminated from these versions of achieved selfhood" (49–50).

28. Knights 1978, 17.

29. For further analysis of this idea, see Balbus 1986, 110–27.

"Ministers of the Interior": The Political Economy of Women's Manuals

In the present day we are fairly flooded with female magazines and receptacles of divers kinds. . . .

—*Woman as She Is*

(1991)

The "Woman Question"

The late 1830s and 1840s in Great Britain saw the beginning of the "woman question," a heterogeneous, often heated, debate on the role of largely middle-class women in postreform England. This "flood" of writing on middle-class women, however, to which the author of *Woman as She Is* refers, should be seen as part of a larger "struggle over signs," a struggle often identified with "moral" or "cultural revolution, in nineteenth-century Britain (Klancher 1987, 3; Corrigan and Sayer 1985, 106). This "revolution," "an attempted organization of consent and incorporation which culminates in a certain kind of admission . . . of labor into society," involved a new machinery of government, new theories of representation, and new lines of exclusion and inclusion as well (Corrigan and Sayer 1985, 106, 115, 143). An emphasis on gender division, upon the separation of domestic and "public" spheres, was a predominant feature of these larger efforts to reconstruct a social world.[1]

Gender division, of course, was central to the very language of reform. The Reform Act of 1832, which enfranchised a portion of middle-class and some working-class men and which served as an emblem at least of the democratic way that lines of inclusion might be redrawn, explicitly excluded women from the vote.[2] And yet, despite the starkness of the lines drawn in this central doctrine of social reconstruction, gender division, in the 1830s, did not operate as a simple polarity or opposition. Discourse excluding women from formal political power and relegating middle-class women to the domestic sphere was very often accompanied by a compensatory rhetoric that blurred the lines between domestic and "public," female and male. In an essay, for example, that emphasizes the necessity of excluding women from formal political power, the *Edinburgh Review* characterizes middle-class women as "ministers of the interior" (Empson 1833, 1). The phrase insinuates as many parallels between women and men, domestic and public, as it does differences, and, as part of an argument for excluding women from formal political power, it also politicizes the domestic sphere.[3] The woman question, therefore, seems more properly called the gender question, involving as it does complex negotiations in regard to gender sameness and difference; while the "gender question," in turn, seems best understood within a set of larger questions over social realignment and reform. It is in these wider contexts that the "flood" of writing on women must be read.

The Political Economy of "Woman's Mission"

Just as writing ostensibly devoted to questions of class or political economy was profoundly "about" gender relations among the genteel, so writing ostensibly about middle-class women was about other lines of exclusion and inclusion than those of gender. Discourse on the woman question was also about class and national identity, imperialism, the nature of "history," social relations, and value. This was the case, moreover, for women writing in what would seem to have been the most feminized of discursive worlds, that of middle-class women writing manuals for other middle-class women.

Two of the most popular manuals, Sarah Lewis's *Woman's Mission* and Sarah Ellis's *Women of England*, were published in 1839 and quickly went through several editions. Although radicals and Owenite socialists had been writing articles on women's education and the political role of women in British society for several years, although Harriet Martineau's liberal feminist *Society in America* had been published in 1837, it was the two manuals by Ellis and Lewis that mark the beginning of what one reviewer was to describe as a "sudden inundation of tabby-bound volumes, addressed in superguilt letters to the 'Wives of England'—the 'Daughters of

England'—the 'Grandmothers of England" (Anon. 1844, 199). The "Grandmothers of England" was a joke, but *Women of England* was indeed followed by Ellis's *Wives of England* (1843), *Mothers of England* (1843), and *Daughters of England* (1845) and by related publications such as *Women's Rights and Duties* (1840), Marion Reid's feminist *Plea for Women* (1843), *Woman, Her Character and Vicissitudes* (1845), and by numerous periodical articles having to do with "Woman and Her Social Position." Manuals written by middle-class women for other middle-class women clearly constitute one part of an explicit struggle over the representation of genteel femininity in the 1830s. Ellis and Lewis, for example, take vigorous issue with feminist texts on women, which often advocated extension of the franchise to women in the 1830s and, in some cases, also proposed that middle-class femininity was not incompatible with political office. But this rejection of formal political power is accompanied by another brand of "reform." Like feminist tracts, these manuals offer their female readers politicized subjectivities and a politicized community to which to belong:

> we are not one iota behind these fiery champions of womanhood, in exalted notions of its dignity and mission—we are anxious as they can be, that women should be roused to a sense of their own importance. (Lewis 1839, 11)

Women "have much to do with politics; woman has a mission! aye, even a political mission of immense importance" (48).

Manual writers, however, were not simply proposing a different role for middle-class women in dominant understandings of history, although that too was true. They also reconfigured popular understandings of historical development so as to reconcile history with their representation of women. Like Coleridge defining his notion of clerisy and Mill his notion of an educated elite, like political economists constructing themselves as "men of science," manual writers positioned themselves as experts too. Indeed, they consistently recited, reconfigured, and evoked the authority of male experts and of male-authored narratives in order to ground their own claims to cultural authority.

The most familiar of the narratives employed by manuals for women are those of Evangelical religion. Evangelical versions of his-

tory assume a moral and religious telos, are critical of overemphasiz-
ing commercial gain, and stress the centrality of genteel women
within an essentially moral and religious understanding of life.[4] Hannah More, for example, writes that

> the general state of civilized society depends more than those are
> aware who are not accustomed to scrutinize into the springs of
> human action, on the prevailing sentiments and habits of
> women. . . . Even those who admit the power of female elegance
> on the manners of men, do not always attend to the influence
> of female principles on their character. (1799, 15)

But women "will not content themselves with polishing when they
are able to reform, with entertaining when they may awaken, with
captivating for a day when they may bring into action powers of
which the effects may be commensurate with eternity." Thus, More
calls on genteel women "to reanimate the dormant powers of piety"
(4). As for women's "exemption from privileges," "the Christian
hope more than reconciles Christian women to these petty privations
by substituting a nobler prize for their ambition, the prize of the high
calling of God in Jesus Christ" (36–38).

Like More, Ellis and Lewis operate inside a recognizably religious economy in which "moral wealth" and "moral progress" are
what history and English greatness are about (Ellis 1839, 16; Lewis
1839, 18). Commercial progress, moreover, while desirable, is not a
necessary precondition for moral progress, at least not in the way
that writers on political economy sometimes claimed: "It is neither
industry nor science, nor machinery, nor books which can make the
happiness of a people" (Ellis 1839, 16; Lewis 1839, 19). The role of
middle-class women, nonetheless, is distinctly more secular than in
More. Ellis, for example, apologizes "for having written a book on
the subject of morals, without having made it strictly religious" (vii).
And Lewis inserts God in parenthesis: "We claim for them no less
an office than that of instruments (under God) for the regeneration
of the world" (11).

Another narrative that Ellis and Lewis partially engage echoes
that of Owenite socialism, which also enjoyed its heyday in the 1830s.
Like Owenites, for example, Ellis and Lewis, suggest that what is
constructed in the *Review* as a commercial "race" is, in fact, a species

of warfare, and they imply that social relations are more properly conceived of as cooperative and familial than as competitive:[5]

> To unite? alas, there is no union in the great field of action in which he is engaged; but envy, and hatred, and opposition, to the close of the day,—every man's hand against his brothers and each struggling to exalt himself, not merely by trampling on his fallen foe, but by usurping the place of his weaker brother, who faints by his side, from not having brought an equal portion of strength into the conflict, and who is consequently borne down by numbers, hurried over, and forgotten. (Lewis 1839, 45, 46)

As in William Thompson and Anna Wheeler's socialist and feminist *Appeal* (1825), the autonomous, self-interested individuals, the basic actors or subjects of history in the political economy of the *Review*, are represented as a source not of the common good but of social ills.[6] Indeed, they are compared to a destructive "torrent" visited as a judgment upon mankind and "now threatening to undermine the strong foundation of England's moral worth" (Ellis 1839, 51). These same rational, autonomous individuals are represented as controlled rather than controlling and as out of touch with the real ends of history, and with real self-interest too. Thus, men of business are impelled forward by a "system" that no one can control, for the system will have to "correct itself" (48). What might seem the *"omnipotent* consideration of worldly aggrandizement," far from raising men to the height of God the father, "clouds," bribes, and confuses their "mental vision" (46, 47, 46). It also alienates them from humanity now "swallowed up in efforts and calculations relating to their pecuniary success" and debases them to the level of the mechanical "until we almost fail to recognize the man in the machine." And "these are rational, intellectual, accountable, immortal beings, undergoing a course of discipline by which they are to be fitted for eternal existence!" (48, 49).

As in Wheeler and Thompson, the autonomous, self-interested socially beneficial subject of political economy is presented as a construction, a false construction, to be exact, since for Owenites and manual writers both "truth" can be told. This false construction, moreover, is located in the social formation of elite masculinity itself:

Again, men are said to be more selfish than women. How can they help it? No pains are taken with their education to make them otherwise. That pugnacity of spirit which is so admired as proof of *spirit* is the very embodiment of the selfish principle—fighting for their *own rights*—as assertion of their own superiority. They are taught at school to despise the weak and practice the lessons at home in petty domestic torments to the weak of their circle—their sisters, receiving at the same time, from those very sisters, a thousand little services, without consciousness and without gratitude. (Lewis 1839, 29)

Finally, as in Owenite and Saint-Simonian discourses, traditionally genteel feminine qualities, seen as constructed for the most part in Ellis and Lewis, are evoked as more socially desirable than masculine:[7] "We must seek, then, some fundamental principle, some spirit indefatigable, delighting in its task, and which may pervade the whole of society. Such a principle we find in family affection—especially maternal affection" (87).[8]

In pointed contrast to Owenite writers, of course, Ellis and Lewis are far from calling for an end to private property or the capitalist system, a system from which they both received benefits. Indeed, no real intervention in the system is possible, since "the system will have to correct itself." Men in trade, moreover, are ultimately excused from certain forms of responsibility. For in a momentary reversion to the metaphors of political economy, Ellis writes,

If to grow tardy or indifferent in the race were only to lose the goal, many would be glad to pause; but such is the nature of commerce and trade, as at present carried on in this country, that to slacken in the exertion, is altogether to fail. (1839, 48)

The burden of resisting or intervening in competitive market relations falls almost entirely on middle-class women, whose capacity for exerting a beneficial influence on competitive relations is then firmly located in the material situation that competitive market relations make possible. *Women of England*, for example, is addressed specifically to women

who belong to that great mass of the population of England
which is connected with trade and manufactures, that portion
of it who are restricted to the services of from one to four domestics, who, on the one hand, enjoy the advantages of a liberal
education, and, on the other, have no pretension to family rank.
(Ellis 1839, 21)

It is only these women of the commercial middle class who are
"removed from the pressing necessities of absolute poverty," but
who are "admitted to the intellectual privileges of the great" while
not being "exempt from the domestic duties which call forth the
best energies of the female character" (22). Since commercial wealth
produces the material conditions that make middle-class women's
moral insight and moral influence possible, the pursuit of commercial self-interest is retained not just as an individual necessity
but also as a social good. Critiques of and reforming interventions
into competitive market relations are best developed, it would
seem, amid the material construction of middle-class women's lives
and behaviors, which competitive market relations provide. Elements familiar from socialist critique are effectively rewritten here
as a species of political economy, for, in a nice revision of Adam
Smith, the system corrects itself through the "invisible hand" of
woman.

   This recourse to the values of political economy in a document
centrally critical of competition and imbued with a religious and
moral understanding of history might be interpreted in several ways.
It would be plausible, for example, to suppose that Ellis and Lewis
felt their dependence on the capitalist economy, which they also
wished to reform, and that it felt natural to locate themselves within
its values to some degree. One might also speculate that Ellis and
Lewis were responding to the shifting fortunes of dominant and
emergent ideologies. If middle-class women or traditionally feminine
values were to be widely constructed as central to history, as Ellis and
Lewis felt they should, it could not have been, in the 1830s, within
Evangelical or socialist terms. Owenism, in particular, was a marginal
(and in many quarters a despised) discourse, one that Evangelicalism
helped to produce but with which it was also at war, and Evangelical
critiques of commercialism had to contend in the 1830s with more

secular and increasingly popular constructions of commercial society as a necessary prelude to moral progress. Elements of both discourses are reconfigured, therefore, in terms that reconcile them to what was rapidly becoming a dominant narrative of history and social relations, that of political economy.

Engendering History for the Middle Class

In *Women of England* and *Woman's Mission* tensions at the core of nineteenth-century middle-class culture, between narratives promoting and narratives criticizing commercial society, are "resolved" through the figure of the middle-class woman, a figure produced and sustained by a commercial progress that she assumes a superior and correcting relation to.[9] In this way and others the manuals represent feminine virtues as superior to masculine and middle-class women as more central to history than men. This gender treachery, however, may have been palliated or rendered invisible by the fact that the manuals' celebration of women also worked to establish the cultural superiority of "the middle class" and to identify middle-class values with national identity and national identity with successful imperialist ventures.

For if the reading of history and social relations associated with middle-class women—their moral judgment of competitive market relations along with the correcting moral influence that they supposedly expressed in the conduct of domestic life—establish a form of gender superiority, these same feminine virtues are identified as the grounds on which the middle class generally may lay a claim to cultural authority and as the grounds on which "Englishness" and England may lay claim to superiority among nations:

> Every country has its moral *characteristics*, upon which is founded its true title to a station, either high or low, in the scale of nations. The national characteristics of England are the perpetual boast of her patriotic sons; and there is one especially which it behoves all British subjects not only to exult in, but to cherish and maintain. Leaving the justice of her laws, the extent of her commerce, and the amount of her resources, to the orator, the statesman, and the political economists, there yet remains one of the noblest features in her national character, which may not

improperly be regarded as within the compass of a woman's understanding, and the province of a woman's pen. It is the domestic character of England—the home comforts, and fireside virtues for which she is so justly celebrated. (Ellis 1839, 13)

Specifically middle-class values, best represented in women, but made possible by the material conditions produced by men, become generalized here to Englishness itself.

This equation of the middle class with the wealth, intelligence, and morality that are "the glory of the British name" was a familiar theme in the 1830s,[10] and its evocation here, as I have suggested, somewhat mediates the manuals' claims on behalf of middle-class women, smoothing the way rhetorically to a celebration of gender superiority, which Ellis and Lewis shared. The appropriation of this class discourse by Ellis and Lewis, however, has further meanings. Since in *Woman's Mission* and *Women of England* middle-class values are feminine, and middle-class femininity is represented as self-sacrificing and "apolitical," since the self-sacrificing middle-class woman made, in many respects, a more palatable, less threatening national ideal than the self-interested entrepreneur, Ellis and Lewis seem freer than some of their male peers to make direct claims for the superiority of the trading middle-class and to explicitly identify middle-class values not only with the "good" of the nation as a whole but also with the essence of national identity itself.[11]

In the pages of the *Review*, for example, political economy is often identified with the good of the nation as a whole, but the class meaning of that identification is suppressed. Although political economy was a construction of history, social relations, and commerce deeply tied to the economic and social interests of many members of the middle-class, it is represented as a "science," as a form of objective knowledge arrived at and entertained without contamination by class position or investment. The truths about history, social relations, and commerce represented and advocated in *Women of England*, however, are rather overtly and deliberately tied to class position. Middle-class women, that is, especially those whose male relatives are in trade and who make sufficient money to support from "one to four domestics," are presented as the persons best situated to arrive at and maintain a "true" understanding of the laws of history (Ellis 1839, 21).

This middle-class female perspective, moreover, is very carefully distinguished from the position and corresponding perspectives and behaviors of upper- and working-class women:

> It is from the class of females above described, that we naturally look for the highest tone of moral feeling, because they are at the same time removed from the pressing necessities of absolute poverty, and admitted to the intellectual privileges of the great: and thus, while they enjoy every facility in the way of acquiring knowledge, it is their still higher privilege not to be exempt from the domestic duties which call forth the best energies of the female character. (Ellis 1839, 22)

The manuals' appropriation of familiar forms of class discourse, however, does more than include women in what it means to be middle class. It entails significant reconfigurations of the discourse itself. It has been frequently argued, for example, that debate about the Condition of England—the economic and bodily suffering, the social dislocations, of the working poor—was being domesticized in the 1830s.[12] Discourse on the working class, that is, was increasingly focused on issues having to do with the protection of children, the welfare of working wives, and the crucial importance of moral education, sanitation, and good housekeeping. Nancy Armstrong contends that the apolitical nature of the family, anchored in the identification of domesticity with genteel women, supplied a new mythology, or narrative, in which to explain the suffering of the poor and new terms in which to incorporate the poor into British society—through surveillance of their education, regulation of their morality, and cleansing of their domestic environment. This discourse, in turn, helped generate a model of government that emphasized bureaucratic apparatuses and professional expertise for the purposes of surveillance and education of the poor (Armstrong 1987, 20–21). This same apparatus, of course, was useful in launching imperialist ventures.

But this domesticized discourse, it is important to note, was far from unitary. Upper-class reformers such as Lord Ashley evoked an older, paternal construction of social relations in which government reform of factories was called for in the guise of fatherly protection and in which upper-class men such as Ashley himself were identified as heads of the familial state. Political economists such as McCulloch, in contrast, constructed factories as homes and factory owners as loving fathers (McCulloch 1835). Home, in this discourse, is constructed as private terrain within the state and as properly free from state intervention. Thus, the domestication of discourse on the Condition of England is articulated differently by different groups of men. What is equally important to note is that discourses that evoke the domestic and the now traditional links between domesticity and genteel women are, in fact, male centered. The reference point for factory reformers such as Ashley is not maternal but paternal protection or, in the 1840s, the rights of husbands. McCulloch also imagines fathers, not mothers, relieving working-class "parents" from their (unsuccessful) attempts to educate their children and inculcate moral standards. This masculinization of domestic discourse on the Condition of England, indeed, seems a means of asserting (competing) masculine authorities in both the public and the domestic spheres. Thus, this male-centered discourse on the Condition of England might be read as a gender strategy and not merely as a use of gender in the interests of class power.

Masculinized domestic discourse, for example, appears alongside other discourses (those of Saint-Simonians and Owenites, for example) that also domesticize social relations but which grant women, or at least the feminine and the maternal, a central role in public affairs. Masculinized domestic discourse also appears alongside the massive presence of working-class women in public employment, a presence that is seen as a challenge to the ideological equation of woman with the home, the exclusion of middle-class women from an increasingly fluid economy, women's subordination to men, and men's control over women's sexuality. (The marital insubordination of economically independent working-class women was a frequent theme in the discourse of reformers in the early 1840s, as was working-class women's sexual promiscuity.)

Similar kinds of concerns were echoed in relation to genteel women. Resistance to the Child Custody Act of 1837 and 1838, for example, touches upon the dangers that would attend a bill granting separated or divorced mothers custody of their children under age seven. The reassertion of specifically paternal authority and capacity in the language of reformers and political economists, which often focused on the capacity of men to parent the children of the poor or to protect working-class women from corruption, might be read as of a piece with these efforts to assert paternal rights in relation to the wives and children of the genteel. Custody of the children, at least, whether working class or genteel, was a central issue in political discourse of the 1830s.

In Ellis and Lewis, however, it is mothers not fathers who are awarded custody, and the subjects of custody have been changed in a somewhat startling direction. For the threat to England's moral worth is not the working class but, more directly, middle-class men in trade, and the cure is not to educate and parent the working poor but, rather, to revive the moral sensibilities of middle-class entrepreneurs, to reeducate them about the ends of history and to reconstruct the masculinity of the middle-class. The cure is to bring men up all over again. Those best positioned to shoulder this burden, and so to intervene in the Condition of England, are not upper-class reformers and middle-class factory owners but middle-class women in the home.

In place of ruling-class fathers, therefore, pushing for protective exclusion of children and women from factory work, instead of paternal entrepreneurs moralizing working-class children in faculty schools, middle-class mothers would oversee the education, moralization, and household order of men in trade while also setting an example for working-class families. A female sovereign, of course, made this construction of social reform seem all the more "natural," and at times in *Women of England* the public realm itself appears as a kind of glorified sisterhood, with men the absent presence:

> The British throne being now graced by a female sovereign . . . it is surely not a time for the female part of the community to fall away from the high standard of moral excellence. . . . Rather let them show forth the benefits arising from their more enlightened system of education, by proving to their youthful sovereign, that whatever plan she may think it right to sanction for the moral advancement of her subjects . . . will be welcomed by every female heart throughout her realm, and faithfully supported in every British home by the female influence prevailing their. (Ellis 1839, 51)

"Ministers of the Interior"/Mothers of the World

Ellis and Lewis, then, offer a domesticized discourse on public affairs in which the Condition of England hinges less directly on fathering the working class than on mothering middle-class men. But the tensions and contradictions of this strategy, a strategy firmly situated after all in the context of middle-class women's lack of access to other forms of power, should not be overlooked. In the first place manual writers, for all their efforts to assure male and female readers that they were advocating a return to women's traditional roles in the home, register uneasiness about asserting women's domestic power, most particularly with respect to male readers.

In contrast to reviewers, who seem free to position their readers as male in essays on political economy and as gender mixed in essays on women, manual writers more continuously position their readers as male and female both. Although manuals specifically addressed to middle-class women might appear to offer a discursive realm in which one might be excused for acting as if the ordinary restraints of male-dominant society did not apply, publishing was tantamount to entering the public sphere, a terrain that men ostensibly owned. Journals such as the *Review*, moreover, were well established as institutions for the interpretation and critique of female writers, and both Ellis and Lewis were reviewed in its pages.

To isolate the mother rather than the father as the central figure in domestic and public social relations was potentially problematic, therefore, even in the feminized world of the woman's manual. Lewis and Ellis, of course, do define "family affection especially . . . maternal affection" as the spirit of social and spiritual regeneration, but they do so while registering the uncomfortable consciousness that to claim women's power even in the home is to provoke unease. Ellis, for example, apologizes to her male readers for suggesting that women "preside" over the domestic sphere:

> Aware that the word *preside* . . . may produce a startling effect upon the ear of man, I must endeavor to bespeak his forbearance, by assuring him, that the highest aim of the writer does not extend beyond the act of warning the women of England

back to their domestic duties that they may become better wives,
more useful daughters and mothers. . . . (1839, 36)

Women's moral surveillance of men, for all its familiarity, is also
very cautiously handled. Men may "stand" corrected before "the
clear eye of woman as it looks directly to the naked truth and detects
the lurking evil of the specious act he is about to commit," but, when
temptation assaults him in the "public sphere, what he recalls is "the
humble monitress who sat alone guarding the fireside comforts of his
distant home" (47). Here "man" becomes the spectator containing the
image of woman, and the image he contains is not that of an unsettling judge with a correcting eye but, instead, a "humble monitress"
looking after "fireside comforts" that belong to him. In Lewis, by the
same token, woman's image is "inscribed" in the hearts of men,
becoming once again the object of *his* vision (1839, 133).

Still, despite the translation of woman as surveillant into a "humble monitress" that men choose to behold, despite official subscrip-
tion to the doctrine that women have "a narrower circle" and "natural
channels," the metaphoric subtext of these two manuals suggests
that men are dependent on women and that women, in particular
women as mothers, are in some sense everywhere. In a reversal of
the metaphoric subtexts of the *Review,* in which women and nature
both are contained, women and nature are implicitly identified and
appear unbounded. Women, for example, are frequently compared
to water, a medium that loses value in the *Edinburgh Review* because
it cannot be easily controlled. Women emit "floods of human kind-
ness" that "overflow" the innumerable channels" opened up by domestic life (Ellis 1839, 22). Women's love is an "overflowing and
inexhaustible fountain" (19).

But the sphere of middle-class women, and by extension genteel
women in their nurturing and domestic roles, is more unbounded
than floods or fountains, whose power after all may be harnessed to
a cotton mill. Middle-class women's sphere and women in their maternal, feeling role are like the earth itself, which "fosters and nour-
ishes with its lovely bosom the roots of all the plants and trees which
ornament the garden of the world, feeding them from her secret
storehouse with supplies that never fail." Unlike the transient "sun
and showers" that male-engendered industrial progress sends to aristocratic crops, in the pages of the *Review,* woman, as mother earth,

"in the absence of all other favoring circumstances, withholds not its support; but when the sun is shrouded, and the showers forget to fall, and blighting winds go forth, and the hand of culture is withdrawn, still opens out its hidden fountains and yields up its resources, to invigorate, to cherish and sustain" (Ellis 1839, 39).

These metaphors, moreover, suggest men's dependence on women, not vice versa. For they suggest that the material conditions of middle-class life, which produce the middle-class mother and which men supply, are more finite, after all, than the "secret storehouse" of women whose supplies "never fail" and whose plenitude is contrasted in these manuals with men's lack. Women's plenitude is represented, finally, as that of nursing mothers, a primary image of men's dependence on women and an image that goes hand in hand with a historical imagination that conceives the central act of human history not as a moment of autonomy in which male entrepreneurs "miraculously" create themselves but, rather, as an act in which women, through the motherly qualities of their hearts, give birth to men a second time around.

Women of Science

The reconfiguration of domesticized discourse on public affairs, the alternately cautious and abandoned assertion of the plenitude of women and the dependence of men, the centrality of mothers as opposed to fathers in setting social relations right, is the most frequently identified strategy of these manuals, but it is not, I would suggest, the only or even the most dominant one. For if women in trading families are identified as different from and as mothering men of their own social position, they are also constructed as *like* men of their class, as sisters or partners and, implicitly, as competitors. The domestication of public political affairs, for example, is accompanied in *Women of England* and in *Woman's Mission* by a reconstitution of the domestic as entrepreneurial, professional, and scientific. Both Ellis and Lewis celebrate women's "industry," "exertion," "energy," "action," "power," calculation," and the ability to set machinery and systems into motion. Writing from the margins of commercial activity, both writers nonetheless situate middle-class women in trading families within its discourses:

Every passing event, however, insignificant to the eye of the world, has its crisis, every occurrence its energy, every cause its effect; and upon these she has to calculate with precision, or the machinery of household comfort is arrested in its movements, and thrown into disorder. (Ellis 1839, 24)

Once again women's domestic work is recast in terms that assert women's centrality to commercial society and material progress, while entrepreneurial values—work, productivity, rational calculation, the employment of machines—are momentarily recast as women's work and are identified with provisions for others rather than with the pursuit of profit.

Throughout *Women of England,* moreover, women's work is subtly professionalized: though "far from wishing them to interfere with the province of the physician," for example, Ellis asserts that women nonetheless are to be instructed in "the whole science of that delicate and difficult cookery which forms so important a part of the attendant's duty" and to choose "with the skill of the doctor what is best adapted for the occasion, . . . converting a diet to medicine of the most agreeable description" (Ellis 1839, 64, 65). There is also a "science of being agreeable," and Ellis proposes that "the art of conversation might in some measure be reduced to a system (not unlike Botany) taught in our schools and rendered an important part of female education" (118). She begins, indeed, to formulate the rules for conversation and a set of methodologies for teaching them. Like the man engaged in business and bent on scientific improvement of production, the woman "engaged in a higher and more important work" investigates "the most effectual means by which it can be done" (139). There is "a kind of science of good household management" and "a philosophy in this science" (25).

Middle-class women in trading families emerge here as the latest experts in an era of expertise. Their skills, moreover, are not confined to housework but also extend to cultural critique and to the preservation of the nation as a whole. If the domestic middle-class woman, as constructed by *Woman's Mission* and *Women of England,* sounds at times like a romantic poet, calling men back to the springs of their nature, she sounds at others like the men of the clerisy, itself a reworking of romantic ideas. For like women, the clerisy operate through influence, through hidden channels, rather than through coercion to preserve the moral and intellectual well-being of the nation. A clerisy, like middle-class women, as constructed by Lewis and Ellis, sees through shifting phenomenon to the permanent and important things, sees the inadequacy of predominant forms of thought to the current social situation, knows society's needs better than the rulers, and is essential to social health.[13]

At other times the domestic woman, and most particularly her advisors, Ellis and Lewis, appear to be social scientists par excellence. Scientific truth, as I have suggested, became increasingly authorized in the 1830s as a means of social control and as an avenue to cultural authority and social power. Science, moreover, centrally included the study of human nature. Owenism, for example, was identified as "the New Science of society, or social science: the science which determines . . . happiness or misery . . . by circumstances over which each individual has hitherto had little control" (Taylor 1983, 19). This new science was focused on "the influence of circumstances over the whole conduct and proceedings of the human race" (19–20). In Ellis, too, there is a science of human nature, and here women's sphere of observation may be "microscopic," but such "acute vision directed to immediate objects . . . will often discover as much of the wonders of creation, and supply the intelligent mind with food for reflection as valuable as that which is the result of a widely extended view" (1839, 30).

This construction of a large segment of domestic middle-class women as professional, as scientific, as experts on human nature and cultural critique, naturally establishes a basis on which Ellis and Lewis may justify and legitimate their own somewhat different positions. Ellis, at least, in contrast to the women for whom she writes, was not from a trading family, was married to a professional, a missionary, had no children, earned money from her writing, and eventually opened a school for girls. She was essentially a professional, a woman of letters and a teacher. Her penchant for professionalizing women's work in the home, however, blurs the lines that divided her own life from more traditional lives among women of the middle class, thereby normalizing and naturalizing her own somewhat untraditional existence.

In Ellis and Lewis, indeed, the persistent repetition of Evangelical discourse on genteel women's undue ambition seems as much directed to themselves as to housewives in trading families. For despite repeated assurances that women's influence must "flow in its natural channels, viz domestic ones," their equally persistent strategy is not only to imagine women's influence as "boundless in its operations" but also to invest the "narrower circle" with what is "lovely, poetical, and interesting, nay even *heroic*," with what is "great and glorious," "daring" and "adventurous" (Ellis 1839, 44, 47, 36; Lewis 1839, 53, 13). The predominant rhetorical strategy of these manuals, indeed, is to establish boundaries only to cross and blur them. It is a strategy well suited to the tensions in Ellis's and Lewis's position as authors—women of letters ostensibly recalling middle-class women to their domestic roles while staking claims to professional expertise, cultural authority, and impact on public affairs. This crossing of boundaries, moreover, is what best defines their construction of women in these volumes. For although Ellis and Lewis refer to women's "natural" capacities for love and moral influence, their manuals reconfigure middle-class women in so many discourses that the constructed nature of femininity, the instability of gender categories, is continually brought to the fore.

Despite occasional evocations of women's maternal nature, for example, even mothering appears socially constructed. Maternal instinct does not produce a moral mother: "Instinct is no more able to perform the functions of moral maternity than abstract philosophy would be able to supply an infant the want of the necessary attentions dictated by instinctive tenderness" (Lewis 1839, 92). By the same token, women's natural capacity for love does not produce selflessness or moral influence. For woman to be

> individually what she is praised for being in *general* it is necessary for her to lay aside all her natural caprice, her love of self-indulgence, her vanity, her indolence—in short her very *self*—and assuming a new nature which nothing less than watchfulness and prayer can enable her constantly to maintain, to spend her mental and moral capabilities in devising means for promoting the happiness of others, while her own derives a remote and secondary existence from theirs. (Ellis 1839, 40)

It is the constructed nature of femininity, after all, that implicitly justifies the project of writing manuals for women in the first place, and it is that construction of femininity that most secures Ellis's and

Lewis's expertise, an expertise that consists not only of observing but also of refashioning classed femininity.

The cultural resonance one might construct for these manuals is necessarily complex. The professionalization of middle-class women's roles, for example, with its notion of set standards, training, certification in the sciences of cooking, conversation, and household management, pulls in several ways. It pulls, for example, toward continued equation of middle-class women with the domestic sphere, enforcing thereby a major ideological strategy for maintaining the general disempowerment of middle-class women in nineteenth-century culture and toward a consoling and ultimately conservative glorification and modernization of the domestic, which assures middle-class women at home that they too participate in "the career open to talent," a career that, not incidentally, constitutes the greatness of the middle class and the core of national identity.

At the same time, however, this professionalization of women's domesticity rhetorically undermines the division of the domestic and the public spheres, the division between women who worked at home and those who worked or who might work in properly genteel occupations. Ellis and Lewis both, of course, insist that the definition of genteel labor must be widened. Lewis inveighs against "the cruelty of that conventional prejudice which shackles independence of women, by attaching the loss of caste to almost all, nay all, of the very few sources of pecuniary emolument open to them" (Lewis 1839, 81). Ellis proposes that women of the lower middle class be trained as "work people: milliners, drawers of patterns" and notes "a strange paradox" that "degradation of what is vulgarly called *making their own living*" when "this should all the while be the very thing of which they are most in want" (Ellis 1839, 240). We are not far here from the language of feminists such as Anna Jameson or Marion Reid or of later feminists such as Frances Power Cobbe and Barbara Bodichon who argue that most women will continue to find their happiness in domestic life but that professions must be opened for those without families to earn their own way.

More than one profession for women was established, moreover, on the basis of its being like domestic labor. Florence Nightingale, for example, was to translate many of Ellis's claims on behalf of domestic women into a set of claims on behalf of nurses.[14] A similar language of professionalized domestic labor was also frequently employed by women who entered into government on the local level. From the 1870s on women could and did serve on school boards, and by 1889 there were nearly one hundred doing so. From 1875 women became Poor Law guardians (there were eighty in 1889), and intermittently in London women were elected to town councils. Characteristically, these women spoke the language of separate spheres, emphasizing the work that only women could do for other women and children (Hollis 1987, 208). Knowledge of domestic management, familiarity with homes and streets, were cited as a form of expertise, as part of women's qualifications for public service.

This evocation of domestic work as expertise, moreover, permitted women to claim territory from men:

> Now it may seem to be a truism to say that where domestic and household management is concerned, there women should have a place and a power of control ... on the hundreds of large households which are nonetheless such because they represent institutions and not private families. (Hollis 1987, 200)

In answer to the infrequent objection "I don't like a woman to step into a man's sphere, and by appointed guardian," we might say, "It is really men who stepped into woman's sphere—that of dispenser, nurse, and teacher of the poor" (Hollis 1987, 208). The language of separate spheres and of professionalized housework, therefore, could be used in both conservative and radical ways. It could reinforce stereotypes about women's nature, and it could also encourage women to come forward in confidence that domestic and family background was useful and relevant to public service and to men's commercial and business experience (Hollis 1987, 210). Ellis's and Lewis's fusion of commercial and professional values with women's domestic labor helped shape a discourse in which these claims could be made.

Ellis and Lewis also contributed to a discourse by which women might participate in that "scientific social knowledge" that was increasingly to inform bureaucracy and reforming bodies of all kinds. What is striking about Ellis's use of scientific metaphor, however, are the ways in which it differs from that of the *Review* or of statistical societies (or even Owenism). Scientific knowledge, to begin with, is not objective or detached. It arises from benevolent feeling, from love, and produces in turn not dispassionate observation but, rather, connected action much as looking through a microscope results in a discovery of the "wonders of creation" rather than in information by which one can exert control:

> good household management . . . is indeed a science well worthy of attention . . . no woman can reasonably complain of incapacity because nature has endowed the sex with perceptions so lively and acute, that where benevolence is the impulse and principle the foundation upon which they act, experience will soon teach them by what means they may best accomplish the end they have in view. (Ellis 1839, 56, 26)

Connection with others, moreover, rather than detached observation of the laws of human nature, is also a primary source of knowledge. And knowledge, rather than producing a means of control, impacts upon the knower: "It is the strong evidence of truths like these, wrought out of their daily experience, and forced upon them as principles of action, which renders the women of England what they are . . ." (27).

This infusion of scientific objectivity with benevolence and dispassionate surveillance with interactive mutuality rewrites an emerging form of class control—the objective gathering of statistical data and a corresponding emphasis on medicine and sanitation as the answer to the problem of the working poor—as a form of loving attention that is both familiar and desired. A similar rhetoric, of course, is employed to rewrite England's imperial conquest and colonial rule as at once an exercise in surveillance, discipline, and good administration and as "the government of love, . . . superintended by a motherly monarch" (Poovey 1988, 196–97). As Corrigan and Sayer put it: "It took a national culture of extraordinary self-confidence and moral rectitude to construe such imperialism as a 'civilizing mission' (and in fact with surprisingly little use of direct armed force, in comparative terms, from the 'Mother Country'" (1985, 194). Manual writers such as Ellis and Lewis helped consolidate, legitimate, and normalize the symbolic understandings and new system of knowledge that made this imperialist rhetoric possible.

This feminization and domestication of science, however, cannot merely be read as a conservative regulation of consent, just as the professionalization of women's domestic work cannot be interpreted merely as one more argument for keeping women in the home. The manual's feminization and domestication of scientific knowledge and its fusion of surveillance with notions of mutuality and care is recalled to some degree in the efforts of female board members and Poor Law guardians much later in the century to infuse local government with more humanistic boundaries and to extend the limits of what local government did (Hollis 1987, 209). Female board members, in contrast to male, identified special needs among the constituency of women, children, the old, the poor, and the sick. Women also had a more client-centered approach and held themselves accountable to a wider concept of community. Female Poor Law members urged removal of children from the workhouse to a more homey environment and urged provision of baby clinics, school ambulance services, and aftercare of workhouse girls (209). Although women's participation in local government was used as an argument against extending suffrage—Mrs. Humphrey Ward, for example, argued that women now had the "domestic" vote and no longer needed the "imperial" vote— the opposite argument was also made: the vote would educate women into moral responsibility for the local and social questions of the day (192–93). Women's manuals, therefore, contributed to discourses that, in later and reconstructed forms, helped to justify the political emancipation of British women and the inclusion of sometimes radical white women on local education commissions, on prison, school, and Poor Law boards, on workhouse and sanitary committees, and on other forms of local government, in which, as ministers of the interior, they sometimes exerted progressive influence. At the same time, however, women's manuals helped consolidate a focus on education and moralization as "solutions" for the problems of the working class and as justifications for imperialist conquest.

NOTES

1. For the best account of this new demarcation, see Davidoff and Hall 1987, 13–34.
2. On the symbolic value of reform, see Corrigan and Sayer 1985, 148.
3. While scrupulously attentive to the importance of gender in nine-

teenth-century cultural and moral revolution, Corrigan overstates the discursive exclusion of genteel and certainly working-class women from popular understandings of "the public": "Because women were successfully claimed (documented, enumerated, legitimated) to belong within the household, to have a domestic identity . . . they could not be thought of as having a public existence" (Corrigan and Sayer 1985, 133).

4. For an account of the construction of femininity in Evangelical narratives, see Jane Rendall 1985; and Davidoff and Hall 1987.

5. See Taylor 1983, 20–21, on the critique of competition in Owenism.

6. See Thompson and Wheeler 1983 (1820), 187–213.

7. According to Taylor (1983) "the very qualities which were considered quintessentially female were also those which the Owenites wished to see generalized across the population: love, compassion, generosity, charity. A good woman, it was implied, was a born communist" (31). See Moses 1984, 232, on Saint-Simonian conceptions of female virtue.

8. For an account of the feminine in Owenite thinking, see Taylor 1983.

9. On the tensions between religious and commercial values in early-nineteenth-century middle-class culture, see Davidoff and Hall 1987, 21–22, 111–12.

10. See, on this point, Corrigan and Sayer 1985, 129–30.

11. The identification of a superior national identity, of course, was central both to the making of the British state—in that the nation epitomized the fictive community that the state organized and in which we are all citizens—and to the justification of Britain's imperialist ventures (Corrigan and Sayer 1985, 111). Thus, middle-class women are further elevated here through the identification of their ostensible disinterestedness and self-sacrifice with the successful rationalization of imperialist projects:

As far as the noble daring of Britain has sent forth her adventurous sons, and that is to every point of danger on the habitable globe, they have borne along with them a generosity, a disinterestedness, and a moral courage, derived in no small measure from the female influence of their native country. (Ellis 1839, 47)

12. See, on this point, Armstrong 1987, 173–76.

13. Knights 1978, 1–18.

14. Poovey 1988, 169.

Learning Not to Curse; or, Feminist Predicaments in Cultural Criticism by Men: Our Movie Date with James Clifford and Stephen Greenblatt

With Judith Stacey

(1992)

Portrait of Man with a Book

As *Dances with Wolves,* Kevin Costner's wildly celebrated film, reaches its emotional climax, Smiles a Lot, his proud, young face glistening with reverential tears, returns to Lt. John Dunbar the damaged leatherbound journal in which the latter has recorded fieldnotes on the Lakota tribe, from which he and Stands with a Fist, his newly acquired wife, are about to take their poignant departure. Novice film critics, we scribble scarcely legible notes about the musical crescendo and heavenly light that mark this pivotal return of the book from a Native American boy to a white man, noting how the white man's gratitude is mirrored and magnified in a close-up image of his wife's beatified expression. All three—white woman, native boy, and white man—seem gratified by the restoration of this white man's words.

Two Men and Their Books

Our path to this celluloid wilderness had been blazed by other images of natives and of white men with books. During the 1991 season of Costnermania the authors of this essay had been reading the work of James Clifford and Stephen Greenblatt in preparation for a collabo-

149

rative study of the politics of contemporary cultural criticism by U.S. men. The former, director of the Center for Cultural Studies at the University of California, Santa Cruz, and a historian of ethnography, is a metatheorist of what others have termed the "new," or "postmodern," ethnography; the latter, a founding editor of *Representations* and a literary critic in Renaissance studies, is generally recognized as the central fashioner of an approach to cultural criticism called "new historicism." Both are widely cited as important figures on the frontiers of U.S. cultural studies, that increasingly favored site of discourse in the embattled academy, now frequently identified with the renewed political relevance and multicultural commitments of Left/liberal academics.[1]

It was in Clifford's and Greenblatt's books, *The Predicament of Culture* (1988) and *Learning to Curse* (1990), both of which sport cover photos of white men with their books,[2] that we found treatments of Native Americans that piqued our curiosity about other white male representations of America's first colonial victims. Although generally wary of westerns as a field for male dreams, we took our versions of Clifford's and Greenblatt's modes of cultural critique to the movies, where they served as valuable, inspiring, but also, at times, troubling film companions in our critical reception of this Oscar-winning artifact of popular culture, an artifact both touted and condemned, in our local newspapers, as an exercise in the "new politics" of multiculturalism (Grenier 1991; Jacobs 1991; and Baltake 1991).

Viewing *Dances with Wolves* through our attempt to simulate Clifford's and Greenblatt's sensibilities, we could produce what we regarded as insightful but also disappointing readings of the film, readings marked by the kinds of insights and disappointments we have often found in Clifford's and Greenblatt's work. Their work, for example, prompted us to readings of the film as a redemptive Western allegory of the kind Clifford finds in the ethnographies that he subjects to his incisive, influential form of cultural critique and as a form of linguistic colonialism of the kind that Greenblatt explores in his complex and likewise influential analyses of Renaissance culture. In a move that the authors of both texts might appreciate their cultural critique also helped us to read *them*. Through the lens of our enhanced analysis of Costner's film we were sensitized to ways in which their own work might be said to reinscribe some of the allegorizing and colonizing strategies that they had already enabled us to perceive in *Dances with Wolves*.

Clifford's and Greenblatt's work, however, contributed little to our analysis of the film as a masculine allegory in which, as in much of the cultural criticism they have published so far, gender politics are accommodated but also marginalized and/or contained. This move in relation to gender politics, we will suggest, is complexly related to the racial politics in Clifford and Greenblatt, just as it is in Costner's film. Read in relation to one another, indeed, Costner's film, Clifford's and Greenblatt's recent books, aspects of the current men's movement, the canon war, and some discourse on cultural studies in the United States suggest recurring lines along which gender and racial critique have and have not become part of the "new" politics, multicultural commitments, and reinvented masculinities of Left-leaning white men.

Two Women and a "Nagging Text"

We begin this essay with an awkward mixture of trepidation, humility, and hope. Deeply troubled by the orchestrated, full-scale, campaign against "PC" (political correctness) inside and outside the academy, our goal is to impede rather than encourage the enemies of multiculturalism. The anti-PC campaign, which is serving as an ideological shield for racist and sexist assaults on affirmative action and multicultural curricular reforms, indiscriminately positions cultural critics such as Clifford and Greenblatt alongside feminists, ethnic studies scholars, deconstructionists, Marxists, other critical theorists, and gay and lesbian scholars.[3] It positions as subversive, that is, the very projects many cultural studies advocates subsume under the cultural studies umbrella, and it links them with all other forms of dissidence from the New (or Old) World Order.[4] Indeed, Kevin Costner himself has been attacked, in the pages of *Commentary* and elsewhere, for having reproduced a politically correct, countercultural, quasisocialist, "antiwhite," "new politics" in *Dances with Wolves* (Grenier 1991, 26).[5] Under such Orwellian political conditions the etiquette of fraternal critique among fellow "subversives" is of no trivial concern. Our goal here is to strengthen oppositional cultural critique, not to undermine it.

But "we," of course, are not fellows, and the etiquette for sororal critique of radical brethren is underdeveloped and fraught.[6] Throughout the 1970s and 1980s white feminists mainly nurtured our own theoretical fields without seeking, or welcoming, much fraternal assistance. In the process we felt free to rake over, appropriate, and critique literature by (largely white) men for our own pressing purposes. In a political climate as unsettling as the present one, however, cooperative, multivocal alliances are crucial, and these may require, if not kinder and gentler, then at least scrupulously constructive forms of criticism. Our goal, like Clifford's and Greenblatt's, is to rewrite stories of cultural difference for a less oppressive future, and to do so we need to rewrite some of the stories of cultural difference we discover in their work. But in critically reading their work and in rereading the film with and apart from them, we hope to produce something closer to a collegial revision than to what Meaghan Morris has identified as that impotent feminist genre—the "nagging text" (1988, 15).

As white feminists in women's studies, moreover, we have been humbled by two decades of criticism by feminists of color exposing the exclusions and colonizing gestures of white feminist genealogies and the institutionalization of feminist work in the academy.[7] Like white, middle-class men of the 1960s, accustomed to feeling at the center of an important political and intellectual movement, white feminists have been called upon to relinquish privilege within "the feminist movement," within institutions, within women's studies programs, and within "feminist theory."[8] Our hope is that continued reflection upon these contradictions and self-indulgences, while deepening our alliance with feminist and antiracist women and men of color, will also foster not less incisive but, rather, less self-righteous critique of those progressive white male colleagues with whom we also share a commitment to cultural critique, multiculturalism, and a less unjust future.

We are fully aware, finally, that a critic's published work can never encapsulate his or her politics. Oral interviews with Clifford and Greenblatt, conducted after this essay was in draft, suggest a far deeper engagement with gender and domestic race politics—in relations with students and colleagues, in campus politics, in new research, in domestic life—than is suggested in much of the work they have published so far. Further dialogues have reminded us that their work, like ours, continues to evolve and may now be moving in directions that will render our critique dated. In future essays we plan to focus upon material from these interviews and from interviews with other academic men, both white and of color, and to reflect upon the ways that interviews and other forms of ethnographic work challenge and complicate the reflections we offer here upon the mainly textual political trajectories of Left-leaning white male critics.[9]

Postcolonial Cultural Poetics

James Clifford and Stephen Greenblatt, in our view, are among the most influential and stimulating of these critics. Clifford's distinctive contribution has been to historicize and decode the rhetorical strategies and political effects of Western ethnography. In the essays collected in *The Predicament of Culture* and in *Writing Culture*, the discourse-setting collection of essays he co-edited with George Marcus, Clifford has honed a narrative that identifies the collapse of empire as the primary source of anthropological crisis, theoretical ferment, and textual experimentation in the West. Anticolonial struggles and native ethnographers have challenged the legitimacy and the conceptual foundations of the classic anthropological endeavor of representing native societies deemed too weak to represent themselves, while a global world marked by incessant and unequal forms of cultural contact and exchange explodes those coherent and stable concepts of self, other, and culture upon which traditional ethnographies depend.

Clifford regards the neocolonial challenge as the enabling condition for his reflexivity about the textual means through which classic ethnographers crafted their authority and for the kinds of experimental efforts to textualize the syncretic cultural subjects of the neocolonial world that he has done so much to canonize. Thus, the postcolonial predicament of culture provides an opportunity for anthropology to reinvent itself as well. Clearing the ground for such renewal, Clifford decodes the textual strategies through which classic ethnographies constructed authoritative cultural accounts that served, however inadvertently, not only to establish the authority of the Western ethnographer over native "others" but also to sustain Western authority over colonial cultures.

Primary among these rhetorical strategies is allegory. Indeed, Clifford insists that ethnographic writing is inescapably allegorical "at the level both of its content (what it says about cultures and their histories) and of its form (what is implied by its mode of textualization)" (1986, 99). What Clifford believes ethnographers *can* and *should* try to escape, however, is the recurrent allegorical genre of colonial ethnography—the pastoral, a nostalgic, redemptive text that preserves a primitive culture on the brink of extinction for the historical record of its Western conquerors. The narrative structure of this "salvage text" portrays the native culture as a coherent, authentic, and lamentably "eroding past," while its complex, inauthentic, Western successors represent the future. What this structure obscures, Clifford suggests, are the specific historical struggles of peoples caught in contact situations.

Like Clifford, Greenblatt responds to a crisis of representation that challenges the conceptual foundations of his discipline, most particularly in Renaissance studies, in which new critical assumptions about the objectivity of the critic, the historical transcendence of the artist, the stability of meaning in free-standing literary texts, and the unity and stability of culture have been especially entrenched. Greenblatt finds in this crisis both a form of loss, in that it challenges familiar forms of power and authority that he, like so many critics trained in the 1960s, stood to inherit, and as an opportunity to reinvent literary critical practice.[10]

Greenblatt, in contrast to Clifford, does not specifically locate this crisis of representation and authority in a particular set of political developments such as the collapse of empire or the development of a global world. In *Learning to Curse,* however, he does insist upon the political entanglements of his own work. For Greenblatt, and for many of his critics, his emphasis upon the syncretic, contestatory nature of identity, texts, culture, and literary criticism, his insistence on reading literary texts in relation to non-literary texts and other phenomena such as institutions and political events, his fondness for homologies that link past to present, his interest in power, and, most particularly, his focus on imperialist themes, signal a continuation of 1960s-style energy (see Cohen 1987; Howard and O'Connor 1987; Boose 1987).[11] In "Resonance and Wonder," indeed, the most recent essay in *Learning to Curse,* Greenblatt describes his critical practice as having been "decisively shaped by the American 1960s and early 70s, and especially by the opposition to the Vietnam War" (166–67).

The phrase "learning to curse," which alludes to the linguistic colonization of Caliban in Shakespeare's *The Tempest*, signals a thematic focus on New World imperialism and on imperializing forms of representation, which does recall the political interests and investments of the antiwar 1960s and early 1970s.[12] Perhaps the central theme of *Learning to Curse*, moreover, is the inescapably colonizing force of all representation. The dramatist, and by implication the literary critic and all who textualize, are metaphorically colonists: "His art penetrates new areas of experience, his language expands the boundaries of our culture and makes the new territory over in its own image" (Greenblatt 1990, 24).

If this focus on imperialist themes recalls the politics of the 1960s, however, it recalls post-1960s liberation politics as well. For the critique of linguistic colonialism that emerged in the antiwar and student movements and in postcolonial politics, in which it was directed for the most part against imperialist governments, was later turned by feminists, black and other ethnic nationalists, and lesbians and gays against the white, Left/liberal, heterosexual male students who had themselves been engaged in the earlier critique. In turning the critique of linguistic colonialism against all who textualize, including the literary critic himself, Greenblatt, like Clifford, might be said to apply it not just to "the usual suspects"—imperialist governments, the establishment, the "fathers" of the 1960s—but, through a series of displacements, to himself, an erstwhile student of the 1960s, a "son," who is now a father of new historicism.[13]

Hollywood Pastoral (or Costner and Custer)

On first viewing *Dances with Wolves* immediately after reading Clifford's essay "On Ethnographic Allegory," it was hard to resist the fantasy that Costner had himself perversely misread this essay as a how-to guide for staging a "salvage text" within a salvage text. Costner plays Lieutenant John Dunbar, the film's white protagonist, a disillusioned Civil War military officer turned lay ethnographer.[14] Alone on the vanishing frontier, Dunbar keeps a journal in which he records the customs, costumes, mores, and language of the Lakota

Sioux as well as his own process of personal redemption. The journal inscribes a prototypical instance of what Clifford has called an ethnographic "fable of rapport," and it keys viewers to empathetically witness a full-scale anthropological "gone native" event in which a former Union military man reinvents himself as a Lakota warrior. Thus, as in the classical tradition of colonial ethnography, Dunbar's textualization of Lakota experience (and Costner's cinemagraphic record of this textualization) aims to rescue their "vanishing primitive culture" from historical oblivion. And in the same ingenious, and, as Clifford's work suggests, inescapable, ethnographic stroke, Dunbar-Costner constructs his own authority as ethnographer-redeemer as well as the triumph of Western technology and artifice over the "authentic," traditional Lakota, who are thereby encoded as incapable of representing themselves.

The much vaunted, and occasionally disputed, "authenticity effects" achieved in *Dances with Wolves* actually do depend partly on the textual legacy bequeathed by a nineteenth-century lay anthropologist and portrait painter, George Catlin.[15] But they depend even more on the hired counsel of living Native Americans who recall the sort of hybrid, heteroglossic subjects of a postmodern world that James Clifford theorizes far more than they resemble the extinct "authentic" Lakota heroes of the film, Kicking Bird and Wind in His Hair.[16]

We credit Clifford's work with sharpening our awareness that cinematic ethnographer Kevin Costner, a white outsider, had to employ syncretic twentieth-century Native Americans in business suits (and several in Indian renewal movements) in order to successfully mis-represent their "authentic" nineteenth-century ancestors. Under the neocolonial conditions of late-twentieth-century America, Native Americans still lack the power to represent their history by themselves, whether on the screen or in the courts. And so, the protagonist of *Dances With Wolves*, like its producer (the identical hybrid person), is a white outsider.

Native American reviewers had divided reactions to the film, which turn on this question of self-representation. Some Native Americans, such as Frank Evans and Michael Dorris, condemned the film for stereotyping Indians as "savages" or "ecological saints" while allowing Costner to act out "every white boy's fantasy of being Indian" and for relegating "good Indians—the only Indians whose causes and needs we can embrace" safely to the past (Evans 1991;

Dorris 1991). Other Native Americans, such as Ed Castillo and Marilou Awiakta, were enthusiastic about *Dances With Wolves*, expressing gratitude to Costner for inviting an unusual level of Indian participation in the cast and crew, for the film's unusual bilingual dialogue, and, of course, for portraying Lakota culture in such positive terms (see Castillo 1991; Awiakta 1991; Valente 1991; Landon 1990). Still others, such as Ines Hernandez, fully registered the film's (all too familiar) colonizing gestures but felt they had been decentered by Native American actors, who effectively took the movie over, filling the screen with their humor and significant silence (1991).

Our reading of the film, which has its own stakes and limitations, intersects with these readings in different ways. We too were impressed by the film's employment of Native American actors, its sympathy with the Sioux, its use of Lakota subtitles, and by the presence and power of Native American actors. At the same time, however, for us, as white feminists, prone to feeling that their race privilege implicates them in the film's colonizing gestures, and as critics recently attending to the images of white men and Native American others produced in contemporary cultural critique, a reading of the film that foregrounds its complex and sometimes contradictory colonialism seems more resonant. Costner's positive representation of the Lakota *is* remarkable in the context of Hollywood's dismal prior record in portraying and employing Indians, but our attention was drawn, nonetheless, to what Frank Evans characterizes as the film's "final form of colonization" and what David Seals aptly dubs the "New Custerism—General George sporting velvet gloves" (Evans 1991, 2; Seals 1991, 637).[17]

Our reading of James Clifford's work also encouraged us to perceive *Dances with Wolves* as a colonial ethnography. Costner's depiction of the Lakota as noble savages, for example, struck us as a caricature of the genre of redemptive anthropology, a genre that, no matter how well intended, perennially reinscribes Western domination over "natives."[18] In sensitizing us to the narrative structure and effects of such sugar-coated, imperialistic poetics and politics, Clifford's approach to cultural studies makes a contribution that we deeply value. Unnervingly, however, viewing Costner's film from this perspective, we perceived certain unexpected continuities between his and Clifford's treatment of natives.

For, in a sense, Clifford is busy redeeming natives too, although the natives he prefers to salvage are syncretic, late-twentieth-century survivors and reinventors. If Lieutenant Dunbar absorbs Lakota traits and wisdom into himself, augmenting them with superior Western knowledge (in the form of rifle power), and if Costner redeems the Hollywood western for liberal neocolonial audiences, Clifford attempts the more difficult task of recuperating the culture, struggles, and texts of hybrid survivors through his own theoretical tools.

Central to Clifford's redemptive project in *The Predicament of Culture* are the Cape Cod Mashpee. The Mashpee, as construed by Clifford, are a cultural inversion of Costner's Lakota Sioux, but they serve analogously to ground an ethnographic allegory. Instead of representing an irretrievable, authentic past, the Mashpee sign Clifford's, admittedly utopian, attempt to envision multiple routes through modernity to heterogeneous futures. Clifford certainly sympathizes with the courtroom struggle for tribal identity and land rights that is the subject of, or rather the occasion for, "Identity in Mashpee," his partially ethnographic and experimental essay. But he constructs his interpretation of this fraught neocolonial contest not as an intervention on behalf of the Mashpee but, rather, as an intervention in cultural studies. In a world seemingly threatened by global cultural homogenization and technological "progress," the Mashpee stand for the reinvention of cultural difference. Their court battle provides a complex discursive site that Clifford, as "positioned observer," reads from a self-consciously distant, theoretical vantage point.[19]

Clifford views the trial as "an experiment in translation" between cultures (1988, 289). Embedded in this translation, however, is a contest between history and anthropology, between written and oral texts, which Clifford, as a historian of anthropology, is unusually well-positioned to resolve. His solution (ironically, of course, achieved through *writing*) is, appropriately enough, a syncretic one that fuses and renovates both disciplines. Clifford constructs and deconstructs alternative narratives about cultural identity that were presented to the Boston jurors: "History I" is Clifford's recounting of the version of Mashpee history presented in the successful legal case against Mashpee claims to tribal identity; Clifford represents this as a flawed, linear, primarily *historical* account based exclusively on written documents. "History II" Clifford presents as a better, but still inadequate, more *anthropological* account that the Mashpee lawyers culled from a mixture of oral and written evidence. This narrative, in Clifford's view, suffered not only from the constraints of adversarial courtroom rules but also from a flawed concept of continuous culture. Having partially cast the struggle in these disciplinary terms, Clifford finds that it was anthropology's concept of culture that proved more fragile in the trial: "This cornerstone of the anthropological discipline proved to be vulnerable under cross-examination." Clifford's redemptive role is to historicize and rewrite that concept in a manner that reinvents cultural difference for postcolonial society; thereby, Clifford's work offers to rescue the endangered enterprise of ethnography that he has so perceptively criticized and chronicled.

Linguistic Colonialism or Tatanka/Buffalo: Same Difference

If reading Clifford prompted us to construct *Wolves* as an ethnographic allegory, reading Greenblatt supplied us with critical tools for further deconstructing the liberal humanist assumptions that ground this allegory and obscure its colonizing tendencies. Like Greenblatt's own work, *Dances with Wolves* might profitably be read as a 1990s reinvention of 1960s-style political critique. Although the film is set in the period of the Civil War, the battle scenes with which the film opens recall nothing so much as Vietnam, a conflict seemingly without purpose, in which officers are incompetent and out of touch with what is going on and acts of intended suicide are construed as heroism. Like so many young men of the Vietnam period, Lieutenant John Dunbar attempts to cut his ties with this bankrupt establishment, the U.S. government and its military, which are, once again, engaged in imperialist conquest—this time of Native American land. In so doing, he throws in his lot with the ostensible enemy, the Lakota Sioux.

Dunbar's rejection of his structural relation to U.S. imperial power is located in and guaranteed by his class position, a position that is most centrally represented by his literacy and education, by the fact that he is, for most of the film, a man writing a book. Writing is the record but also the sign of Dunbar's ability to see beyond his culture's racist constructions of cultural difference—"nothing I had heard about these people was correct." It is this book-writing student of Sioux culture who enters into a brotherhood with Sioux males and

in the process disowns imperialist agendas. This escape from complicity is further guaranteed by a series of contrasts that the film
constructs between this textualizing middle-class male and a series
of dirty, badly dressed, physically unhealthy, and illiterate, lower-
class white male figures, who become increasingly identified with the
brutalities of imperialist power. The distance between these figures
and the middle-class Dunbar is recurrently signaled, in fact, by the
vulgarities they perform in relation to his text. There is the crude,
slovenly mule-driving guide, for example, who farts and then quips
to the earnest, scribbling Dunbar, "Put that in your book." And there
is the lower-class soldier who scornfully wipes his ass with a page
torn from Dunbar's journal.

In the meantime Dunbar himself becomes increasingly clean,
well-groomed, and well-dressed, qualities that the film identifies
with the nineteenth-century Sioux but that struck us as also redolent
of twentieth-century middle classes. In becoming like the Sioux,
therefore, Dunbar becomes not a bicultural subject but, instead, what
he regards as his own true self. Thus, after learning that his adoptive
Sioux relatives had renamed him *Dances with Wolves*, he writes, "I
knew for the first time who I really was." In the end, despite Costner's obvious sympathy with Native Americans, the Sioux are rewritten as the white hero, who bears their shared virtues into the future.
Dunbar's superior literacy and technology, of course, smooth the
way for this colonizing translation.

Having recently read Greenblatt's *Learning to Curse*, we were
particularly sensitized to the colonizing potential of the film's easy
equations between education, belief in a common humanity, non-
complicity, and progress. In the title essay, "Learning to Curse," for
example, textualization of the "other," most particularly by "educated" and "humanist circles," is identified not with transcendence
of imperialist agendas, as it is in Costner's film, but as a central site
on which colonizing processes move forward (Greenblatt 1990, 19).
Greenblatt, moreover, is particularly incisive about the ways in which
not only racist constructions of cultural difference (the notion, for
example, that native others have no language or culture) but also
liberal constructions of cultural sameness (the notion that native others are like "us") may be turned to colonizing purposes. The "sympathetic" and "seductive" assumption that native inhabitants of the
New World were like Europeans and "comfortable in (their) own

modes of thought" may not have caused "the horrors of the Conquest, but it made those horrors easier for those at home to live with" (30).

Costner's film, of course, does reject several stereotypical notions about Native Americans, some of which date back to the sixteenth century—the idea that Native Americans have no family life or political organization, for example, or that Native Americans are sexually degenerate. *Dances with Wolves* also respectfully invokes cultural difference in exposing non-Native American viewers to the experience of hearing Lakota spoken and of having to rely on subtitles for obviously broken translation. At the same time, however, the film ultimately collapses cultural difference into cultural sameness by suggesting that the two languages translate into each other—Tatanka/Buffalo, same difference.

The humanist implications of this suggestion, increasingly manifest in the film, that languages are transparent, that there is a common reality and humanity, facilitate Dunbar's brotherhood with the Sioux, but they also prepare the ground for Costner's rewriting of the Sioux as his white hero and as a figure for himself. At the end of the film Dunbar and Kicking Bird speak one language, English, Dunbar's own, while Dunbar is given permission—through the return of his diary by Smiles a Lot, a Native American boy—to represent Lakota culture and values, now transparently reinscribed in Dunbar's text and in himself. As in Renaissance culture, in which, as Greenblatt observes, Europeans rehearsed their encounter with the peoples of the New World through their constructions of the legendary "wild man," the wild man appears at the end of Costner's film to be an upper-class white man who has gotten lost (Greenblatt 1990, 21). We have met the other, and he is us—those of us, that is, who are literate, white, middle-class males.

It would come as no surprise to Greenblatt, we imagine, that his work on the colonizing force of representation and of liberal humanist assumptions provides tools for reading his own textualizations. A major feature of his work, after all, has been to identify homologous relations between seemingly unconnected cultural sites. Thus, despite his emphasis upon the inescapably colonizing force of all representation, Greenblatt too suggests that textualization can put distance between us and colonizing activities. In contrast to Costner, of course, whose presentation of cultural difference is collapsed into a celebration of cultural sameness in the end, Greenblatt locates himself between these two modes of constructing the other, as like us and as different. This ability to hold sameness and difference in suspension, moreover, is identified with resistance to assimilation by dominant forms of power.

In "Filthy Rites," for example, Greenblatt first locates this capacity in the nineteenth-century Zuñi, whose ritual dance is read as a form of mocking white colonizers, acknowledging submission, and producing powerful medicine. This balance of unlike elements in Zuñi ritual defies "hierarchical organization," and "in this indifference to unity, this refusal of conceptual integration, we may grasp one of the sources of the Zuñis' dogged resistance, to this day, to assimilation" (Greenblatt 1990, 64). In the title essay, "Learning to Curse," a similar capacity to sustain the simultaneous perception of likeness and difference, "the very special perception we give to metaphor," is located in Shakespeare, whose *Tempest* tests our capacity to sustain metaphor in relation to colonial themes (312).[20] The same capacity, however, is most powerfully located in Greenblatt himself, whose literary critical mode throughout these essays is characterized by the practice of establishing homologies between different cultures and cultural phenomena, homologies attended by rigorous attention to the ways in which these phenomena are the same and different.

Like Clifford's, then, Greenblatt's meditation on imperialist themes focuses upon the reinvention of a discursive practice, representation of native others. One might quarrel here with this focus, as tending to narrow the field of colonizing practices being considered, but it is Greenblatt's own representation of native others that seems most problematic. In contrast to Clifford's essay, in which syncretic others are refigured along with ethnographic authority, in *Learning to Curse* native others tend to disappear. Despite the careful identification of "culture" with the oral as well as the written, the private as well as the public, Greenblatt's essays here concentrate, for the most part, on delivering readings of public written texts and, through them, of the educated, publishing (and in Renaissance culture, elite, white, male) colonizers. There is much less of a focus on offering, say, constructions of or speculations about the cultural practices of oral, often illiterate, colonized others.[21] Culture, therefore, tends in practice, if not in theory, to be most richly represented by the productions of elite, white men.[22] Since Greenblatt makes little use of his characteristic homologies to link native others in the past with native others in the present, native others in this book appear to exist almost entirely in the past and to leave almost no impact on "culture" as it is constructed here. Inevitably, "most of the people of the New World will never speak to us. That communication, with all that we might have learned, is lost forever" (Greenblatt 1990, 32).

Learning Not to Curse

It is because of the critiques that Greenblatt and Clifford enable us to make of their own work that we are far from wishing to denigrate their projects. If in both *The Predicament of Culture* and *Learning to Curse* the representation or thematization of native others is also an occasion for establishing the author's or white elite men's cultural authority, Clifford and Greenblatt provide powerful tools for scrutinizing their own authorizing moves, for uncovering narratives of salvage and the ways in which privilege, in the words of Elizabeth Spelman, finds "ever deeper places to hide" (1988, 183). In thinking through this essay, indeed, we have tried to turn these tools against ourselves. For our project, too, has redemptive agendas. It seeks, for example, to find space for the authority of critical work on gender and domestic race issues in white, male-centered cultural studies and space for white male authority in feminist cultural work. To what degree do we seek to enhance our own authority in this critical reading of Clifford's and Greenblatt's representation of native others? In making this critique we too evoke and displace others at least partially for our own ends. Few among us can claim clean hands, and in critically reading Clifford and Greenblatt we hope to become better readers of our own indulgences and dodges.

We also value Greenblatt's and Clifford's genuine contributions to envisioning multicultural and less unjust futures, for academic and lay concepts of cultural difference and sameness sorely need reconstruction, and not just for the sake of conceptual currency. The image of a culture, David Seals reminds us,

> is as important, especially in this high-tech world of instant global telecommunications, in the perception of it, or of a race of people as whatever lies in the *actual* truth of that culture. Indians have often been victims of stereotyping—Custerism, I

call it—and this reduction of the image of a people kills as surely as any real-life, Wounded Knee–type massacre. (1991, 635)

In the wake of the demonization of Khadafy, Noriega, and Saddam Hussein and the "orientalizing" of Arabs, the lethal consequences of reductive images in the New World Order should be all too obvious. And closer to our academic "home," the reactionary media epithet "PC thought police," applied indiscriminately by the media, and by some of our colleagues as well, to all who criticize the Eurocentric humanities curriculum, makes crucial the forging of cooperative, multivocal alliances among all of its targets. Working alliances, however, as opposed to theoretical or mythical ones, require something more than a compelling cause. They require the acknowledgment and working through of tensions and divisions. As we turn our race and gender glasses first on Costner's film and then on Clifford's and Greenblatt's work, we hope to foster, not hamper, resistance to the reactionary discourses now dominating the decline of the twentieth century.

Iron John Dunbar

Gendered as well as racial others are subjugated in *Dances with Wolves*, in which masculinist and imperialist representational strategies are mutually dependent. Costner's movie, to be sure, does evince a superficial patina of awareness and sympathy with feminist criticism of cinematic representations of women. The film, for example, does not portray women primarily as sexual objects, nor as frail nor foolish. Indeed, in a promotional video trailer that hypes the film for potential cable television audiences, Costner recounts his victory over conventional Hollywood standards in casting a woman "with lines in her face" for the role of the white woman, reared by the Sioux, who becomes Dunbar's linguistic translator and bride. Likewise, the filmscript challenges gender conventions in its character-naming strategies and elsewhere. Lieutenant Dunbar becomes the nature dancer of the film's title, while his future bride, who "Stands with a Fist," also shoots with a rifle—and with courage and accuracy. And while the Lakota wife of Dunbar's mentor and double, Kicking Bird, is more stereotypically named "Black Shawl," she displays wisdom and more than quiet strength.

If *Dances with Wolves* does not portray women rapaciously or disrespectfully, however, it scarcely portrays women, especially Native American women, at all. As in the conventional western genre that the film attempts to invert, women are utterly tangential to its overt narrative interests, interests that have to do with the reinvention of the white hero's masculinity in relation to activities conventionally associated with men—hunting, waging war, governing a community, and bonding with other males. Yet Costner's film, to give it credit, makes a point of reinventing masculinity in relation to women as well.

Native American women, for example, though minimally represented in the film, provide hints of a gender order in which the contributions of women are more overtly validated than in nineteenth-century, white, middle-class culture. Although they do not hunt, for example, we do see Native American women at work, skinning hides. Although excluded from tribal counsel, native women speak at community gatherings, where they are accorded honor by the men (and by the camera as well), and Black Shawl gives her husband, Kicking Bird, direct criticism and pointed advice.[23] These hints of self-assertion, status, and power on the part of Native American women suggest a set of domestic relations that Dunbar will enter into as he assimilates to Sioux culture. But white men and women, we are to learn, are not the same as Native Americans.

Stands with a Fist, for example, is assertive too, as her name indeed suggests, but her assertiveness is directed toward Native American women and men and not toward her white suitor. Her other moments of agency, moreover, either serve to facilitate men's relation to one another (as in her translating activities for Dunbar and Kicking Bird), or they mark her as more comfortable than Native American women with Western male technology (as when she, not Black Shawl, shoots a Pawnee warrior with one of Dunbar's rifles). As an evocation of the feminist new woman, moreover, Stands with a Fist is ultimately rewritten as that familiar woman, a submissive wife. For at the end of the movie, when Dunbar proposes to leave the Sioux, Stands with a Fist assures him,"You made a decision; my place is with you; I go where you go."

This recoding of spunky frontier woman as adoring wife is facilitated by the fact that Native American women are relegated to the background of this film and by the fact that self-assertion on their part often acts to foreground the white heroine. (Both instances of Black Shawl's critical advice to Kicking Bird are interventions on Stands with a Fist's behalf.) The traditional recoding of the white heroine, who, as the lone female survivor of the film, represents the only "new woman" with whom the future must engage, is also facilitated by Costner's extended focus on Dunbar's political and personal reinvention of himself in relation to the male Sioux, the official cultural other in this film, and by ethnocentric evocations of cultural difference between Dunbar and Native American men. For throughout the film the white, middle-class hero is represented as less harshly patriarchal than Native Americans.

Dunbar, for example, arrives at the Sioux camp tenderly cradling the unconscious woman in his arms, but angry, suspicious Wind in His Hair retrieves her from the white intruder by dragging her by her arm and dumping her in the care of Lakota women. In this first transfer scene, as in several later scenes with Kicking Bird, Lakota men are portrayed as more authoritarian and less civil to women than Dunbar, and it is Dunbar's implied racial superiority in this domain that justifies the domestication and later the transfer of patriarchal rights from native Kicking Bird back to white Dunbar. Thus, when Stands with a Fist falls in love with Dunbar, white audiences have been well prepared to agree with the Lakota villagers that "it makes sense": "They are both white."

If racial superiority is evoked in the service of traditional gender relations, however, Dunbar's superior performance of patriarchy, in turn, prepares the way for the colonizing transfer of the future to this white hero. The film, in this respect, evokes the more polarized and more extreme codings of the Gulf War, in which Western men were represented by the U.S. government and its censored mediaservants as both liberators and protectors of women, while native male others were represented as callous and patriarchal or, in the case of Saddam, as rapists of a feminized Kuwait. At the same time, those privileged objects of Western male liberation, female soldiers, were turning up on the frontier of "Indian country" only to be studiously recoded, in the media, as in *Dances with Wolves*, as mothers and wives. This gender coding of the war, of course, helped paper over real divisions between U.S. white men and men of color both in the war and as citizens in the New World Order, an order that they are ostensibly to inherit.[24]

Despite its patriarchal politics, however, *Dances with Wolves*, like some strands of the men's movement today, contends that "men can change."[25] Ed Castillo accurately locates the chief source of the movie's popularity in the audience appeal of Dunbar's character, "precisely because his is a 1990s man, not an 1860s man." Echoing elements of the men's spiritual movement, à la Robert Bly, the movie suggests that traditional forms of masculinity wound, and even castrate, men. Like the wounded boy in Bly's masculine mythology, *Iron John*, John Dunbar enters into the wilderness of the frontier to be healed among other men, the male Sioux. "Going native," he may be seen as getting in touch with the "wild man" within, a process most dramatically suggested by his ecstatic fireside dance, which evokes the contemporary phenomenon of men's drumming societies.[26] Castillo notes that "powerful drum beats rhythmically signal a deeper transformation of Dunbar as he joins in the rhythm of the earth and perhaps harks back to a race memory of his own neolithic ancestors" (1991, 10).

Reading the film as a modern Native American man committed to contemporary Native American struggles, Castillo probably perceives political advantage to the cultural association of Native Americans with ecological values.[27] We can appreciate this view, but, as Euro-American white feminists, whose reading strategies have been influenced by feminists of color, we cannot overlook subtle dimensions of colonial discourse intermingling with male chauvinism in Costner's postfeminist masculine fantasy. For Costner's 1990s man contains feminist threats to white male hegemony not only by maintaining patriarchal power relations but also by selectively absorbing feminine traits, just as he does male Native American ones. While his stolid, unfluid woman stands with her fist, Dunbar becomes the sensitive, communicative, and playful yet also virile man, shaving his facial hair, wearing Sioux jewelry and dress, and becoming more beautiful than the heroine in every frame.[28]

This gender recoding is consistent with a recent report on network programming strategies for "Children's TV, Where Boys Are King." ABC, for example, has dropped all children's programs with female central characters, because boys refuse to watch these, while girls will watch male leads, and to compensate for the absence of female leads, the networks now "give the male characters attributes considered to be 'female'" (Carter 1991, A1). Costner makes a similar co-optive concession to white feminism when he syncretically rein-vents Dunbar as embodying the best of white femininity and native masculinity. Costner, that is, while reinscribing gender and racial superiority, also seems, wistfully, or defensively, to have displaced onto white men those far more visible processes of cultural reinven-tion recently undertaken by feminist, lesbian and gay, and Native American and other racial and ethnic liberation movements. White men can change, as *Dances with Wolves* demonstrates, but individual, psychological change, while welcome, is hardly enough. Authority for some groups is "easily compatible with the expression of soft and tender emotions" (Segal 1990, 284), as with other signs of cultural reinvention, like "the dream of limitless multiple embodiments," which Susan Bordo calls the *"dance* from place to place and self to self" (1990, 145). What is required, of course, is a greater challenge to patriarchal power relations than that of performing them with greater sensitivity and better grace.

Feminist Predicaments

Of course, neither James Clifford nor Stephen Greenblatt succumb to simplistic masculine allegories about rediscovering the wild man within. Nonetheless, it unsettles us to find more sophisticated margi-nalizations and/or displacements of feminist and other forms of cul-tural reinvention in most of their published work. Clifford directs and teaches in a vanguard cultural studies program and campus in which the presence of feminist scholars is unusually prominent. Greenblatt teaches in a department in which feminist scholarship is also strong. Both scholars, moreover, are not only overtly sympathetic with femi-nism and its intellectual contributions to ethnography and literary criticism, but both have demonstrated their own capacity for feminist analysis, as in Clifford's discussion of the male gaze that William Carlos Williams turns on the disparaged figure of "Elsie" and Greenblatt's analysis of Martin Guerre.

Disappointingly, however, in *The Predicament of Culture* and in *Learning to Curse*, both authors still marginalize feminist contributions to cultural criticism, even though their own projects might be strengthened by including the kinds of emphases that have consis-tently characterized critical gender and antiracist work—emphases on the investigation of familial life and other nontextual cultural practices outside the officially public sphere. Clifford, for example, might have buttressed his argument for a syncretic understanding of Mashpee cultural identification had he pursued the possibility that Mashpee women bore disproportionate responsibility for negotiating that hybrid identity. In a passing reference, Clifford mentions the prevalence of intermarriage during the late eighteenth century between Mashpee women and freed black slaves, which was "encouraged by a common social marginality and by a relative shortage of men among the Indians and of women among the Blacks" (1988, 297). Greater attention to the history of Mashpee kin and gender arrangements might have strengthened the case for Mashpee tribal status as well as Clifford's case for cultural reinvention, because women may have been the primary cultural carriers of the continuous tribal identity that the Mashpee lawsuit sought to establish, or the primary cultural reinventors and syncretists for their "tribe." Greenblatt, as various of his critics have observed, tends in practice if not in theory to equate culture with a discursive field defined by the published texts of elite white men. This representation of culture might be broadened by the more extensive employment of strategies that have marked the work of feminists and of ethnic studies men: the insistence on a larger definition of the discursive domain, one that takes into greater account heterogeneous cultural spaces—the oral, the nonliterate, the familial.[29]

A similar tendency to foreground the texts and activities of male public spheres informs Greenblatt's and Clifford's textual relations to feminist work. Both, for example, have tended to confine their references to feminist labor to the literal margins of their texts, placing them in parenthetical comments and footnotes, where they fail to revise otherwise androcentric metanarratives, genealogies, or characterizations of what constitutes a discursive field. Clifford, for example, makes an explicit decision to bracket gender (and class) analysis while exploring "emergent possibilities" represented by "Natives." He sets out, in "The Pure Products Go Crazy," to liberate Elsie from symbolic exploitation by Carlos Williams, who has submerged her particularity into the general decaying condition of modernity. Clifford instead asks Elsie to stand for marginalized, silenced groups—"'Natives,' women, the poor"—and the syncretic possibilities of postmodernity he hopes they represent. Ironically, however, Clifford's decision to bracket Elsie's gender and class locations reduces her to a monological script of race-ethnicity, even though, in a footnote, he registers awareness of literature by feminists that demonstrates systematic interrelationships among ideological constructions of race, gender, and class.[30]

Greenblatt, too, has been roundly and sometimes harshly criticized, both for his exclusions and for his use of feminist insights.[31] *Learning to Curse* provides further ground for feminist critique. If in Clifford's revisionary ethnography few feminists are cited as among those up against the predicament of culture, in *Learning to Curse* feminists are marginally alluded to as persons who seem not to have gotten things, particularly fluid and syncretic things, right. Thus, in a footnote to "Resonance and Wonder" Greenblatt notes that "the discourse of the appropriating male gaze is itself in need of considerable qualification" (1990, 183). This may be true, but largely feminist work on the male gaze is critiqued here without citation or even identification as feminist. In the same essay, moreover, feminists seem foregrounded among those whose gaze is problematic: "A criticism that never encounters obstacles, that celebrates predictable heroines and rounds up the usual suspects, that finds confirmation of its values everywhere it turns is quite simply boring" (168). Like Stands with a Fist, feminist new women seem implicitly rewritten here as an even more familiar feature of the cultural landscape, not the adoring but,instead, the nagging wife.

In Greenblatt's *Learning to Curse*, therefore, as in Clifford's *The Predicament of Culture* and in some of the discourse on cultural studies as a whole, feminist work by women, despite its multiple reinventions of itself over the last thirty years, is, at best, marginally represented as experimental or is presented as fixed. Cultural criticism by (largely white) men, however, along with the author's persona, often appear syncretic, fluid, postmodern, or playful. Thus, Clifford occasionally depicts himself as a rootless, syncretic, Westerner, while Greenblatt enacts the "lie" of any single narrative of himself by imposing and reimposing not identities but critical positions. In *Learning to Curse*, indeed, in which he adapts and critiques multiple critical approaches and engages a whole catalog of cultural themes, Greenblatt seems a figure for U.S. cultural studies itself, with its multiple themes, its syncretic borrowing and perpetual critique of all critical positions.[32] Self-characterizations such as these may challenge traditional masculine authority and suggest a refreshing capacity for change, but they imply unsettling polarities with the representations of feminist scholars presented in these works. Feminist scholars, that is, sometimes appear to be standing stolidly with their fists, while male cultural critics are fluidly dancing with wolves.

Predicaments of Cultural Studies

More troubling analogies may be at hand in the texts of some male cultural critics who represent cultural studies as the fluid, syncretic repository of the best of what has been thought and said since 1968, for, like *Dances with Wolves*, these representations have the potential to marginalize and/or absorb the discourse of the other into a common, and dominant, language.[33] Indeed, an essay on cultural studies published in 1985 maintains that feminist studies, black studies, and American studies have failed and that cultural studies now stands alone on the political frontier. In this formulation cultural studies becomes the lone voice in the wilderness, having absorbed the voices of those who did not get it right, arguing for "the necessity of a counter-disciplinary praxis" and "introducing the notion of the resisting intellectual as an educational formation necessary to restore academics to their roles as intellectuals" (Giroux et al. 1985, 473). It is disturbing that syncretism and multiplicity appear here not as conflicting and identifiable voices but, instead, as a new improved discourse, as one heteroglossia for all of us.

The reinscription or reinvention of a specifically white masculine authority and privilege that accompanies the efforts by some male cultural studies critics to reinvent "real-world" politics for their work may be difficult to see because of the way "politics" is often coded. Politics, that is, may be coded, as in Costner's film, as critique of imperialist, other-world ventures, while any critique of white male authority is carried on as a textual repositioning of the self vis-à-vis distantly colonized (male) others. Introducing a special issue of *Cultural Studies* on "Chicano/a Cultural Representations," for example, Rosa Linda Fregoso and Angie Chabram find it ironic that the ubiquitous image of the other in much postmodern cultural criticism is so abstract, despite the physical proximity of so many tangible others to postmodern or white male cultural studies theorists:

As Raymond Rocco points out, "they are no longer out there, but are instead an integral part of the theorist's everyday life, serving their food, driving their cars, cleaning their homes or offices." And it is doubly ironic that we remain an abstraction when we are now in fact challenging their theoretical formulations as well. (1990, 210)

Anxiety about direct confrontations seems one likely source for these ironies and contradictions. Representing visions of distant male natives may appear a safer "Field of [Men's] Dreams" than representing more proximate others.[34] This caution is all the more ironic, of course, given the "political anxiety" of many cultural studies scholars and their insistence on looking at the power relations that construct present critical discourse.[35]

The new war on political correctness, however, in offering an opportunity for "humanists" to gain a "real-world political relevance in which the left finally has a cause not only against academic conservatives but against statist ones also" (Marcus n.d., 8), offers the possibility for reinventing relations between domestic others as well, between Left-leaning men, white feminists, feminists of color, and U.S. antiracist men of color in the academy. It is crucial, however, that sufficiently complex narratives emerge about what is at stake and who the interested parties are. The emerging battle, for example, is sometimes figured in relation to a political paradigm that no longer seems adequate to our construction of present political realities. Debate about the canon, according to George Marcus, "reproduces the fiction of the old categories [Left and Right] and has great nostalgic appeal. There is a conservative, orthodox authority which various liberal/left positions can resist" (Marcus n.d., 8). Race and gender divisions that position the Left/liberal allies in this struggle rather more complexly are obscured by the reassertion of this 1960s-style political paradigm in the 1990s wardrobe of cultural studies.

We would not have written this piece, however, if we did not believe that different narratives of our political histories and alliances were possible. One aim of this essay, indeed, is to shift our own discursive strategies, to enter into a differently constructed dialogue with a wide spectrum of our male colleagues, as we continue to engage in and construct dialogue and alliance with feminists, especially feminists of color. The dialogue we have aimed at here and that we envision for the future is one that involves the sort of criticism that also includes appreciation and fosters exchange. We are aware that in shifting strategies we will please very few. We will inevitably be read, depending on the "positionalities" of our readers, as having been too critical or too kind, of having given white, male colleagues too much credit or too little, of having acted like the feminist police or like deferential wives, as having positioned ourselves, once again, inside a nagging text. Shifting strategies, however fashionably postmodern, is not a comfortable, reassuring, or ingratiating move.

Alliance, however, would seem to require a willingness to experiment, to be tentative, and to encounter risk, lessons we are learning as we work with our colleagues of color to build a multicultural women's studies program on our campus. The voice we present here, moreover, is only one of many that might be registered, just as our focus here on domestic others is one of many and is meant not to displace but rather to augment the postcolonial focus that Clifford and Greenblatt favor. Resistance to the monovocal, after all, is what Clifford and Greenblatt advocate, and hearing the discourses of the "'Other'—of all the others," is the announced aim of cultural studies as it is sometimes currently defined (Brantlinger 1990, 3). Both seem key to the political alliances we really need, alliances that, in practice as well as in theory, are polyvocal, syncretic, and reflective, alliances that help us to hear and to see the other and in the process help us to investigate that spot the size of a quarter that, as Virginia Woolf points out, we cannot see on the back of our own heads.

Fields of Dreams

Clifford and Greenblatt were not with us when we unenthusiastically accompanied male relatives to *Field of Dreams,* an earlier Costner movie. Had they been, they might have enhanced our own understanding of its allegorical properties, while we might have urged them to attend equally to its masculinist script. Then bell hooks might have inspired us all further to decode the liberal, hierarchical race relations between Costner and the retired black reporter he conscripts to realize his baseball fantasy. In a genuinely multivocal alliance with critical friends like these we might resolve some predicaments in cultural criticism and better weather the right-wing assault on all of us.

NOTES

We want to thank the following for helpful and sometimes vigorously challenging responses to this piece: Emily Apter, Wini Breines, Bob Connell, Rosa Linda Fregoso, Maggie George-Cramer, Susan Gerard, Julie Haase, Ines Hernandez, Tom Laqueur, Louis Montrose, Mike Rogin, Roger Rouse, Debby Rosenfelt, Kamala Visveswaren, and Judy Walkowitz.

We also wish to thank James Clifford and Stephen Greenblatt for their forthright and generous responses to an earlier draft.

1. See Giroux, Shumway, Smith, and Sosnoski 1985. On some of the perceived tensions between new historicism and cultural studies, see Kuenzli 1991; Veeser 1991.

2. The men on Clifford's cover are, however, black men masquerading as white ethnographers, an image that conveys a self-consciously critical and ironic stance toward the politics of racial and colonial relations.

3. These categories are, in fact, complexly overlapping. They are retained in much anti-"politically correct" discourse, although this discourse constructs members of each category as subversive in the same way. They are also retained in much academic discourse, in which their usefulness as categories seems increasingly problematic.

4. Examples of the voluminous media attacks on campus "political correctness" include Bernstein 1991; Taylor 1991; Will 1991b; and the *Newsweek* cover story provocatively entitled "Thought Police" (1990). President George Bush made the PC issue the focus of his commencement address at the University of Michigan in May 1991; see Dowd 1991. Not in the popular media but particularly vicious is Barbara Epstein (1991). Numerous essays have analyzed and responded to this campaign, but these have received far less attention in the popular media. See, for example, Beers 1991; Carton 1991; Graff 1991; Martinez 1991; and Wiener 1991. Two new organizations, *Teachers for a Democratic Culture* and *Union of Democratic Intellectuals*, have formed to counter the offensive spearheaded by the *National Association of Scholars* and right-wing think tanks and foundations.

5. While Costner's recent movies and starring roles including *Robin Hood* and *JFK* might suggest a liberal political orientation, Costner refuses to discuss his political views and is a recurrent dinner and golf companion of President Bush. For an illustrative expression of his reluctant, ambiguous political views, see Wuntch 1991.

6. One, not entirely successful, attempt to initiate a dialogic approach to such a discourse that by Jardine and Smith (1987). Boone (1990) provides a sensitive critique of that volume's formulation of the subject as men *in* feminism and attempts to carve a less polarizing frame for male feminism.

7. Among the most influential of these critiques have been hooks 1984; Moraga and Anzaldúa 1981; Hull and Smith 1982; Asian Women United of California 1989; Anzaldúa 1990; and Mohanty, Russo, and Torres 1991.

8. The quotation marks suggest the problematic status of these terms,

which have, in the past, very often been equated with white feminist politics and scholarship.

9. An initial discussion of these issues appears in Newton and Stacey 1992.

10. Among those forms of power, for example, is that of identifying and celebrating a "numinous literary authority" that appeared to "bind and fix the energies we prize, to identify a stable and permanent source of literary power, to offer an escape from shared contingency" (Greenblatt 1988, 3).

11. Cultural studies is also sometimes characterized as a resurgence or reinvention of 1960s-style political energy or modes of thought. See Brantlinger 1977, 25; Marcus n.d., 8.

12. On the cover of *Learning to Curse*, which bears the portrait of an elite white man holding a book, the phrase does not appear to refer to native others but, if anything, to the critic himself. Perhaps cursing has to do here with the burden of being elite, a representer, a colonizer of others. Perhaps it has to do with the burden of understanding how elite cultures operate. One review of the book reads the phrase in this light. See McLeod 1991.

13. "The usual suspects" is a phrase from Greenblatt 1990, 168.

14. For an essay that intersects at some points with our own, see Padget 1992.

15. The costumes were modeled on the drawings in Catlin. According to Castillo 1991, Catlin's drawings were of formal and ceremonial Sioux attire, which *Dances with Wolves* inaccurately presents as daily garb.

16. For example, Doris Leader Charge, a linguist at Sinte Gleska Indian College in South Dakota, translated the screenplay's dialogue into Lakota and coached the "authentic" Lakota actors, "none of whom spoke Lakota fluently." The role of Kicking Bird was played by a Canadian-born Oneida, that of Wind in His Hair by an Omaha, while the Lakota who played Chief Ten Bears is also a folksinger and activist. See Castillo 1991.

17. Although not himself a Native American, Seals is a South Dakota resident and author deeply immersed in and identified with contemporary Indian cultures and struggles, particularly those of the Lakota. His essay quotes divided reactions from his Lakota friends to Costner and the film.

18. Clifford explicitly criticizes the elegiac view of vanishing Indians in "Identity in Mashpee" (1988, 284; also see Clifford 1986.) *Dances with Wolves* has also been criticized for exploiting Lakota culture and people to enhance Kevin Costner's authority and coffers at their expense. See Seals 1991; and Harrison 1991.

19. "Overall, if the witnesses seem flat and somewhat elusive, the effect is intentional. Using the usual rhetorical techniques, I could have given a more intimate sense of peoples' personalities or of what they were really trying to express; but I have preferred to keep my distance" (Clifford 1988, 291).

20. This reading of *The Tempest* has been attacked by anti-PC forces. See Will 1991. See also Greenblatt's response ("Literary Politics").

21. For an example of this approach, see Davis 1986; see also "Family Fortunes" in this volume for a comparison and contrast of Davis and Greenblatt.

22. See Porter 1988 for a detailed and rigorous reading of these tendencies.

23. Awiakta 1991: 70–71 notes this aspect of the movie.

24. For compatible feminist analyses of the Gulf War, see the symposium "Watching the War," especially Jeffords 1991.

25. For some recent reflections on men and change, see Segal, "Can Men Change?" and Connell, "The Big Picture." See also Segal 1990; Connell 1988. For an overview of various strands of the "men's movement," see Clatterbaugh 1990.

26. See Adler, Springen, Glick, and Gordon 1991. For an account of the wild man and of Bly's other contributions to the spiritual wing of the men's movement, see Clatterbaugh 1990.

27. We are grateful to Linda Collins for suggesting this association to us.

28. On the general phenomenon of "sensitive men" in current Hollywood movies, see Maslin 1991. On related deconstructions of masculinity in mass culture, see Modleski 1991; Hanke 1990; and Segal 1990.

29. Porter (1988) makes a similar argument.

30. We are, of course, not the first feminists to object to these practices. White feminists have launched several challenges to Clifford's explanation for excluding feminists from the *Writing Culture* conference and volume that has come to define what ethnographic poetics "are." See, for example, Mascia-Lees, Sharpe, and Cohen 1989; Gordon forthcoming; Lutz 1991. Feminists of color have broadened this critique; see hooks 1990; Fregoso and Chabram 1990.

31. See, for example, Boose 1987; Waller 1987; Neely 1988; Newman 1991.

32. For a reading of Greenblatt that sees nothing redeeming in his "self-referentiality," see McLeod's review of *Learning to Curse*. McLeod (1991, 101–2) reads Greenblatt's storytelling, playful self as a form of "self-centeredness" that goes hand in hand with the "denial of ideological responsibility."

33. Several recent essays on feminism and cultural studies cite the marginalization of feminism and feminist theory in cultural studies discourse. See Schwichtenberg 1989; Rakow 1989; Long 1989; Radway 1991. Meaghan Morris 1988 discusses and disrupts the analogous marginalization of feminism in postmodernist discourse more broadly. For related critiques with respect to Chicano studies, see Lipsitz 1991; and with relation to African-American studies, see hooks 1990.

34. The interviews of male cultural critics that we have begun conducting have already begun to challenge and complicate this thesis.

35. See Rooney 1990. On the political nature of cultural studies, see Nelson 1991.

Starting Over:
An Afterword

The following essay, as I explain in my Preface, is an attempt to tell one story of myself as author of this book. I wrote it because not to do so seemed a contradiction and a blatant evasion in a critic who has so often emphasized the importance of connecting personal life and desires with public discourse. I am intensely, and sometimes painfully, aware of many things this narrative reveals and of the many that it glosses over. In telling this partial and imperfect story I do not mean to suggest that my life has been unusually interesting, different, or dramatic. The narrative I construct for myself in these pages intersects with the narratives of many other first generation feminists that I know, and that is part of the reason for its telling. I tell this story as well because I am a materialist-feminist, because the investigation of the personal, the familial, the psychoanalytical are part of what women's and ethnic studies have contributed to our sense of "the material," and because, in teaching the nineteenth-century British past, I have always felt convinced by a central feature of Raymond William's thought, that "great social and historical changes . . . altered not only outward forms—institutions and landscapes—but also inward feelings, experiences, self-definitions."[1] This process, of course—always assuming the constructed nature of the categories—goes both ways.

Excerpt from an Application for a Sabbatical, University of California, Davis, Winter, 1991

. . . I am especially interested in reading strategies that assume a fluid relation between "public" and "private" and that explore the bearing of familial relations, domestic investments, sexual anxieties, and desires on the construction of dominant forms of cultural knowledge and expertise.

California Dreaming

I began this book in the spring of 1981 while I was living in California, first in Laguna Beach and then in the Fairfax district of Los Angeles. I had come to California the summer before to get a better grip on a relationship (a long-distance relationship that had "failed" some months earlier). But having reinserted myself in the landscapes of my childhood (I had grown up in Compton, at the southern tip of South Central Los Angeles) and being habitually open to new beginnings, I had decided that I would try to stay on the West Coast anyway, that I would return "home." That spring, in due course, I sent to Philadelphia, where I actually lived, for my cast-iron pots, my records, and my cat—I have never traveled light—and book by book, box by box, I began to feel that I was starting over.

In the winter of that year my first book, *Women, Power, and Subversion*, had been published (it had focused on nineteenth-century female writers and a subculture both of resistance and participation in dominant forms of power), and I was thinking about a second, a book that would focus on gender rather than on women and that would deal rather less with subversion and rather more with the construction of dominant discourses of gender and class. In preparation for that project I decided I should think through the theoretical and methodological underpinnings of my previous work and try to establish where they lay in relation to other literary critical work that I cared about. In the process, I hoped, I would carve out a set of revised strategies for myself. But I had other agendas as well, some of them having to do with relationships of a different order, not failed relationships to be exact but ones I hoped to improve or indeed pursue.

I was at that time national coordinator of the Marxist Literary Group (MLG), a task for which my social skills perhaps better suited me than my theoretical commitments or expertise. I was on the editorial board of *Feminist Studies*, as well, and I was beginning to feel that my theoretical and personal home was with this latter collective of women rather than with the somewhat embattled feminists in the largely male MLG. Not that I disliked men or working with men, most particularly the men in MLG, with whom I shared many interests and concerns. (I liked men, if anything, too well, and when a critic I admired once read my essay on Charlotte Bronte as an example of "Marxist aestheticism," as an undervaluation of "sexual and romantic longings," I had to laugh. Any asceticism I might have exercised in the construction of that text had been a feminist reaction against myself, an effort to curb my overinvestment in the discourses of heterosexual romance at the time.)

My energies, then, were about to shift directions. After my years in California I would give up my position as national coordinator of MLG and stop attending its summer institutes—not out of disillusionment or rancor, I should be clear. Although I had participated in, and even helped to lead, some MLG struggles over gender and then gay politics, I continued to feel allied with the community that MLG represented. But eventually I came to understand—I construct this looking back—that the pioneering work linking gender, class, race, and sexual identity was being carried on elsewhere, a lot of it by *Feminist Studies*. I wanted to invest my energy on that frontier. That was later, however, and in another county. In the spring of 1981 I was in California, and I was frustrated by the relation or lack of relation that I saw between my field, mainstream feminist literary criticism, and the work being carried on in the MLG.

The lines between these communities seemed most palpable to me at Modern Language Association (MLA) meetings, where each December I attended MLG sessions and saw only a few (and the same) feminists and where I also attended mainstream feminist sessions and saw almost no one from the MLG. (A few feminists crossed over like myself but no men that I recall.) The concerns of these discursive communities, moreover, did not seem much to intersect. MLG sessions, for the most part, had little to say about gender (unless they were officially feminist sessions, in which case they were often sparsely attended), and mainstream feminist literary critical sessions (which were massively attended) had very little to say about economics, the state, or class, although they had much to say about gender and literary texts. Race, as I recall, played a small role in both kinds of sessions but was mainly discussed in sessions on writers of color. I was frustrated by the cleavage between worlds—and exhausted as well since the MLG sessions, largely white, feminist literary, critical sessions, and the race sessions were inevitably scheduled against each other. It was tough going to keep up.

I had been trying, of course, with many others, to bridge these divisions in my classrooms for some time. Race had been central to my teaching since 1967 when, as a graduate student at UC-Berkeley, I began to teach Composition (Subject A) and to read and teach the writings of radical black men, the more radical the better in those days. (This was an outcome of my involvement early on in the politics and discourses of civil rights and a continuation of my muddled first attempts to deal with the confusing mix of race privilege, guilt, patronizing sympathy, racism, and secret, cross-race identification that had attended my growing up as a lower-middle-class white girl in a city and school system becoming largely black and increasingly poor.) I began to deal with class a year later when I took my first job, and, desperate for a handle on the nineteenth-century novel, read Raymond Williams and found in him not only a way to understand and a reason to teach the nineteenth-century past, but also a way of constructing my own class longings and insecurities.

Gender entered later still when I became a feminist in 1971. (And I was one of those for whom an initial consciousness-raising session turned the world upside down. What had seemed private, idiosyncratic, my own neurosis at 7:00 P.M. appeared systematic and political by 9:30). Like other feminists on the left, therefore—I had begun to think, in reading Raymond Williams, that I was at heart a "socialist"—I drew upon what I had already learned about race and class relations in beginning to think through the newly constructed and to me astonishing set of social relations implied by gender. (Astonishing and also painful since it was at the site of my gendered sexuality that I first experienced failed relations, that my childhood sense of an acceptable self was first dissolved, and that my automatic association of home with well being and protection was dislodged. It was at the site of home and self-identification, indeed, that I made my first conscious efforts at "starting over").

It was in the MLG, however (ironically enough), that class and gender analysis came together for me in a new way. It was the summer of 1977, I was writing *Women, Power, and Subversion*, and I had dropped in on the institute after its first week in order to visit a man with whom I was then in a (problematic) relationship (MLG Institutes at the time were three weeks long and a prime site, for many of us, in which to explore the intersection of politics with other passions). What I encountered there, in that hot St. Cloud June was a deluge of post-Marxist theory—Althusser, Macherey, Jameson, Eagleton,

Spivak, Derrida. I went home, reeling from paradigm shock (and with my adrenalin slightly elevated by the struggles over gender that had taken place in the last few days), and changed directions in my book. Writing *Women, Power, and Subversion* became an exercise in patchwork quilting or, more fashionably put, in bricolage, as I tried to merge insights from mainstream feminist literary criticism, history, and anthropology with what I could manage in the way of this new (new to me) post-Marxist theory, mainly Althusser, Eagleton, and Macherey.

Having begun this experiment, rather by accident, in my first book, I wanted to continue and improve upon it in a second, and I thought that, if I mapped the relations between mainstream feminist, antiracist, and post-Marxist literary critical work, I might clarify what bridging work most needed to be done. In the process, I thought (in some of the more utopian moments to which native Californians are sometimes given), this mapping might draw the communities represented by at least mainstream feminist literary criticism and the MLG closer together and in the process help create a critical and political community more in line with my own mix of politics, intellectual interests, and also desires. The essay that came out of that moment in 1981 when I was most concerned with relationship, with making a relationship that didn't properly exist, became "Toward A Materialist-Feminist Criticism," the first essay in this book. It was, in its first version, a talk that I wrote in my head as I drove the L.A. freeways between Fairfax and U.C.-Irvine, where I was a visiting instructor (ostensibly in the English department but actually in history, where I felt much more at home). I delivered the talk that fall at a women's studies conference on a panel with Barbara Christian and arranged by Debby Rosenfelt, two of the lasting relationships I forged during my sojourn in the West. Some years later, when we were both on the board of *Feminist Studies* (Barbara Christian was to join the board in 1985), Debby and I reworked and enlarged the talk as the introduction to a collection of "materialist-feminist" literary critical essays. Our interest by then was less in mapping out a set of relations between post-Marxist and feminist criticism than in intervening in mainstream feminist criticism itself and in constructing, through describing, naming, and so partially creating it, a critical community or configuration of feminist literary critics on the Left, one that included white feminists and feminists of color. We both were in that other country by then, and our relation to other feminist women was what most concerned us.

The term *materialist-feminist criticism*, which was our own coinage, a recycled term borrowed from British feminists like Michele Barrett and Annette Kuhn, aimed at conveying the problematic and fluid relation between feminist and post-Marxist work, especially in the United States. Hyphenated terms like *socialist-* or *Marxist-feminist*, we felt, drew the lines too cleanly for the work of the white women we had in mind (including our own). *Socialist-* or *Marxist-feminist*, moreover, would barely have allowed us to include, or allude to, work by many women of color, women whose scholarship seemed to us to be informed by similar but also different kinds of bridging movements, women who we knew would not have identified themselves by those terms. We spent a long time, however, debating what formulation to use, weighing the political implications, as we saw them, for each. *Materialist-feminist criticism* stuck, and, though we were criticized by more Marxist-identified feminists, the relative fluidity of the term seems to have made it serviceable for some time. (Feminists, of course, were not the only critics on the Left to find terms like *materialist* helpful. Many white male critics who were also reinventing their relation to the Left began, by the 1980s at least, to identify themselves in similar terms, as "cultural materialists" or "materialist critics." In that way and others many male leftists entered their own "other countries.")

Letter from a Former Lover to the National Coordinator of the MLG, July 16, 1980

On the Marxist Union . . . the crowd was young, white, New Yorkish, many women, academic (lots of grad students) many other familiar faces. Pretty clearly it was a New American Movement affair, but the New Left people always have had trouble moving out socially toward others, and so every lobby gathering was a lot of small isolated knots of people (two or three) and no sense of communality. . . . I gave up, finally, in the middle of an organizational workshop during which it became clear to me that whoever was in charge of all this didn't know anything about political process. You can't invite 150 talkers (academics, no less), Marxists, sectarians, special-issue folks, and ask them to voice their positions willy-nilly when you have an hour to come to a decision. I would prefer to have a program rammed down my throat, take-it-or-leave-it, than sit through such a meeting again. And who was a major instigator of this mayhem? Dr. X (and I half-suspect enjoying the destructiveness because it made Y so confused). So I gave up with a pretty clear sense that nothing will come of this. I think the Left, at the moment, is totally fucked. The New Left is old, tired, flabby, sentimental, idiotic. I prefer isolation and retreat into scholarly stuff. Until the next turn of this wheel everything else Left is preposterous.

Excerpt from a Preface to *Feminist Studies*, Vol. 6,
Spring 1980

The editorial board, our collective, meets on the average of five times a year on the East Coast; West Coast editors fly, or are flown, in perhaps twice. We meet early—usually in New York but sometimes in Philadelphia—and always at someone's apartment or house. We meet all day and work through a long agenda, making collective decisions about the content and shape of upcoming issues, about policies, about the latest refinements in our round robin process. We drink coffee. We eat a lot of fruit and (even more) carbohydrates. We schedule longer meetings, meetings that last a day and a half, meetings that are three-day retreats, because there is never enough time, not for business only, but for thinking, for being creative, and for finding out the shape of one another's lives. (We long for time, after the work is over, simply to drink wine together at twilight!)

In Another Country

I did not stay in California after all. There were no jobs for me there, and in time, in the spring of 1982, I returned to Philadelphia, living quite contentedly for awhile with my gay ex-husband and his lover(s). In 1983–84 I had a grant from the National Endowment for the Humanities. I was working with *Feminist Studies*, having more or less let go of MLG, and I was having a hard time with my nineteenth-century book. Indeed, although I drafted several chapters of this book, including the two that appear in this volume, I found myself focusing instead on the materialist-feminist anthology. Part of this diversionary move might be explained by the fact that, somewhere between my trip West and my return East, I had decided that the book would focus on discourses by white, middle-class, nineteenth-century men. (I had developed, perhaps in MLG, a new interest in the discourses of this "other.") When I pursued this tack in 1983, however, I began to feel that I was staring at a blank wall. I could not "see" the discourses of men in isolation. I felt, moreover, something I can only call "depressed." It was depressing to study the discourses of white middle-class men and only those. White middle-class, male-authored texts came alive for me, fed my imagination, only in relation to those of women.

There was a connection perhaps between my inability (but also my desire) to focus on the discourses of men and the fact that I was now solely immersed in academic communities of women. Certainly, I belonged to many such communities, including two or three study groups in Philadelphia that were ongoing at the time. My most passionate intellectual and political ties, moreover, were with the editors and associates of *Feminist Studies*. Indeed, my most passionate friendships were there as well. (I once complained to a sister editor, whom I rather envied for being married to an interesting academic man, that *my* whole intellectual life was with women, that I almost never had really gripping conversations with a man, most especially those I was in relationships with. "That's true of every feminist I know," she replied.) At any rate it took me several months of false starts to see that I had to work the discourses of women back in.

I was also troubled at that time by what had become the dominant discourse in what I, now more tenuously, still thought of as my "field," literary criticism. I was troubled, that is, by deconstruction, by what I saw of its most dominant forms. I disliked and disapproved of the inaccessibility of its language, its focus on isolated, written, high-cultural texts, its insistence on polarities everywhere (an insistence that seemed to me to be convincing to a point, in written texts, but that ultimately struck me, despite the baroque complexities of deconstructive readings, as a simplification). Much deconstructive work, indeed, reminded me, despite considerable differences in theoretical complexity and assumption, of my formalist graduate training, a training I had resisted—by reading and assimilating Raymond Williams—as soon as I was safely out of graduate school. (I had picked up the idea, in the Berkeley English department of the 1960s, that Marxist criticism was "vulgar" and that most things outside the text were a kind of crutch that really good close readers didn't need.)

I had, of course, assiduously learned and spoken the language of my training for many years, even when it did not make sense to me (which was, unfortunately, often) for, like a good student, I understood that it was necessary to speak that language, to do well, to be approved of, to be heard. Besides, I had no other language of literary criticism to put in its place. Now I felt pressured, once again, compelled even, to speak the language of another dominant, uncongenial, and often baffling discourse to be taken seriously, to be heard, and, once again, more practiced now in shifting registers, I resisted. I resisted by trying to name, to authorize, a different (though related) discourse—that of materialist-feminist criticism, one I saw as focused not only on public written representation but also on social texts and one less given to the critique of binaries than to the analysis of untidy intersections.

All this time, of course, I was also shifting positions. I was reading new feminist theory and feminist work on the nineteenth century, and I was taking in many things. I was becoming influenced by poststructuralism, especially by critics who combined it with Marxist categories and so reinflected it and broadened the uses to which it might be put. Little by little, I changed vocabularies to some degree, changed the inflection of my own "discourse," picked up different ways of reading, and thought differently about "language," "identity," "experience," and "history," along with many others. But there were several years in the mid-1980s when the dominance of the most popular forms of U.S. poststructuralist literary critical work drove me not just to publish anthologies of differently oriented scholarship but also to entertain persistent fantasies of having pursued a career in Hollywood.

Excerpt from "A Matter of Life and Death,"
Cornell West. 1992

For me identity is fundamentally about desire and death. How you construct your identity is predicated on how you construct desire and how you conceive of death. . . . And so in talking about identity we have to begin to look at the various ways in which human beings have constructed their desire for recognition, association, and protection over time and in space and always under circumstances not of their own choosing.

Matters of Life and Death

During the academic year of 1983–84 I started over. I got married, bought a different house, and moved into a small collective—my ex-husband, my new husband, and my new husband's old friend, a visiting British historian, a Marxist of the old school, with whom I argued endlessly over dinner about the role of "ideology," until by mutual, unspoken agreement we stopped talking theory at the dinner table and meals proceeded more smoothly. I continued to pursue my book on the nineteenth century, teaching my eight courses a year, and helping to plant the half-acre on which we all lived, but *Starting Over*, as you have by now gathered, is not that book, or only a small piece of it, a fact that has as much to do with daily life and with nonacademic life events—the birth of my daughter and the death of my ex-husband—as with the vagaries of theoretical discourses and my discontents.

After the birth of my daughter, Anna, that is, I could no longer work in British archives, unless I left her, which I was not prepared to do. (I did persist for a while, however, in trying to combine some of my other habitual, and obsessive, modes of work with motherhood. During my ninth month, for example—it was August, a Philadelphia August with 90 percent humidity—I developed high blood pressure and was ordered by my doctor to stay in bed. Day after day I lay on my left side, facing away from the dogwood tree outside, sweating into the white comforter, and rewriting the nineteenth-century chapters of this book. For a few weeks after my daughter's birth I tried to continue this regime, nursing her while holding a book open with my other hand or composing a talk in my head out of material from the chapters on women's manuals and the *Edinburgh Review*, but it would not do. I was teaching again, and my daughter had trouble nursing as it was. I laid my writing aside for the following summer.)

In the spring of the following year, 1986, my ex-husband, and best friend for twenty years, was diagnosed as having AIDS. (It was not a nervous breakdown, as we had supposed and hoped, when he began to lose his way at night on familiar streets.) I continued to write, my work a refuge, through the trips with him to the National Institutes of Health, the experimental drugs, the returns home, the sudden recoveries, the frightening turns for worse. (Once in late October we sat up in the kitchen long past midnight, drinking champagne and talking about how Hamlet wasn't tragic. A few days later, standing puzzled in the light of a November morning, Dick had forgotten the relation between a box of cereal and a bowl. Two weeks after, as he lay mute and in a coma, I was to learn the terrible resistance of flesh to needle as I tried to give him shots. I was to learn, near dawn Thanksgiving morning, how strangely firm, how quickly chilled, a long-loved hand becomes in death.)

When I returned to writing a year later I had lost my taste somewhat for studying the nineteenth-century past, but in an effort to begin again, I decided to take stock. I went to MLA, saw that critical tides had shifted, once again, this time to more historically engaged literary work, and felt at once that the current conversations were ones I cared about and desired to enter. The essays "History as Usual?" "*Family Fortunes*," and "Historicisms New and Old" were first drafted in that year, that year of recovery, of assessing where my field and I had gone. And though the thrust of these essays is nothing if not interventionist and critical, the very energy of the critiques and of the interventions I tried to make was deeply rooted in celebration and renewal.

**Excerpt from "Looking for Love in All the Wrong Places,"
a talk delivered at the Marxist Feminist Session of the
MLG, MLA, December 1988**

Having written several essays on the relationship between materialist feminism and the "new historicism" and having read far more, I propose to end my talk by telling you why we should talk about the relationship less and ourselves more. My strategy, therefore, is not unlike that of certain nineteenth-century social activists who advertised tent meetings devoted to religious awakening only to convert those meetings by degrees, once the crowd had assembled, to the topic of abolition and still later, of course, to the topic of women's rights. Let me begin, however, by saying a few words about the proposed topic before I refer more critically to the politics of examining and reexamining this relationship or any of the others we have focused on in the past. ("What are you majoring in?" someone asks the heroine of a recent film, *Everybody's All American*. "I'm majoring in Gavin and me," she replies, "or should it be Karl and me, Michel and me, Mikhail and me, me and Jacques?")

Relocations

I did not stay in this place for very long, as "Learning Not to Curse," the penultimate essay in this book, might suggest. Nor did I stay very long in my present home. It was 1988 when I delivered this salvo against focusing too much on our relation to male critical others, and I was about to move into a new house and a new academic community, for in January of 1989 I was hired as director of women's studies at U.C.-Davis, and the following May I was in California, surrounded once by unpacked boxes, my iron pots, my records, my daughter's toys, my own and my husband's books, many of which were still in cartons three years later. I began my term as director expecting to move in a larger, more varied, more racially and ethnically mixed version of the female communities in which I had spent the last ten years, although, having immersed myself during this same period in the flood of writing by women of color that had emerged since 1981, I had come to my new post with an agenda for starting over from a different place. It was no accident that the only book I read that June was Gayatri Spivak's *In Other Worlds*. I wished, very deliberately, to begin from "other worlds" in developing women's studies. I wished to help construct a different kind of community, a different and differently managed collective, community, home. I began in the simplest way I knew, though fueled by theory. I made a list of every feminist of color in the university and of every ethnic studies director (all male), and I went out day by day for coffee, for tea, and for lunch. By the end of June I had gained several pounds, and women's studies had applied for money with the four ethnic studies programs to host a series on Comparative Feminist Perspectives for the following year.

I spent most of the next three years doing what directors usually do, holding meetings, writing reports and documents of supplication to white male administrators, hiring, revising curriculum, submitting proposals for new courses, having lunch, and, in my case, cooking and baking. (Had I picked up in *Feminist Studies*, or first at my mother's table, this persistent association of successful community, of the desire for it, with tasty, carbohydrate-rich food?) What emerged out of these three intense, sometimes painful, often euphoric (distinctly fattening), years were some of the most deeply satisfying accomplishments of my career. When I arrived at Davis there was a large feminist community but only one faculty in women's studies, myself. In three years, through a combined effort of many hands, the faculty had been increased to eight, four white women and four women of color. There was a differently articulated mission for the program, that of working across categories and cultures and of pursuing cross-race, cross-gender alliances. There was a newly organized major and minor, a multiracial and cross-cultural curriculum, a program in graduate-level study, and newly strengthened ties to the ethnic studies programs.

What also emerged for me, personally, during those initial years was a revised sense of who alliance might be with, a more complex sense of how alliances are built, and a better grip on the multilayered ways that what Sandra Harding calls "traitorous identities" are constructed. I came to see in a more specific way than before that the bases for alliance is more than shared politics and intellectual interests, although these were vital. I came to see, in the most material of ways, the importance of daily behaviors—acts of loyalty, generosity, and support, exchanges of gossip, warmth, and jokes, offerings of chicken with cilantro pesto and polenta almond cake, and the practice of inviting ever larger groups of friends and potential allies home.

Of course, I also came to see in a daily way how alliances, like other relationships, fail, fall short, or involve starting over. The history of those initial years, like most histories, was uneven. I am thinking, for example, of the white feminists who answered questionnaires about what women's studies should be doing with angry comments like "There's too much emphasis on race" and "White women exist too." But I am thinking as well of the senior white feminists who devoted hours and days to negotiating (in absurdly secret committees) the successful tenure or promotion of other feminists—sometimes white feminists and more often feminists of color. I am thinking about Chicana colleagues who bothered to tell me they were "touched" that I had looked up the ethnic studies faculty first, to whom it mattered that I served up asiago cheesecake, black bean salad, and lemon tart at day-long committee meetings. I am thinking of a Native American colleague who responded with such unexpected anger to an early version of "Learning Not to Curse," that the presumption and folly of presuming on past credit was painfully inscribed in my consciousness.

I am thinking of the white liberal men who rarely if ever engaged with race or gender or sexuality in their work but who consistently said yes to our requests for faculty lines, for joint hires with ethnic studies, for a lesbian to teach our course on sexualities, for space, for funds, the same liberals who thought that, now that we mentioned it, it *would* be a good thing for women's studies to hire a gay man. I am thinking of the ethnic studies director of whom I said (to angry students, white feminists, and feminists of color), "Think of him as a brother whom we must bring along." I am thinking of the same director saying once to me, "We know you mean well, but there are things you just don't see."

It is out of this unevenness, these complexities and contradictions, that "Learning Not to Curse," the penultimate essay in this volume, was to emerge and with it the larger project for which it stands as an exploratory first beginning.

Excerpt from a (Unsuccessful) Proposal to the Spencer Foundation Spring 1992

We are applying to the Spencer Foundation for support that would enable us to complete a collaborative, cross-disciplinary investigation of the comparative impact on antiracist and leftist academic men of the goals and perspectives associated with women's and ethnic studies. Combining textual criticism with oral history and participant-observation, our project takes as the object of its investigation our subjects' scholarship as well as their teaching, their collegial relations, their institutional practice and behaviors, the development of their cultural knowledge, the intellectual and political milieus in which they move, and their personal lives. . . . In playing the narratives derived from published texts against narratives offered in oral interviews . . . we hope to complicate the way academics characteristically read their relations to one another. In so doing we hope to promote a more various, more multilayered, more fully human knowledge of the others with whom our own intellectual, political, and personal lives are entwined. In focusing, moreover, on the complex conditions that produce "traitorous identities," a willingness to "betray" the traditional privileges of one's group and one's own position, we hope to produce understandings that will enable us as educators to "hail the most progressive tendencies" in our colleagues, our students, and ourselves and to build dialogues and alliances across historical boundaries.

Starting Over: 538 Isla Place, Election Day, 3 November 1992

I am writing this as the workmen tear out my daughter's bathtub in our latest home. The tub is so grainy now after seventeen years of scouring, by other hands than mine, that it is permanently dirty. (I imagine a series of children like my daughter, refusing to come out, making a game of smearing gummy soap along its surfaces, prolonging the period before bed. "But, Mom, I'm cleaning the tub!") I have moved, and a marriage that "failed" nine years ago, several months before the wedding, has finally ended. It is testimony to our mutual hunger for, our immersion in multiple discourses, of home, family, community, connection, alliance, and solidarity—my ex-husband is a leftist of the oldest school—that we have sustained this failure for so many years. I am trying to settle in here, to feel "at home," though, in fact, home has always been a tenuous place (and even more so after the death of my first husband, for, if Dick could leave this world abruptly, then so could I).

My friend Susan tells me, "Life is change. The trick is in how you meet it." I meet it with iron pots (new pots, white pots, for a new beginning—I am professional now, I am middle class, and I feel the privilege of my access to the materialities of home), with cartons of books, my own and now my daughter's, with an archaeology of fraying couches and bowing tables from different relations, different locations, of my life, with a new (but aging) cat. I am starting over. "We" are starting over. (I have just turned on the news.) "We" have a gift, perhaps, for starting over. I think most survivors of the 1960s do, and we have been waiting twelve years for this beginning, for this chance to move more swiftly on. I want to slow this moment down. I want to savor it before it (also) passes. I have never traveled light. Have you?

U.C. Santa Barbara, 13 November 1992

I am sitting in a conference room at U.C.–Santa Barbara, one day into a conference on the Future of Multiculturalism, which is slated to go on for three and a half days. I am impressed by this conference that has gathered some forty-eight participants largely from California and the U.C. system. I note with interest that there are some thirty-three speakers, sixteen women of color, nine men of color, five white men, and three white women. I am trying to imagine what I would have felt at a conference like this three years ago, before I had taken residence in California. Would I have felt that I was on someone else's ground? Would I have been here on this ground at all? I note these things: that this is "radical multiculturalism" not "cultural studies," that the emphasis here is on politics rather than on methodologies, that postmodernism is very little mentioned while being radically rewritten, that several interventions with respect to class and economic exploitation have been structured in, and that gender is less often mentioned for the two days I am there. I note, with interest, that having worked at Davis to make gatherings like this happen, I have fashioned a sense of my belonging. Later, in the conference hotel, sitting in front of a well-burning fire with colleagues from my campus, I reflect on the fact that the organizers of this conference are a young, white, heterosexual, middle-class, feminist woman and a young, white, heterosexual, middle-class, feminist man. They are a couple. They belong, quite actively, to MLG.

Postscript: O'Hare Airport, 26 June 1993

Flying home from Pittsburgh, where I have been attending the Summer Institute for the Study of Culture and Society—this institute is still being held by the MLG some sixteen years later—my plane is grounded by a summer storm. I am beginning to be hungry, having eaten last seven hours before, but there is nothing to eat, so I decide to review my notes. Of most interest to me is a discussion on "The Current Conjuncture," which the institute engaged in two days before. The discussion, which lasted several hours, is summarized near the end by one of the panelist participants as having turned on "the strategic implications of the differences between those referring to a strictly Marxist mode of production and those who see it needing revision because of determinations of race, gender, and culture."

What I am struck by as I read my notes are these two things. The first is a sense of the dogged familiarity of this debate. Although certain valences are new, although as individuals many of the participants have moved beyond this impasse in their work, the debate inevitably emerges when we meet together on this ground, under the sign of MLG. (I think of a young, white, male participant who owned, my first day there, that he had delivered an economistic paper because he felt it was appropriate to the MLG. Privately, and later on, I learn that he is keenly interested in writing on the intersection between the theories of a well-known Marxist intellectual and the personal, familial, also gendered dynamics of his life.)

The second thing I note is this. I feel the need, once more, for starting over. I review my notes and finish two of the readings proposed for this discussion, several chapters from Robert Reich's *The Work of Nations* and Mike Davis's "Who Killed L.A.?" I am deeply disturbed by the first and stricken by the second, a recent account of the racialization and social, political, and economic abandonment of inner cities, an account of interethnic strife and of the bipartisan state and national subsidization of white flight and metropolitan resegregation. (Another essay I will read, Susan Willis's "Sweet Dreams," suggests that inner cities have been feminized as well.) I am struck, in particular, by the essay's account of The Weed and Seed program, which channels funds for job training programs and community development through the Justice Department's war on gangs, a tendency, according to Davis, that prefigures the absorption of the welfare by the police state.

I am hungry now, and my stomach twists, but part of the constriction has to do with this essay on our "current conjuncture" and with the fact that my younger brother, my only ally in the long struggle of our childhood, is now a member of a task force on gangs, a merger of the Los Angeles Police Department and the FBI. (We have come to terms, but to different terms, with the multiple impoverishments of our early lives, I through the continuities and changes, the "startings over," that I have partially described, and he by working his own way—steadfastly, patiently—from nightbeat to vice squad to detective, LAPD, South Central Los Angeles, Watts.)

I stare out the rectangle of my window and I try to think—how I can better take this on? And what I think of first is almost entirely governed by what I am accustomed to, by what I do best, by what is most at hand. I sit on the ground in the Chicago airport (my ground time is to last three hours), making rough notes and thinking how can I teach this, in its terror, in its complexity?—how can I teach this with hope, with something approaching hope, to the students in my two courses, "Gender and Cultural Representation" and "Problems in Feminist Research," this fall?

NOTES

1. Williams 1970, 11.

Works Cited

Adler, Jerry, Karen Springen, Danile Glick, and Jeanne Gordon. 1991. "Drums, Sweat and Tears." *Newsweek* 24, June: 46–53.

Alarcon, Norma. 1990. "The Theoretical Subjects of *This Bridge Called My Back* and Anglo-American Feminism." In *Making Face, Making Soul, Haciendo Caras: Creative and Critical Perspectives by Women of Color*, ed. Gloria Anzaldúa, San Francisco: aunt lute foundation.

Alexander, Sally. 1984. "Women, Class and Sexual Difference in the 1830s and 1840s: Some Reflections on the Writing of Feminist History." *History Workshop Journal* 17:125–49.

Allen, Paula Gunn. 1975. "The Sacred Hoop: A Contemporary Indian Perspective on American Indian Literature." In *Literature of the American Indians*, ed. Abraham Chapman. New York: New American Library.

———. 1986. *The Sacred Hoop: Recovering the Feminine in American Indian Traditions.* Boston: Beacon Press.

Althusser, Louis. 1971. *Lenin and Philosophy, and Other Essays.* London: New Left Books.

Anon. 1834. "Mrs. Jameson's *Characteristics and Sketches.*" *Edinburgh Review* 60:180–201.

———. 1835. *Woman as She Is and as She Should Be.* London: James Cochrane and Co.

———. 1844. "A Bewailment from Bath; or, Poor Old Maids." *Blackwood's Magazine* 15: 199–201.

Anzaldúa, Gloria, ed. 1990. *Making Face, Making Soul, Haciendo Caras: Creative and Critical Perspectives by Women of Color.* San Francisco: aunt lute foundation.

Armstrong, Nancy. 1987. *Desire and Domestic Fiction: A Political History of the Novel.* New York: Oxford University Press.

Aronowitz, Stanley. 1992. "Reflections on Identity." *October* 61: 91–107.

Asian Women United of California, ed. 1989. *Making Waves: An Anthology of Writings by and about Asian American Women.* Boston: Beacon Press.

Atkinson, Jane Monnig. 1982. "Review Essay: Anthropology." *SIGNS* 8, no. 2 (Winter): 236–58.

Auerbach, Nina. 1982. *Woman and the Demon: The Life of a Victorian Myth.* Cambridge: Harvard University Press.

Awiakta, Marilou. 1991. "Red Alert! A Meditation on *Dances with Wolves.*" *Ms.* March–April): 70–71.

Balbus, Isaac D. 1982. *Marxism and Domination: A Neo-Hegelian, Feminist, Psychoanalytic Theory of Sexual, Political, and Technological Liberation.* Princeton: Princeton University Press.

———. 1986. "Disciplining Women: Michel Foucault and the Power of Feminist Discourse." In *Feminism as Critique: The Politics of Gender*, ed. Seyla Benhabib and Drucilla Cornell. Minneapolis: University of Minnesota Press.

Baltake, Joe. 1990. "Plains of Magic." *The Sacramento Bee* 21 November, sc. 1, 5.

———. 1991. "It was anything but 'Costner's Last Stand'" *Sacramento Bee*, 21 November, F1, 4.

Barrett, Michele. 1980. *Women's Oppression Today: Problems in Marxist Feminist Analysis.* London: Verso.

Beale, Francis. 1970. "Double Jeopardy: To Be Black and Female." In *The Black Woman,* ed. Toni Cade. New York: Signet.

Beers, David. 1991. "PC? B.S." *Mother Jones,* September–October, 384–87.

Behar, Ruth. 1990. "Rage and Redemption: Reading the Life Story of a Mexican Marketing Woman." *Feminist Studies* 16, no. 2 (Summer): 223–58.

Behar, Ruth, and Deborah Gordon, eds. Forthcoming. *Women, Writing Culture: A Reader in Feminist Ethnography.* Berkeley: University of California Press.

Bell, Roseann P., Bettye J. Parker, and Beverly Guy-Sheftall, eds. 1979. *Sturdy Black Bridges: Visions of Black Women in Literature.* Garden City, N.Y.: Anchor Books.

Belsey, Catherine. 1980. *Critical Practice.* London: Methuen.

———. 1986. "Constructing the Subject: Deconstructing the Text." In *Feminist Criticism and Social Change: Sex, Class, and Race in Literature and Culture,* ed. Judith Newton and Deborah Rosenfelt. New York: Methuen.

Bennett, Tony. 1979. *Formalism and Marxism.* London: Methuen.

Berman, Morris. 1978. *Social Change and Scientific Organization: The Royal Institution, 1799–1844.* Ithaca: Cornell University Press.

Bernstein, Richard. 1991. "The Rising Hegemony of the Politically Correct." *New York Times,* 28 October, D4.

Bethke Elshtain, Jean. 1981. *Public Man, Private Woman: Women in Social and Political Thought.* Princeton: Princeton University Press.

Blain, Virginia. 1985. "Double Vision and the Double Standard in *Bleak House:* A Feminist Perspective." *Literature and History* 11:31–46.

Bly, John. 1987. *The Pillow and the Key: Commentary on the Fairy Tale of Iron John, Part One.* St. Paul, Minn.: Ally Press.

Boone, Joseph A. 1990. "Of Me(n) and Feminism: Whose Is the Sex That Writes?" In *Engendering Men: The Question of Male Feminist Criticism,* ed. Joseph A. Boone and Michael Cadden. New York: Routledge.

Boose, Lynda E. 1987. "The Family in Shakespeare Studies; or—Studies in the Family of Shakespeareans; or—The Politics of Politics." *Renaissance Quarterly* 40:707–42.

Bordo, Susan. 1990. "Feminism, Postmodernism, and Gender- Skepticism." In *Feminism/Postmodernism,* ed. Linda J. Nicholson. New York: Routledge.

Braidotti, Rosa. 1987. "Envy: Or, with My Brains and Your Looks." In *Men in Feminism,* ed. Alice Jardine and Paul Smith. New York and London: Methuen.

Brantlinger, Patrick. 1977. *The Spirit of Reform: British Literature and Politics, 1832–1867.* Cambridge: Harvard University Press.

———. 1990. *Crusoes' Footprints: Cultural Studies in Britain and America.* New York: Routledge.

Breines, Wini. 1989. "A Couple of White Guys . . ." *Nation* 27 (November): 630–32.

Brewster, David. 1834. "Mrs. Somerville on the Physical Sciences." *Edinburgh Review* 59: 154–77.

Brownstein, Rachel. 1982. *Becoming a Heroine: Reading about Women in Novels.* Harmondsworth: Penguin.

Bulwer-Lytton, E. G. E. 1831. "Spirit of Society in England and France." *Edinburgh Review* 52:375–87.

Butler, Judith. 1990. *Gender Trouble: Feminism and the Subversion of Identity.* New York: Routledge.

———. 1992. "Contingent Foundations: Feminism and the Question of 'Postmodernism'." In *Feminists Theorize the Political*, ed. J. Butler and Joan Scott. New York: Routledge.

Butler, Judith, and Joan W. Scott, eds. 1992. *Feminists Theorize the Political*. New York: Routledge.

Cade, Toni. 1970. *The Black Woman: An Anthology*. New York: New American Library.

Carby, Hazel V. 1987. *Reconstructing Womanhood: The Emergence of the Afro-American Woman Novelist*. New York: Oxford University Press.

Carter, Bill. 1991. "Children's TV, Where Boys Are King." *New York Times*, May 1, A1, B6.

Carton, Evan. 1991. "The Self Besieged: American Identity on Campus and in the Gulf." *Tikkun* 6, no. 4 (July-August): 40–47.

Castillo, Edward D. 1991. "Dancing with Words: Reflections On the Shadow Catcher Kevin Costner." *Film Quarterly* 44, no. 4:14–23.

Catlin, George. 1989. (1844) *North American Indians*. Ed. Peter Matthiessen. New York: Penguin.

Chabram-Dernersesian, Angie. 1992. "I Throw Punches for My Race, But I Don't Want to Be a Man: Writing Us—Chica-nos (Girl, Us)/Chicanas—into the Movement Script." In *Cultural Studies*, ed. Lawrence Grossberg, Cary Nelson, and Paula A. Treichler. New York: Routledge.

Chodorow, Nancy. 1978. *The Reproduction of Mothering: Psychoanalysis and the Sociology of Gender*. Berkeley: University of California Press.

Christ, Carol. 1980. *Diving Deep and Surfacing: Women's Spiritual Quest*. Boston: Beacon Press.

Christian, Barbara. 1980. *Black Women Novelists: The Development of a Tradition*. Westport, Conn: Greenwood Press.

———.1987. "The Race for Theory." *Cultural Critique* 6 (Spring): 51–63.

Clatterbaugh, Kenneth. 1990. *Contemporary Perspectives on Masculinity: Men, Women, and Politics in Modern Society*. Boulder: Westview Press.

Clausen, Jan. 1982. *A Movement of Poets: Thoughts on Poetry and Feminism*. Brooklyn: Long Haul Press.

Clifford, James. 1986. "On Ethnographic Allegory." In *Writing Culture: The Poetics and Politics of Ethnography*, ed. James Clifford and George E. Marcus. Berkeley: University of California Press.

———. 1988. *The Predicament of Culture: Twentieth-Century Ethnography, Literature, and Art*. Cambridge: Harvard University Press.

Cohen, Walter. 1987. "Political Criticism of Shakespeare." In *Shakespeare Reproduced: The Text in History and Ideology*, ed. Jean E. Howard and Mary F. O'Connor. London: Methuen.

Collins, Patricia Hill. 1990. *Black Feminist Thought: Knowledge, Consciousness, and the Politics of Empowerment*. New York: Routledge.

Connell, R. W. 1987. *Gender and Power: Society, the Person, and Sexual Politics*. Stanford: Stanford University Press.

———. Forthcoming. "The Big Picture—a Little Sketch. Changing 'Western' Masculinities in the Perspective of Recent World History." *Theory and Society*.

Cooter, Roger. 1984. *The Cultural Meaning of Popular Science: Phrenology and the Organization of Consent in Nineteenth-Century Britain*. Cambridge: Cambridge University Press.

Corrigan, Philip, and Derek Sayer. 1985. *The Great Arch: English State Formation as Cultural Revolution*. London: Basil Blackwell.

Coulson, Walter. 1831. "McCulloch's Principles of Political Economy." *Edinburgh Review* 52:338–39.

Coward, Rosalind, and John Ellis. 1977. *Language and Materialism: Developments in Semiology and the Theory of the Subject.* London: Routledge and Kegan Paul.

Dale, Peter Allan. 1977. *The Victorian Critic and the Idea of History: Carlyle, Arnold, Pater.* Cambridge: Harvard University Press.

Dance, Daryl C. 1979. "Black Eve or Madonna? A Study of the Antithetical Views of the Mother in Black American Literature." In *Sturdy Black Bridges: Visions of Black Women in Literature,* ed. R. Bell, B. Parker, and B. Guy-Sheftall. Garden City, N.Y.: 123–32.

Davidoff, Leonore. 1979. "Class and Gender in Victorian England: The Diaries of Arthur J. Munby and Hannah Cullwick." *Feminist Studies* 5 (Spring): 87–141.

———. 1990. "'Adam Spoke First and Named the Orders of the World': Masculine and Feminine Domains in History and Sociology." In *The Politics of Every Day: Continuity and Change in Work, Labour and the Family,* ed. H. Corr and L. Mamieson. London: Macmillan.

Davidoff, Leonore, and Catherine Hall. 1987. *Family Fortunes: Men and Women of the English Middle Class, 1780–1850.* London: Hutchinson.

Davis, Angela. 1971. "Reflections on the Black Woman's Role in the Community of Slaves." *Black Scholar* 3, no. 4 (December): 2–15.

———. 1981. *Women, Race, and Class.* New York: Random House.

Davis, Mike. 1993. "Who Killed L.A.? A Political Autopsy." MS.

Davis, Natalie. 1986. "Boundaries and the Sense of Self in Sixteenth-Century France." In *Reconstructing Individualism: Autonomy, Individuality, and the Self in Western Thought,* ed. Thomas C. Heller, Morton Sosna, and David E. Wellbery. Stanford: Stanford University Press.

De Alva, J. Jorge Klor. 1990. "Chicana History and Historical Significance." In *Between Borders: Essays on Mexicana and Chicana History,* ed. Adelaida R. Del Castillo. Encino, Calif.: Floricanto Press.

De Beauvoir, Simone. 1961 (1949). *The Second Sex.* New York: Bantam Books.

De Lauretis, Teresa. 1984. *Alice Doesn't: Feminism, Semiotics, Cinema.* Bloomington: Indiana University Press.

———. 1986. "Feminist Studies / Critical Studies: Issues, Terms, and Contexts." In *Feminist Studies / Critical Studies,* ed. T. de Lauretis. Bloomington: Indiana University Press.

———. 1987. *Technologies of Gender: Essays on Theory, Film, and Fiction.* Bloomington: Indiana University Press.

"The Derisory Tower." 1991. The *New Republic,* 18 February, 5–47.

Dews, Peter. 1987. *Logics of Disintegration: Post Structuralist Thought and the Claims of Critical Theory.* London: Verso.

Diamond, Irene, and Lee Quinby, eds. 1988. *Feminism and Foucault: Reflections on Resistance.* Boston: Northeastern University Press.

Dickens, Charles. 1960 (1852). *Bleak House.* New York: Bantam Books.

Dill, Bonnie Thornton. 1983. "Race, Class, and Gender: Prospects for an All-inclusive Sisterhood." *Feminist Studies* 9, no. 1 (Spring): 131–50.

Dinnerstein, Dorothy. 1976. *The Mermaid and the Minotaur: Sexual Arrangements and Human Malaise.* New York: Harper and Row.

DiStefano, Christine 1991. *Configurations of Masculinity: A Feminist Perspective on Modern Political Theory.* Ithaca: Cornell University Press.

Dollimore, Jonathon. 1985. "Introduction: Shakespeare, Cultural Materialism and the New Historicism." In *Political Shakespeare: New Essays in Cultural Materialism.* ed. J. Dollimore and Alan Sinfield. Ithaca: Cornell University Press.

Donovan, Josephine, ed. 1975. *Feminist Literary Criticism: Explorations in Theory.* Lexington: University Press of Kentucky.

Dorris, Michael. 1991. "Indians in Aspic." *New York Times,* 24 February, E17.

Dowd, Maureen. 1991. "Bush Sees Threat to Flow of Ideas on U.S. Campuses." *New York Times,* 5 May, A1.

Dubois, Ellen Carol, and Vicki L. Ruiz, eds. 1990. *Unequal Sisters: A Multicultural Reader in U.S. Women's History.* New York: Routledge.

Eagleton, Terry. 1976. *Marxism and Literary Criticism.* Berkeley: University of California Press.

———. 1978. *Criticism and Ideology: A Study in Marxist Literary Theory.* London: Verso.

———. 1983. *Literary Theory: An Introduction.* Minneapolis: University of Minnesota Press.

———. 1985. *Myths of Power: A Marxist Study of the Brontës.* New York: Barnes and Noble.

Echols, Alice. 1983. "The New Feminism of Yin and Yang." In *Powers of Desire: The Politics of Sexuality,* ed. Ann Snitow, Christine Stansell, and Sharon Thompson. New York: Monthly Review Press.

Edwards, Paul, ed. 1972. *Encyclopedia of Philosophy.* vol. 3. New York: Macmillan.

Eisenstein, Zillah. 1985. *The Radical Future of Liberal Feminism.* Boston: Northeastern University Press.

Ellis, Kate. 1984. "I'm Black and Blue from the Rolling Stones and I'm Not Sure How I Feel about It: Pornography and the Feminist Imagination." *Socialist Review* 75–76 (May–August): 103–26.

Ellis, Mrs. [Sarah Stickney]. 1839. *The Women of England: Their Social Duties, and Domestic Habits.* New York: D. Appleton.

Elshtain, Jean Bethke. 1981. *Public Man, Private Woman: Women in Social and Political Thought.* Princeton: Princeton University Press.

Empson, William. 1833. "Mrs. Marcet—Miss Martineau." *Edinburgh Review* 57:3–39.

English, Deirdre, Barbara Epstein, Barbara Haber, and Judith Mcclean. 1985. "The Impasse of Socialist-Feminism." *Socialist Review* 79 (January-February): 93–110.

Epstein, Barbara. 1991. "'Political Correctness' and Collective Powerlessness." *Socialist Review* 91, nos. 3–4:13–36.

Epstein, Joseph. 1991. "The Academic Zoo: Theory—In Practice." *The Hudson Review.* 44:9–30.

Evans, Frank. 1991. "'Dances' Trips on Its Image." *Sacramento Bee,* 13 January, Encore sec. 2.

Faure, Christine. 1981. "Absent from History." *SIGNS* 7, no. 1:71–80.

Fausto-Sterling, Ann. 1986. *Myths of Gender.* New York: Basic Books.

Felperin, Howard. 1985. *Beyond Deconstruction: The Uses and Abuses of Literary Theory.* Oxford: Oxford University Press.

Fetterley, Judith. 1978. *The Resisting Reader: A Feminist Approach to American Fiction.* Bloomington: Indiana University Press.

Fish, Stanley. 1980. *Is There a Text in This Class? The Authority of Interpretive Communities.* Cambridge: Harvard University Press.

Flax, Jane. 1978. "The Conflict between Nurturance and Autonomy in Mother-Daughter Relationships and within Feminism." *Feminist Studies* 4 (June): 171–91.

———. 1987. "Postmodernism and Gender Relations in Feminist Theory." *SIGNS* 12, no. 4: 622–25.

———. 1992. "The End of Innocence." *Feminist Theorize the Political*, ed. Judith Butler and Joan W. Scott. New York: Routledge.

Fontana, Biancamaria. 1985. *Rethinking the Politics of Commercial Society: The 'Edinburgh Review,' 1802–1732*. Cambridge: Cambridge University Press.

Fraser, Nancy. 1990. "Rethinking the Public Sphere: Toward a Socialist Feminist Theory of Democracy." Paper presented at a conference on "Negotiations, Strategies, Tactics: Discourse and Praxis in the Humanities and Social Sciences," University of California, Davis.

Fraser, Nancy, and Linda Nicholson. 1988. "Social Criticism without Philosophy: An Encounter between Feminism and Postmodernism." In *The Institution of Philosophy: A Discipline in Crisis?* ed. Avner Cohen and Marcelo Descal. Totowa, N.J.: Rowman and Littlefield.

Fregoso, Rosa Linda, and Angie Chabram. 1990. "Introduction. Chicana/o Cultural Representations: Reframing Alternative Critical Discourses." *Cultural Studies* 4:203–12.

Fuss, Diana. 1989. *Essentially Speaking: Feminism, Nature and Difference*. New York: Routledge.

Gallagher, Catherine. 1985. *The Industrial Reformation of English Fiction: Social Discourse and Narrative Form, 1832–1867*, Chicago: University of Chicago Press.

———. 1986. "Critics of Power: Marxists and The New Historicists." Paper presented at Modern Language Association meeting, New York, December.

Gallop, Jane. 1987. "French Theory and the Seduction of Feminism." In *Men in Feminism*, ed. Alice Jardine and Paul Smith. New York and London: Methuen.

———. 1992. *Around 1981: Academic Feminist Literary Theory*. New York: Routledge.

Gallop, Jane, Marianne Hirsch, and Nancy K. Miller. 1990. "Criticizing Feminist Criticism." In *Conflicts in Feminism*, ed. Marianne Hirsch and Evelyn Fox Keller. New York: Routledge.

Gayle, Addison, Jr., ed. 1971. *The Black Aesthetic*. New York: Doubleday.

Gilbert, Sandra, and Susan Gubar. 1979. *The Madwoman in the Attic: The Woman Writer and the Nineteenth-Century Literary Imagination*. New Haven: Yale University Press.

Gilligan, Carol. 1982. *In a Different Voice: Psychological Theory and Women's Development*. Cambridge: Harvard University Press.

Giroux, Henry, David Shumway, Paul Smith, and James Sosnoski. 1985. "The Need for Cultural Studies: Resisting Intellectuals and Oppositional Public Spheres." *Dalhousie Review* 64:472–86.

Glenn, Evelyn Nakano. 1980. "The Dialectics of Wage Work: Japanese-American Women and Domestic Service, 1905–1940." *Feminist Studies* 6, no. 3 (Fall): 432–71.

Gluck, Sherna Berger, and Daphne Patai, eds. 1991. *Women's Words: The Feminist Practice of Oral History*. New York: Routledge.

Goldberg, Jonathan. 1982. "The Politics of Renaissance Literature: A Review Essay." *English Literary History* 49:514–42.

Goldman, Lawrence. 1983. "The Origins of British 'Social Science': Political Economy, Natural Science, and Statistics, 1830–35." *Historical Journal* 26, no. 3:587–616.

Gonzalez, Deena J. 1988. "The Widowed Women of Santa Fe: Assessments on the Lives of Unmarried Women, 1850–1880." In *On Their Own: Widows and Widowhood in the American Southwest, 1848–1939*, ed. Arlene Scadron. Urbana: University of Illinois Press.

Gordon, Deborah. Forthcoming. *Gender in the Field: The Politics of Cultural Description, 1967–1990.* Ann Arbor: University of Michigan Press.

Gordon, Linda. 1974. "Voluntary Motherhood: The Beginnings of Feminist Birth Control Ideas in the United States." In *Clio's Consciousness Raised: New Perspectives on the History of Women,* Mary S. Hartman and Lois Banner, ed. New York: Harper Torchbooks.

———. 1986. "What's New in Women's History?" In *Feminist Studies/Critical Studies,* ed. Teresa de Lauretis. Bloomington: Indiana University Press.

Graff, Gerald. 1983. "The Pseudo-Politics of Experience." In *The Politics of Experience,* ed. W. J. T. Mitchell. Chicago: University of Chicago Press.

———. 1991. "The Nonpolitics of PC." *Tikkun* 6, no. 4 (July–August): 50–52.

Greenblatt, Stephen. 1987. "Friction and Fiction." In *Reconstructing Individualism: Autonomy, Individuality, and the Self in Western Thought,* ed. Thomas C. Heller, Morton Sosna, and David E. Wellbery. Stanford: Stanford University Press.

———. 1988. *Shakespearean Negotiations.* Berkeley: University of California Press.

———. 1990. *Learning to Curse: Essays in Early Modern Culture.* New York: Routledge.

———. N.d. "Literary Politics: A Response." MS.

Grenier, Richard. 1991. "Wolves in Sheep's Clothing?" *San Francisco Examiner,* 31 March, 26.

Griffin, Susan. 1978. *The Roaring Inside Her.* New York: Harper.

Hall, Catherine. 1981. "Gender Divisions and Class Formation in the Birmingham Middle Class, 1780–1850." In *People's History and Socialist Theory,* ed. Raphael Samuel. London: Routledge.

———. 1992. *White, Male and Middle-Class: Explorations in Feminism and History.* New York: Routledge.

Hanke, Robert. 1990. "Hegemonic Masculinity in *thirtysomething.*" *Critical Studies in Mass Communication* 7:231–48.

Haraway, Donna. 1983. "A Manifesto for Cyborgs: Science, Technology and Socialist Feminism in the 1980s." *Socialist Review* 80:65–107.

———. 1988. "Situated Knowledges: The Science Question in Feminism as a Site of Discourse on the Privilege of Partial Perspective." *Feminist Studies* 14, no. 3 (Fall): 575–600.

Harding, Sandra. 1986. *The Science Question in Feminism.* Ithaca: Cornell University Press.

———. 1987. "Feminism, Science and the Anti-Enlightenment Critiques." Paper delivered at the Penn Mid-Atlantic Seminar for the Study of Women in Society.

———. 1989. "The Instability of the Analytical Categories of Feminist Theory." In *Feminist Theory in Practice and Process,* ed. Micheline R. Malson, Jean F. O'Barr, Sarah Westphal-Wihl, and Mary Wyer. Chicago: University of Chicago Press.

———. 1991. "Reinventing Ourselves as Other: More New Agents of History and Knowledge." *New Feminist Issues* 468–513.

Harrison, Eric. 1991. "For Lakota 'Dances' Can't Keep Wolf from the Door." *Los Angeles Times,* 29 July, A1, A14, A15.

Hartsock, Nancy M. 1985. *Money, Sex, and Power: Toward A Feminist Historical Materialism.* Boston: Northeastern University Press.

Hennessy, Rosemary. 1993. *Materialist Feminism and the Politics of Discourse.* New York: Routledge.

Hernandez, Ines. 1991. Conversation.

Heyck, T. W. 1982. *The Transformation of Intellectual Life in Victorian England.* London: Croom Helm.

Hill Collins, Patricia. 1990. *Black Feminist Thought: Knowledge, Consciousness, and the Politics of Empowerment.* New York: Routledge.

Hoffman, Leonore, and Deborah Rosenfelt, eds. *Teaching Women's Literature from a Regional Perspective.* New York: Modern Language Association.

Hoffman, Nancy, Cynthia Secor, and Adrian Tinsley, eds. 1976. *Female Studies,* vol. 4: *Closer to the Ground; Women's Classes, Criticism, Programs.* Old Westbury, N.Y.: The Feminist Press.

Hollis, Patricia. 1987. "Women in Council: Separate Spheres, Public Space." In *Equal or Different: Women's Politics, 1900–1914,* ed. Jane Rendall. London: Basil Blackwell.

hooks, bell. 1984. *Feminist Theory from Margin to Center.* Boston: South End Press.

———. 1989. *Talking Back: Thinking Feminist, Thinking Black.* Boston: South End Press.

———. 1990. *Yearning: Race, Gender, and Cultural Politics.* Boston: South End Press.

———. 1992. *Black Looks: Race and Representation.* Boston: South End Press.

Houghton, Walter E. 1957. *The Victorian Frame of Mind, 1830–1870.* New Haven: Yale University Press.

Howard, Jean E. 1986. "The New Historicism in Renaissance Studies." *English Literary Renaissance* 16:13–43.

Howard, Jean E., and Marion F. O'Connor, eds. 1987. *Shakespeare Reproduced: The Text in History and Ideology.* London: Methuen.

Howard, June. 1983. "Informal Notes toward 'Marxist-Feminist' Cultural Analysis." *Minnesota Review* 20:77–92.

———. 1988. "Feminist Differings: A Recent Survey of Feminist Literary Theory and Criticism," *Feminist Studies* 13, no. 1:167–90.

Howe, Florence. 1972. "Feminism and Literature." In *Images of Women in Fiction: Feminist Perspectives,* ed. Susan Koppleman Cornillon. Bowling Green, Ohio: Bowling Green University Press

———. 1984. *Myths of Co-education: Selected Essays, 1964–1983.* Bloomington: Indiana University Press.

Hull, Gloria, and Barbara Smith. 1982. "The Politics of Black Women's Studies." In *All the Women Are White. All the Blacks are Men. But Some of Us Are Brave: Black Women's Studies,* ed. Gloria Hull, Patricia Bell Scott, and Barbara Smith. Old Westbury, N.Y.: The Feminist Press.

Inkster, Ian. 1983. "Introduction: Aspects of the History of Science and Science Culture in Britain, 1780–1850 and Beyond." In *Metropolis and Province: Science in British Culture, 1780–1850,* ed. Ian Inkster and Jack Morrell. London: Hutchinson.

Jacobs, Joanne. 1991. "And Now, It's 'Indian Chic.'" *Sacramento Bee,* 8 April, B7.

Jacobus, Mary. 1979. "The Buried Letter: Feminism and Romanticism in *Villette.*" In *Women Writing about Women,* ed. Mary Jacobus. London: Croom Helm.

Jameson, Fredric. 1971. *Marxism and Form: Twentieth-Century Dialectical Theories of Literature.* Princeton: Princeton University Press.

Janeway, Elizabeth. 1975. "On the Power of the Weak." *SIGNS* 1, no. 1:103–10.

Jardine, Alice A. 1985. *Gynesis: Configurations of Women and Modernity.* Ithaca, N.Y.: Cornell University Press.

Jardine, Alice, and Paul Smith, eds. 1987. *Men in Feminism.* New York: Methuen.

Jay, Martin. 1984. *Marxism and Totality: The Adventures of a Concept from Lukacs to Habermas.* Berkeley: University of California Press.

Jeffords, Susan. 1991. "Protection Racket: The 'Rape' of Kuwait." *Women's Review of Books,* July, 7.

Jeffrey, Francis. 1803. Letter to Francis Horner, 11 May, cited in *Rethinking the Politics of Commercial Society: The 'Edinburgh Review,' 1802–1832,* by Biancamaria Fontana. Cambridge: Cambridge University Press, 1985.

———. 1825. "Political Economy." *Edinburgh Review* 43:13.

———. 1966. *Contributions* 1:xi. Cited in "The Edinburgh Review, 1802–1900." In *Wellesley Index to Victorian Periodicals,* ed. Walter Houghton, vol. 1. Toronto, 1966.

Jensen, Joan. 1990. (1977). "Native American Women and Agriculture: A Seneca Case Study." In *Unequal Sisters: A Multicultural Reader in U.S. Women's History,* ed. Ellen Carol Dubois and Vicki L. Ruiz. New York: Routledge.

Jones, Ann Rosalind. 1981. "Writing the Body: Toward an Understanding of 'L'écriture féminine'." *Feminist Studies* 7, no. 2:247–63.

Jones, Jacqueline. 1982. "'My Mother Was Much of a Woman': Black Women, Work, and the Family under Slavery." *Feminist Studies* 8, no. 2:235–70.

Kampf, Louis, and Paul Lauter, eds. 1972. *The Politics of Literature: Dissenting Essays on the Teaching of English.* New York: Random House.

Kaplan, Cora. 1986a. *Sea Changes: Culture and Feminism.* London: Verso.

———. 1986b. "*Aurora Leigh.*" In *Feminist Criticism and Social Change: Sex, Class, and Race in Literature and Culture,* ed. Judith Newton and Deborah Rosenfelt. New York: Methuen.

Kaplan, E. Ann. Forthcoming. "Cultural Studies, Film and Discursive Constructions." In *Cultural Studies,* ed. E. Ann Kaplan and T. Brennan.

Keller, Evelyn Fox. 1979. *Reflections on Gender and Science.* New Haven: Yale University Press.

Kelly-Godal, Joan. 1976. "Did Women Have a Renaissance?" In *Becoming Visible: Women in European History,* ed. Renate Bridenthal and Claudia Koontz. Boston: Houghton Mifflin.

Kennedy, Valerie. 1979. "*Bleak House:* More Trouble with Esther." *Journal of Women's Studies in Literature* 330–47.

Kessler-Harris, Alice. 1992. "The View from Women's Studies." *SIGNS* 17, no. 4:794–805.

Kettle, Arnold. 1960 (1951). *An Introduction to the English Novel: Defoe to George Eliot.* Vol. 1. New York: Harper Torchbooks.

Kim, Elaine H. 1982. *Asian American Literature: An Introduction to the Writings and Their Social Context.* Philadelphia: Temple University Press.

Klancher, Jon. 1987. *The Making of English Reading Audiences, 1790–1832.* Madison: University of Wisconsin Press.

Knights, Ben. 1978. *The Idea of the Clerisy in the Nineteenth Century.* London: Cambridge University Press.

Kolodny, Annette. 1975. *The Lay of the Land: Metaphor as Experience and History in American Life and Letters.* Chapel Hill: University of North Carolina Press.

———. 1980. "Dancing through the Minefields." *Feminist Studies* 6, no. 1:1–25.

Kondo, Dorinne K. 1990. *Crafting Selves: Power, Gender, and Discourses of Identity in a Japanese Workplace.* Chicago: University of Chicago Press.

Koppelman Cornillon, Susan, ed. 1972. *Images of Women in Fiction: Feminist Perspectives.* Bowling Green, Ohio: Bowling Green University Press.

Kuenzli, Rudolf. 1991. Introduction to the special issue on "Cultural Studies and the New Historicism." *Journal of the Midwest Modern Language Association* 24, no. 1 (Spring): 1–2.

Kuhn, Annette. 1978. "Structures of Patriarchy and Capital in the Family." In *Feminism and Materialism: Women and Modes of Production,* ed. Annette Kuhn and Ann Marie Wolpe. London: Routledge.

————. 1982. *Women's Pictures: Feminism and Cinema.* London: Routledge.

LaCapra, Dominick. 1983. *Rethinking Intellectual History: Texts, Contexts, Language.* Ithaca: Cornell University Press.

————. 1986. Remarks on panel "The New Historicism: Political Commitment, and the Post-Modern Critic." Modern Language Association meeting, New York, December.

Landon, Susan. 1990. "In Another's Man's Moccasins." *Sunday Journal* (Albuquerque), 16 December, A1, A3.

Lauter, Paul. 1980. "Working-Class Women's Literature—An Introduction to Study." *Radical Teacher* 15 (March): 16–26.

————. 1983. "Race and Gender in the Shaping of the American Literary Canon: A Case Study from the Twenties." *Feminist Studies* 9, no. 3: 435–63.

————. 1984. "Society and the Profession, 1958–83." *PMLA* 99 (May): 414–26.

Lazreg, Marnia. 1988. "Feminism and Difference: The Perils of Writing as a Woman on Women in Algeria." *Feminist Studies* 14, no. 1:81–107.

Lebsock, Suzanne. 1982. "Free Black Women and the Question of Matriarchy: Petersberg, Virginia, 1784–1820." *Feminist Studies* 8, no. 2:271–92.

Lentricchia, Frank. 1980. *After The New Criticism.* Chicago: University of Chicago Press.

————. 1988. "Foucault's Legacy—A New Historicism?" In *The New Historicism,* ed. H. Aram Veeser. New York: Routledge.

Lerner, Gerda. 1975. "Placing Women in History: Definitions and Challenges." *Feminist Studies* 3, nos. 1–2: 8.

Lesage, Julia. 1979. "One Way or Another: Dialectical, Revolutionary, Feminist." *Jump Cut* 29 (May).

Lewis, Sarah. 1839. *Woman's Mission and Woman's Influence.* 10th American ed. New York: International Book Co.

Lister, T. H. 1830. "Mrs. Gore's *Women as They Are; or, The Manners of the Day.*" *Edinburgh Review* 51:444–62.

Long, Elizabeth. 1989. "Feminism and Cultural Studies." *Critical Studies in Mass Communication* 6:427–35.

Lugones, Maria C., and Elizabeth V. Spelman. 1983. "Have We Got a Theory for You! Feminist Theory, Cultural Imperialism and the Demand for the Woman's Voice." *Women's Studies International Forum* 6, no. 6:573–81.

Lutz, Catherine. 1991. "The Gender of Theory." Paper presented at the American Anthropological Association, Chicago, November.

McCulloch, J. R. 1835. "Philosophy of Manufacturers." *Edinburgh Review* 61:453–72.

Macherey, Pierre. 1978. *A Theory of Literary Production.* London: Routledge.

McLeod, Bruce. 1991. Review of *Learning to Curse. Journal of the Midwest Modern Language Association* 24:100–103.

Malson, Micheline R., Jean F. O'Barr, Sarah Westphal-Wihl, and Mary Wyer, eds. 1989. *Feminist Theory in Practice and Process.* Chicago: University of Chicago Press.

Mani, Lata. 1992. "Cultural Theory, Colonial Texts: Reading Eyewitness Accounts of Widow Burning." In *Cultural Studies,* ed. Lawrence Grossberg, Cary Nelson, and Paula A. Treichler. New York: Routledge.

Marcus, George E. N.d. "A Broad(er) Side to the Canon: Being a Partial Account of a Year of Travel among Textual Communities in the Realm of Humanities Centers and Including a Collection of Artificial Curiosities," MS.

Martin, Biddy. 1988. "Feminism, Criticism, and Foucault." In *Feminism and Foucault: Reflections on Resistance,* ed. Irene Diamond and Lee Quinby. Boston: Northeastern University Press.

Martin, Biddy, and Chandra Talpade Mohanty. 1986. "Feminist Politics: What's Home Got to Do with It?" In *Feminist Studies/Critical Studies*, ed. Teresa de Lauretis. Bloomington: Indiana University Press.

Martineau, Harriet 1837. *Society in America*. 3 vols., London: Saunders and Otley.

Martinez, Elizabeth. 1991. "Willie Horton's Gonna Get Your Alma Mater." *Z Magazine* (July–August): 126–30.

Marxist-Feminist Literary Collective. 1978. "Women's Writing: *Jane Eyre, Shirley, Villette, Aurora Leigh.*" *Ideology and Consciousness* 3:27–48.

Mascia-Lees, Frances E., Patricia Sharpe, and Colleen Ballerino Cohen. 1989. "The Postmodernist Turn in Anthropology: Cautions from a Feminist Perspective." *SIGNS* 15:7–33.

Maslin, Janet. 1991. "Give Him a Puppy. And Get the Lady a Gun." *New York Times*, 21 July, B1.

Meese, Elizabeth. 1986. *Crossing the Double-Cross: The Practice of Feminist Criticism.* Chapel Hill: University of North Carolina Press.

———, ed. 1989. *Coming to Terms: Feminism, Theory, Politics.* London: Routledge.

Merchant, Carolyn. 1980. *The Death of Nature: Women, Ecology and the Scientific Revolution.* San Francisco: Harper and Row.

Merivale, Herman. 1837. "Definitions and Systems of Political Economy." *Edinburgh Review* 66:73–99.

Mill, J. S. 1831. "The Spirit of the Age." In *Mill's Essays on Literature and Society*, ed. J. B. Schneewind. New York: Collier Books, l965.

Miller, D. A. 1981. "The Novel and the Police." *Glyph* 8:127–47.

———. 1983. "Discipline in Different Voices: Bureaucracy, Police, Family, and *Bleak House.*" *Representations* 1 (February).

———. 1988. *The Novel and the Police.* Berkeley: University of California Press.

Miller, Nancy. 1991. *Getting Personal: Feminist Occasions and Other Autobiographical Acts.* New York: Routledge.

Millett, Kate. 1970. *Sexual Politics.* New York: Doubleday.

Mitchell, Juliet, and Jacqueline Rose, eds. 1982. *Introductions to Feminine Sexuality: Jacques Lacan and the Ecole Freudienne.* New York: W. W. Norton.

Modleski, Tania. 1986. "Feminism and the Power of Interpretation." In *Feminist Studies / Critical Studies*, ed. Teresa De Lauretis. Bloomington: Indiana University Press.

Moers, Ellen. 1973. "*Bleak House:* The Agitating Women." *Dickensian* 69:13–24.

Mohanty, Chandra Talpade. 1988. "Under Western Eyes: Feminist Scholarship and Colonial Discourses." *Feminist Review* 30:61–88.

———. 1990. "On Race and Voice: Challenges for Liberal Education in the 1990s." *Cultural Critique* (Winter): 179–208.

Mohanty, Chandra, Ann Russo, and Lourdes Torres, eds. 1991. *Third World Women and the Politics of Feminism.* Bloomington: Indiana University Press.

Montrose, Louis. 1986. "Renaissance Literary Studies and the Subject of History." *English Literary Renaissance* 16 (Winter): 6–12.

Moraga, Cherríe, and Gloria Anzaldúa, eds. 1981. *This Bridge Called My Back: Writings by Radical Women of Color.* New York: Kitchen Table Press.

More, Hannah. 1799. *Strictures on the Modern System of Female Education.* 4th ed. London: T. Cadell Jun and W. Davies.

Morgan, Robin, ed. 1970. *Sisterhood Is Powerful: An Anthology of Writings from the Women's Liberation Movement.* New York: Vintage.

Morris, Meaghan. 1988. *The Pirate's Fiancé.* London: Verso.

Moses, Claire Goldberg. 1984. *French Feminism in the Nineteenth Century.* Albany: State University of New York Press.

Mouffe, Chantal. 1992. "Citizenship and Political Identity." *October* 61:28–32.

Neale, R. S. 1972. *Class and Ideology in the Nineteenth Century.* London: Routledge.

Neeley, Carol Thomas. 1988. "Constructing the Subject: Feminist Practice and the New Renaissance Discourses." *English Literary Renaissance* 18, no. 1:5–18.

Nelson, Cary. 1987. "Men, Feminism: The Materiality of Discourse." In *Men in Feminism,* ed. Alice Jardine and Paul Smith, 153–172. New York: Methuen.

———. 1991. "Always Already Cultural Studies: Two Conferences and a Manifesto." *Journal of the Midwest Modern Language Association* 24, no. 1:24–38.

Newman, Karen. 1991. *Fashioning Femininity and English Renaissance Drama.* Chicago: University of Chicago Press.

Newton, Judith Lowder. 1986 (1981). *Women, Power and Subversion: Social Strategies in British Fiction, 1778–1860.* New York: Methuen.

Newton, Judith, and Deborah Rosenfelt, eds. 1986. *Feminist Criticism and Social Change: Sex, Class, and Race in Literature and Culture.* New York: Methuen.

Newton, Judith, and Judith Stacey. 1992. "Ms.representations: Postmodern/Feminist Dilemmas in Studying Men." Paper presented at the Society for the Study of Social Problems, Pittsburgh, August.

Nicholson, Linda J. 1986. *Gender and History: The Limits of Social Theory in the Age of the Family.* New York: Columbia University Press.

Norton, Eleanor Holmes. 1970. "For Sadie and Maude." In *Sisterhood Is Powerful: An Anthology of Writings from the Women's Liberation Movement,* ed. Robin Morgan. New York: Vintage.

O'Brien, D. P. 1970. *J. R. McCulloch: A Study in Classical Economics.* New York: Barnes and Noble.

———. 1975. *The Classical Economists.* Oxford: Clarendon Press.

O'Brien, Mary. 1981. *The Politics of Reproduction.* Boston: Routledge.

O'Connor, Alan. 1988. "The Problem of American Cultural Studies." *Critical Studies in Mass Communication* 6, no. 4:407.

Olsen, Tillie. 1978. *Silences.* New York: Delacorte.

Ong, Aihwa. 1987. *Spirits of Resistance and Capitalist Discipline: Factory Women in Malaysia.* Albany: State University of New York Press.

Ordoñez, Elizabeth. 1982. "Narrative Texts by Ethnic Women: Rereading the Past, Reshaping the Future." *Melus* 9, no. 3 (Winter): 19–28.

Padget, Martin. 1992. "Film, Ethnography, and the Scene of History: 'Dances with Wolves' as Participant Ethnography." Paper presented at the University of California Film Studies Conference, Berkeley, February.

Pearson, Carol, and Katherine Pope. 1981. *The Female Hero in American and British Literature.* New York: R. R. Bowker.

Pechter, Edward. 1987. "The New Historicism and Its Discontents: Politicizing Renaissance Drama." *PMLA* 102:292–309.

Perkin, Harold. 1968. *The Origins of Modern English Society, 1780–1880.* London: Routledge.

Piercy, Marge. 1970. "The Great Coolie Damn." In *Sisterhood Is Powerful: An Anthology of Writings from The Women's Liberation Movement,* ed. Robin Morgan. New York: Vintage.

Poovey, Mary. 1988a. "Feminism and Deconstruction." *Feminist Studies* 13, no. 1:51–66.

———. 1988b. *Uneven Developments: The Ideological Work of Gender in Mid-Victorian England.* Chicago: University of Chicago Press.

Porter, Carolyn. 1988. "Are We Being Historical Yet?" *South Atlantic Quarterly* 87, no. 4:743–86.

Pratt, Annis, ed. 1981. *Archetypal Patterns in Women's Fiction.* Bloomington: University of Indiana Press.

Rabine, Leslie. 1988. "A Feminist Politics of Non-Identity." *Feminist Studies* 14, no. 1: 11–32.

Radway, Janice. 1983. "Women Read the Romance: The Interaction of Text and Context." *Feminist Studies* 9 (Spring): 53–78.

———. 1991. "Antidisciplinary Logic of Culture Studies." Paper presented at Modern Language Association meeting, San Francisco, December.

Rajchman, John. 1992. "Introduction: The Question of Identity." *October* 61:5–7.

Rakow, Lana F. 1989. "Feminist Studies: The Next Stage." *Critical Studies in Mass Communication* 6:209–15.

Rapp, Rayna. 1979. "Review Essay: Anthropology." *SIGNS* 4, no. 3 (Spring): 497–513.

Reich, Robert B. 1991. *The Work of Nations: Preparing Ourselves for Twenty-First Century Capitalism.* New York: Vintage.

Rendall, Jane. 1985. *The Origins of Modern Feminism: Women in Britain, France and the U.S., 1780–1960.* New York: Schocken.

Rich, Adrienne. 1979. *On Lies, Secrets, and Silence: Selected Prose, 1966–1978.* New York: W. W. Norton.

———. 1980. "Compulsory Heterosexuality and Lesbian Existence." *SIGNS* 5, no. 4: 631–60.

Richards, Paul. 1988. "State Formation and Class Struggle, 1832–48." In *Capitalism, State Formation and Marxist Theory,* ed. Phillip Corrigan. London: Quartet Books.

Riley, Denise. 1988. *"Am I That Name?": Feminism and the Category of "Women" in History.* Minneapolis: University of Minnesota Press.

Robinson, Lillian. 1978. *Sex, Class and Culture.* Bloomington: Indiana University Press.

Rooney, Ellen. 1990. "Discipline and Vanish: Feminism, the Resistance to Theory, and the Politics of Cultural Studies." *differences* 2:15.

Rosaldo, Michelle Z. 1980. "The Use and Abuse of Anthropology: Reflections on Feminism and Cross-Cultural Understanding." *SIGNS* 5, no. 3:389–417.

Rose, Jacqueline. 1983. "Femininity and Its Discontents." *Feminist Review* 14 (Summer).

Rosenberg, Karen. 1984. "Peaceniks and Soldier Girls." *Nation,* 14 [April].

Rubin, Gayle. 1975. "The Traffic in Women: Notes on the 'Political Economy' of Sex." In *Toward an Anthropology of Women,* ed. Rayna R. Reiter. New York: Monthly Review Press.

Ruehl, Sonja. 1986 (1982). "Inverts and Experts: Radclyffe Hall and the Lesbian Identity." In *Feminist Criticism and Social Change: Sex, Class, and Race in Literature and Culture,* ed. Judith Newton and Deborah Rosenfelt. New York: Methuen.

Russo, Mary. 1986. "Female Grotesques: Carnival and Theory." In *Feminist Studies/ Critical Studies,* ed. Teresa de Lauretis. Bloomington: University of Indiana Press.

Ryan, Mary P. 1981. *Cradle of the Middle Class: The Family in Oneida County, New York, 1790–1865.* Cambridge: Cambridge University Press.

Ryan, Michael. 1982. *Marxism and Deconstruction: A Critical Articulation.* Baltimore: Johns Hopkins University Press.

Sandoval, Chela. 1991. "U.S. Third World Feminism: The Theory and Method of Oppositional Consciousness in the Postmodern World." *Genders* 10 (Spring): 1–24.

Schwichtenberg, Cathy. 1989. "Feminist Cultural Studies." *Critical Studies in Mass Communication* 6:202–8.

Scott, Joan Wallach. 1987. "On Language, Gender, and Working-Class History." *International Labor and Working-Class History* 31 (Spring): 1–13.

———. 1988. *Gender and the Politics of History.* New York: Columbia University Press.

Scrope, G. Poulett. 1833. "Miss Martineau's *Monthly Novels.*" *Quarterly Review* 49:136–52.

Seals, David. 1991. "The New Custerism." *Nation,* 13 May, 637.

Segal, Lynne. 1990. *Slow Motion: Changing Masculinities, Changing Men.* London: Virago Press.

———. Forthcoming. "Can Men Change? Masculinities in Context." *Theory and Society.*

Senf, Carol. 1973. *"Bleak House:* Dickens, Esther and the Androgynous Mind." *Victorian Newsletter* 64 (Fall): 21–27.

Showalter, Elaine. 1975. "Literary Criticism." *SIGNS* 1, no. 2:435–60.

———. 1987. "Critical Cross-Dressing: Male Feminists and the Woman of the Year." In *Men in Feminism,* ed. Alice Jardine and Paul Smith. New York and London: Methuen.

Showalter, Elaine, and English Showalter. 1973. "Victorian Women and Menstruation." In *Suffer and Be Still: Women in the Victorian Age,* ed. Martha Vicinus. Bloomington: Indiana University Press.

Simpson, David. 1988. "Literary Criticism and the Return to 'History.'" *Critical Inquiry* 14 (Summer): 726–39.

———. 1991. "Introduction: The Moment of Materialism." In *Subject to History: Ideology, Class, and Gender,* ed. David Simpson. Ithaca: Cornell University Press.

Smith, Barbara. 1970. "Toward a Black Feminist Criticism." *Conditions Two* 25–44.

Smith, Paul. 1988. *Discerning the Subject.* Minneapolis: University of Minnesota Press.

Smith, Valerie. 1987. *Self-Discovery and Authority in Afro-American Narrative.* Cambridge: Harvard University Press.

Smith-Rosenberg, Carroll. 1974. "Puberty to Menopause: The Cycle of Femininity in Nineteenth Century America." In *Clio's Consciousness Raised: New Perspectives on the History of Women,* ed. Mary S. Hartman and Lois Banner. New York: Harper Torchbooks.

———. 1975a. "The Female World of Love and Ritual: Relations between Women in Nineteenth Century America." *SIGNS* 1, no. 1:1–30.

———. 1975b. "The New Woman and the New History." *Feminist Studies* 3, nos. 1–2:185–98.

———. 1985. "Introduction." *Disorderly Conduct: Visions of Gender in Victorian America.* New York: Knopf.

Spelman, Elizabeth V. 1988. *Inessential Woman: Problems of Exclusions in Feminist Thought.* Boston: Beacon Press.

Spender, Dale. 1981. "Introduction." In *Men's Studies Modified: The Impact of Feminism in the Academic Disciplines,* ed. Dale Spender. Oxford: Pergamon Press.

Spivak, Gayatri Chakravorty. 1983. "The Politics of Interpretation." In *The Politics of Interpretation,* ed. W. J. T. Mitchell. Chicago: University of Chicago Press.

———. 1988. *In Other Worlds: Essays in Cultural Politics.* New York: Routledge.

———. 1990. *The Post-Colonial Critic: Interviews, Strategies, Dialogues.* Ed. Sara Harasym. New York: Routledge.

Stacey, Judith. 1990. *Brave New Families: Stories of Domestic Upheaval in Late Twentieth Century America.* New York: Basic Books.

Stack, Carol. 1970. *All Our Kin.* New York: Harper.

Stansell, Christine. 1987. "A Reply to Joan Scott." *International Labor and Working-Class History* 31 (Spring): 224–29.

Stewart, Robert. 1985. *Henry Brougham, 1778–1868: His Public Career*. London: The Bodley Head.

Stimpson, Catherine R. 1981. "Zero Degree Deviancy: The Lesbian Novel in English." *Critical Inquiry* 8 (Winter).

Stoker, Fraya Katz. 1972. "The Other Criticism: Feminism versus Formalism." In *Images of Women in Fiction*, ed. Susan Koppelman Cornillon. Bowling Green, Ohio: Bowling Green State University Press.

Stuard, Susan Mosher. 1981. "The Annales School and Feminist History: Opening Dialogue with the American Stepchild." *SIGNS* 7, no. 1:135–43.

Taylor, Barbara. 1983. *Eve and the New Jerusalem: Socialism and Feminism in the Nineteenth Century*. New York: Pantheon Books.

Taylor, John. 1991. "Are You Politically Correct?" *New York*, 21 January, 33–41.

Thompson, E. P. 1983. "Class Consciousness." In *History and Class: Essential Readings in Theory and Interpretation*, ed. R.S. Neale. Oxford: Basil Blackwell.

Thompson, Noel W. 1984. *The People's Science: The Popular Political Economy of Exploitation and Crises, 1816–34*. Cambridge: Cambridge University Press.

Thompson, William, and Anna Wheeler. 1983 (1820). *Appeal of One Half the Human Race, Women, against the Pretensions of the Other Half, Men, to Retain Them in Political, and Thence in Civil and Domestic Slavery*. London: Virago Press.

"Thought Police." 1990. *Newsweek*, 24 December, 48–54.

Toews, John E. 1987. *The American Historical Review* 92, no. 4:879–907.

Tompkins, Jane P. 1980. *Reader-Response Criticism: From Formalism to Post-Structuralism*. Baltimore: Johns Hopkins University Press.

Valente, Judith. 1991. "For the Sioux, Life Is as Hard as the Dakota Hills." *Sacramento Bee*, 1 April, B6, B8.

Veeser, H. Aram. 1991. "Re-Membering a Deformed Past: (New) New Historicism." *Journal of the Midwest Modern Language Association* 24, no. 1 (Spring): 3–13.

Vicinus, Martha. 1974. *The Industrial Muse*. New York: Barnes and Noble.

Wade-Gayles, Gloria. 1984. *No Crystal Stair: Visions of Race and Sex in Black Women's Fiction*. New York: Pilgrim Press.

Walkowitz, Judith R. 1980. "Introduction." In *Prostitution and Victorian Society: Women, Class and the State*. Cambridge: Cambridge University Press.

———. 1992. *City of Dreadful Delight: Narratives of Sexual Danger in Late Victorian London*. Chicago: University of Chicago Press.

Walkowitz, Judith R., and Daniel J. Walkowitz. 1974. " 'We Are Not Beasts of the Field': Prostitution and the Poor in Plymouth and Southampton under the Contagious Diseases Acts." In *Clio's Consciousness Raised: New Perspectives on the History of Women*, ed. Mary S. Hartman and Lois Banner. New York: Harper Torchbooks.

Waller, Marguerite. 1987. "The Difference It Makes." *diacritics* (Spring): 2–20.

Warnock, Donna. 1982. "Patriarchy Is a Killer: What People Concerned about Peace and Justice Should Know." In *Reweaving the Web of Life: Feminism and Nonviolence*, ed. Pam McAllister. Philadelphia: New Society Publishers.

Washington, Mary Helen. 1975a. "Introduction." In *Black-Eyed Susans: Classic Stories by and about Black Women*, ed. Mary Helen Washington. Garden City, N.Y.: Anchor Books.

———. 1975b. "Introduction." In *Midnightbirds: Stories of Contemporary Black Women Writers*, ed. Mary Helen Washington. Garden City, N.Y.: Anchor Books.

"Watching the War: Seven Perspectives." 1991. *Women's Review of Books*, July, 4–13.

Watson, Barbara Bellow. 1975. "On Power and the Literary Text." *SIGNS* 1, no. 1: 111–18.

Weeks, Jeffrey. 1981. *Sex, Politics and Society: The Regulation of Sexuality since 1800.* London: Longmans.

Weiner, Martin J. 1981. *English Culture and the Decline of the Industrial Spirit 1850–1908.* Cambridge: Cambridge University Press.

West, Cornell. 1992. "A Matter of Life and Death." *October* 61:20–23.

Whelwell, William. 1834. "On the Connexion of the Physical Sciences." *Quarterly Review* 51:54–68.

White, Deborah Gray. 1990 (1983). "Female Slaves: Sex Roles and Status in the Antebellum Plantation South." In *Unequal Sisters: A Multicultural Reader in U.S. Women's History*, ed. Ellen Carol DuBois and Vicky L. Ruiz. New York: Routledge.

Williams, Patricia J. 1991. *The Alchemy of Race and Rights: Diary of a Law Professor.* Harvard: Harvard University Press.

Williams, Raymond. 1970. *The English Novel from Dickens to Lawrence.* Forgmore, St. Albans, Herts: Paladin.

Williams, Sherley Anne. 1982. "Papa Dick and Sister-Woman: Reflections on Women in the Fiction of Richard Wright." In *American Novelists Revisited: Essays in Feminist Criticism*, ed. Fritz Fleischmann. Boston: G. K. Hall.

Willis, Susan. 1991. *A Primer for Daily Life: Is There More to Life than Shopping?* New York: Routledge.

Wollstonecraft, Mary. 1975 (1792). *A Vindication of the Rights of Woman.* New York: Norton.

Wood, Ann Douglas. 1974. "'The Fashionable Diseases': Women's Complaints and Their Treatment in Nineteenth-Century America." In *Clio's Consciousness Raised: New Perspectives on the History of Women*, ed. Mary S. Hartman and Lois Banner. New York: Harper Torchbooks.

Wuntch, Phillip. 1991. "Garrison's Case Weak, Costner Says." *Sacramento Bee*, 3 January.

Yeo, Richard. 1984. "Science and Intellectual Authority in Mid-Nineteenth Century Britain: Robert Chambers and *Vestiges of The Natural History of Creation*." *Victorian Studies* 28:5–31.

Young-Bruehl, Elisabeth. 1991. "Pride and Prejudice: Feminist Scholars Reclaim the First Person." *Lingua Franca* 15–18.